Better Teachers, Better Schools

What Star Teachers Know, Believe, and Do

A Volume in
Urban Education Studies Series

Series Editor:
Nicholas D. Hartlep, *Metropolitan State University*
Thandeka K. Chapman, *University of California, San Diego*
Kenneth J. Fasching-Varner, *Louisiana State University*

Urban Education Studies Series

**Nicholas D. Hartlep, Thandeka K. Chapman,
Kenneth J. Fasching-Varner, Series Editors**

Better Teachers, Better Schools

What Star Teachers Know, Believe, and Do

Edited by

Valerie Hill-Jackson
Texas A&M University

and

Delia Stafford
The Haberman Educational Foundation

Information Age Publishing, Inc.
Charlotte, North Carolina • www.infoagepub.com

Library of Congress Cataloging-in-Publication Data

CIP data for this book can be found on the Library of Congress website:
http://www.loc.gov/index.html

Paperback: 978-1-68123-715-2
Hardcover: 978-1-68123-716-9
E-Book: 978-1-68123-717-6

Printed in the United States of America

CONTENTS

EDITORS' FOREWORD

Nicholas D. Hartlep, Thandeka K. Chapman, and Kenneth J. Fasching-Varner

The *Urban Education Studies* book series was created as a publishing vehicle for sharing the lives and voices of educators, students, and parents connected to urban areas and the experiences of people of color in public schools. We, the series editors, are committed to increasing the visibility of urban issues from the perspectives and documented experiences of the people most affected by them, in order to address issues of equity and justice in complex urban contexts.

Dr. Martin Haberman dedicated his personal and professional life to the advancement of urban teacher effectiveness. Trained at Teachers College, Columbia University, Haberman's career included numerous awards and recognitions for his scholarship around teacher selection. Haberman believed that in order to improve urban schools, time and resources should be spent on teacher "selection," not necessary teacher "preparation." His rationale was influenced by his 50 years of research in teacher effectiveness and teacher retention.

As Jonathan Kozol says in this book's foreword, "The editors of this volume, Valerie Hill-Jackson and Delia Stafford, continue to advance Martin's ideas and theories in *Better Teachers, Better Schools: What Star Teachers Know, Believe, and Do* by sharing the personal narratives of practicing teachers, the latest research that build on his theories, as well as highly referenced and unpublished manuscripts written by Martin" (p. xii). In 2012, it too, was Kozol who eulogized Haberman at the ribbon cutting and opening of the Martin Haberman Library for Social

Better Teachers, Better Schools: What Star Teachers Know, Believe, and Do
pp. vii–viii
Copyright © 2017 by Information Age Publishing

Justice Teaching. The library is housed at the Milwaukee Center for Teaching, Learning, and Public Education and officially opened Friday, September 28, 2012.

Better Teachers, Better Schools: What Star Teachers Know, Believe, and Do excited us because its predecessor, *Better Principals, Better Schools: What Star Principals Know, Believe, and Do* did such a marvelous job at detailing why the leaders of urban K–12 schools are so vital for creating better schools for our children. Using Haberman's framework, *Better Teachers, Better Schools* documents the effective practices of successful urban K–12 teachers. We, the editors of this book series, are mindful that Haberman's criteria for successful teachers is both extensive and rigorous in his expectations for academic, social, and behavioral pedagogical knowledge. We welcome the opportunity to provide readers with tangible examples of quality teaching, across the spectrum of K–12 classrooms, that will help other teachers and educators to support students' academic and social and emotional growth.

We are honored that Dr. Haberman's legacy will continue in the publishing of Hill-Jackson and Stafford's *Better Teachers, Better Schools* volume and hope that the text is utilized by those who, like Haberman himself, continue to develop better practices that enrich the educational experiences of students and parents connected to urban schools.

DR. MARTIN HABERMAN
(1932-2012)

Star teachers are characterized by those who are extremely effective with student achievement among underserved learners even though their district or school may be failing. "[Star teachers] see the need for diverse children in poverty to succeed in school as a matter of life and death for the students and the survival of society."

—**Dr. Martin Haberman**

Star Teachers: The Ideology and Best Practice of Effective Teachers of Diverse Children and Youth in Poverty (Haberman Educational Foundation, 2010, p. 216)

FOREWORD

Standing the Test of Time:
The Martin Haberman Legacy

Jonathan Kozol

Dr. Martin Haberman's (1932–2012) legacy as a staunch advocate for underserved learners, is standing the test of time. I believe in picking battles big enough to matter and small enough to win. Martin dedicated his life's work to the same idea by winning the battle for children living in poverty by working to select the best teachers and principals for them.

The quest for selecting great teachers for the children and youth of public schools is paramount for the spread of justice and democracy in our country; on this front, Martin never wavered. He believed that in urban schools exemplary teaching with direct focus on students must always apply ideals of fairness, equity, and social justice to their world. I see parallels in Martin's life mission and mine. I think we both aim to empower teachers in order to give our children, who are the poorest of the poor, the same opportunity we give our own kids.

Martin, Distinguished Professor Emeritus at the University of Wisconsin's School of Education, was a revered teacher educator who was a longtime University of Wisconsin-Milwaukee education professor and created the Metropolitan Milwaukee Teacher Education Program. He was co-founder of the Urban Doctoral Program at University Wisconsin School of Education, a noted researcher, and the author of seven books and 350

Better Teachers, Better Schools: What Star Teachers Know, Believe, and Do
pp. xi–xii

articles and book chapters on teaching and learning. In his books, *Star Teachers of Children in Poverty* (Kappa Delta Pi, 1995) and *Star Teachers: The Ideology and Best Practice of Effective Teachers of Diverse Children and Youth in Poverty* (Haberman Educational Foundation, 2010), Martin goes to great lengths to describe the divergent ideologies and practices between "star" teachers and quitters. After five decades of meticulous investigations, Martin was able to determine that the character and beliefs of star teachers differ greatly from "quitters/failures" in today's public schools. The ideology of stars is manifested through exceptional performance in underserved classrooms.

To this end, the Haberman Educational Foundation, Inc. (HEF) was chartered in 1994 to further publicize and disseminate his research and writings. HEF provides the Haberman Star Teacher and Star Principal Interview trainings to school districts, universities, and charter schools across the nation. The selection protocols are used to choose the best teachers and principals for the children and youth, especially for those who live in poverty. Moreover, the Milwaukee Teachers' Education Association established the Martin Haberman Library for Social Justice Teaching. The library, housed at the Milwaukee Center for Teaching, Learning, and Public Education, opened Friday, September 28, 2012, and I was honored to be the guest speaker at the ribbon-cutting ceremony. Indeed, Martin's life will be remembered as one dedicated to the promise of children and youth in poverty.

The editors of this volume, Valerie Hill-Jackson and Delia Stafford, continue to advance Martin's ideas and theories in *Better Teachers, Better Schools: What Star Teachers Know, Believe, and Do* by sharing the personal narratives of practicing teachers, the latest research that build on his theories, as well as highly referenced and unpublished manuscripts written by Martin. All of these chapters are extensions of Martin's research, which articulate the third space—or the art of relationship building—expressed by teachers who are committed to learning side-by-side with learners in classrooms.

My friend Martin and I both champion the proposition that it is not content, nor pedagogy, but the capacity of teachers to build relationships with children, parents, as well as classroom and school leaders that ultimately makes a difference in the life chances of underserved learners. I am a fan of Martin's glorious legacy of educational democracy for the urban learner; his academic treasures leave an indelible mark on education and are standing the test of time.

—Dr. Jonathan Kozol
American writer, scholar, and educational activist

PROLOGUE

A Star Teacher for Every Classroom

Valerie Hill-Jackson and Delia Stafford

Everyone cannot be a teacher and only a few are destined to be "star" teachers. Star teachers, characterized by those who demonstrate the extraordinary ability to connect with students and support their achievement even while surviving in failing districts or schools, are exceedingly more effective than "qualified" teachers. This statement buttresses five decades of groundbreaking research on star teachers by Dr. Martin Haberman (1932–2012). Haberman understood that teacher effectiveness becomes especially critical for learners from challenged communities, and this philosophy forms the raison d'etre for *Better Teachers, Better Schools: What Star Teachers Know, Believe, and Do*. This volume contains 10 chapters and includes the most significant and highly demanded works by Haberman (Chapters 1 through 4, 8, and 10), testimonials by scholar-practitioners (Chapters 5 and 6), and the latest empirical research (Chapters 7 and 9), which have been influenced by Haberman's scholarship and help make the case for star teachers.

This prelude to *Better Teachers, Better Schools* is apportioned into two major segments, which combine to provide a blueprint for understanding and weighing the chapters in this edited work. First, we detail the insidious nature of the teacher quality gap and demonstrate how this chasm is magnified in urban schools and classrooms. Second, Haberman's (1995)

Better Teachers, Better Schools: What Star Teachers Know, Believe, and Do
pp. xiii–xxiii
Copyright © 2017 by Information Age Publishing

seven midrange functions of star teachers are summarized and help set the stage for the contents of this book.

THE TEACHER QUALITY GAP

There is an observable disparity in the state and national achievement scores between learners of color and their White counterparts (Howard, 2015). This so-called achievement gap is better understood among critical scholars as a cacophony of gaps, including the income gap (Reardon, 2013); opportunity gap (Carter & Welner 2013; Putnam, 2016); and teacher quality gap (Goldhaber, Lavery, & Theobald, 2015). The variation in academic performance, in terms of the rate of interaction by effective teachers with middle-class students compared to underserved students, is known as the "teacher quality gap." The quality of teachers is inconsistent throughout American cities and school districts (Goldhaber et al., 2015); the outcome is a kind of zip-code education in which the wealthier or advantaged communities are afforded the best resources and teachers (Kozol, 2005).

Often the students who need the best teachers the most are given the worst or most ill-prepared teachers imaginable; the best teacher graduates are recruited by school districts with excellent academic reputations and more visible parents. Further, the frequency of effective teachers often changes from classroom to classroom within the same school. This observation is corroborated by Goldhaber et al. (2015) when they purport:

> There is evidence that principals reserve "favorable" classroom assignments for teachers with greater classroom success and higher exam licensure scores (Player, 2010), perhaps due to rigidities in teacher compensation structures. And in schools that "track" students by performance level, the inequities we observe (particularly at the middle school level) could be due in part to more qualified teachers being assigned to teach more "advanced" courses. (p. 305)

Consequently, the best teachers are siphoned off by the better schools and the more ideal classroom assignments, while the truly needy students are stuck with the leftover batch of educators. Schools are littered with "qualified" teachers; those who were highly successful in their teacher preparation programs but were gone by year 3 or year 5 in their employment because they lacked the attributes to be successful (AEE, 2014). Feng (2010) explains that this problem is intensified in urban classrooms where teachers come and go at a higher rate, in a single academic year.

An important issue often raised with regards to teacher turnover is its dis-proportionate impact on minority and low-income students. According to the National Center for Education Statistics (1998), schools with 50 percent or more minority students experience turnover at twice the rate of schools with lower minority populations. Similarly, Freeman, and colleagues (2002) found that teachers who switched schools were more likely to have served a greater proportion of minority, low-income, and low-achieving students at their previous schools. In relation to income, Ingersoll (2001) found that schools with poverty levels greater than 50% have significantly higher rates of turnover than low-poverty schools (schools with less than 15% poverty). Findings from a study of schools in the Philadelphia School District yielded similar results, with a higher teacher turnover rate in its highest poverty schools, compared to schools with the lower rates of poverty (Useem & Neild, 2002). The study found that in 1999-2000, 46% of teachers in middle schools with the highest poverty rate began teaching at their school within the past 2 years. (cited in Guin, 2004, pp. 3–4)

To exacerbate the issue of attrition in urban teachers, students in underserved schools are at the mercy of poorly equipped learning envi-ronments; nonrigorous curricula and learning experiences that do not prepare them for jobs or college; and teachers who are generally dispas-sionate and uncommitted to the growth and academic success of those they serve (Noguera, 2003).

If teacher quality is one of the most important factors impacting stu-dent achievement, then it is reasonable to suggest that the teacher quality gap is the most deleterious effect on individual learners' academic achievement, and the largest contribution on the overall student achieve-ment gap in the United States. Haberman's conclusions have been sub-stantiated by other scholars in teacher education who agree that effective teachers are the most important indicator for a learner's success in the classroom (Chetty, Friedman, & Rockoff, 2013; Darling-Hammond, 2010; Hightower et al., 2011; NCATE, 2016). Haberman warns that too many teachers who are designated to urban or diverse classrooms do not have the mindset to be an effective teacher.

STAR TEACHERS MAKE A DIFFERENCE

What colleges and universities cannot impart among prospective teachers is the ability to relate to diverse children in poverty and to persist at a job in a failing bureaucracy organized for the benefit of the adults and against the best educational interests of the children. The selection of teachers is infinitely more important than the nature of their training. Just because you get admirable grades in a teacher preparation program and pass the teacher licensure test, does not qualify candidates to teach. There is no correlation between the academic success of teacher candidates (grade point average, teacher licensure exam scores, etc.) and their ability to support academic achievement among learners (Goldhaber, 2006; Ingersoll, Merrill, & Stuckey, 2014). Learning subject matter and pedagogical content in colleges and universities can be readily achieved, but content knowledge by itself cannot predict effective teachers. But the inability to relate to learners does provide some insight into teachers who become quitters/failures (Haberman 1995, 2010).

Teacher effectiveness is determined by the professional triumvirate of knowledge, skills, and dispositions. While teacher knowledge and skills are generally easily understood, the definition for dispositions is often complicated by synonyms such as behaviors, beliefs, characteristics, and perceptions. Therefore, for the purposes of this volume, dispositions are defined as one's beliefs put into action, and Haberman uses the phrase "midrange functions" as a synonym. The rationale for operationalizing dispositions that get to the core of teachers' character is clear, yet the national teaching standards for effective teaching offer *technical* dispositions for the preparation and evaluation of teachers (e.g., InTASC, 2011; NCATE, 2016) as they provide a sterile depiction of teacher traits and professional attitudes. For instance, the National Board for Professional Teaching Standards (NBPTS, 2002) provides the following guidance for professional development of teachers and counselors:

> Proposition 1: Teachers are committed to students and their learning.
>
> Proposition 2: Teachers know the subjects they teach and how to teach those subjects to students.
>
> Proposition 3: Teachers are responsible for managing and monitoring student learning.
>
> Proposition 4: Teachers think systematically about their practice and learn from experience.
>
> Proposition 5: Teachers are members of learning communities. (pp. 3–4)

The standards by these well-meaning teacher advocacy agencies offer suggestions that are more pedantic in nature as they present an idealistic representation of a "qualified" teacher. Additionally, teacher preparation curricula and licensure exams are not clearly aligned to these lofty propositions that inform the NBPTS standards and fail to put forward any viable road map to teachers for how to get there. The field of teacher education continues to offer the same types of dispositional models for effective teaching while expecting different results for student achievement (Villegas, 2007).

Meanwhile, the 16 million miseducated learners in urban schools continue to be underserved in their school districts. Haberman proposes that learners from underserved communities need teachers who can relate to them; he argues that while mastery of one's subject matter is extremely important, it is not enough to affect educational outcomes. Thornton (2006) cites the research of several scholars who make the case for the importance of professional qualities that speak to one's character or personal dispositions:

> A large body of literature related to dispositions centers on the moral and ethical dimensions of teaching. Much of this work focuses on fostering positive dispositions toward diversity (Major & Brock, 2003) and addresses the issue of teacher candidates entering teacher preparation programs with beliefs and dispositions that work against the success of students from diverse backgrounds (Shutz et al., 1996). This field of research addresses worldviews and the mismatch between teachers' and students' backgrounds, experiences, languages and the resulting attitudes of teachers. Such mismatches often lead teachers to see children of diverse backgrounds as children with deficits as learners (Zeichner, 1996). Dispositions within this body of literature are closely intertwined with attitudes, values and beliefs about issues of equity. (pp. 55–56)

Consequently, a star teacher is best defined by *relational* dispositions or midrange functions. This ability to relate to youngsters derives from the ideology and practices of star teachers and are outlined by Haberman's (1995) 7 midrange functions, or dispositions, of great teachers (see Figure 1). A star teacher's midrange functions, or ideology and behavior, become of critical importance for the urban learner because as the teacher thinks, s/he does. A teacher's ideology or mindset is inextricably linked to his or her practice in the classroom. Teacher beliefs are powerful determinants for how they perform in the classroom (Anderson & Stillman, 2013; Hamre et al., 2012; Weiner & Jerome, 2016). If a teacher believes that all students can learn, and these learners have the potential to be successful, s/he will move heaven and earth to ensure that the learners on his or her watch will experience academic success. However, if a teacher feels in his or her heart that there is no hope for learners, then he or she is less likely to implement the practices to support student learning.

Stars stand out among their peers and have that special "it" factor—an approach to teaching that combines the science of teaching with the artistry of relationship building. On the other hand, quitters/failures are those who have left urban schools with unsatisfactory ratings from supervisors or who describe themselves as unable to continue in urban schools. The worst quitters/failures are those who remain shielded by the bureaucracy in overwhelmed, failing schools. These quitters exact the worst type

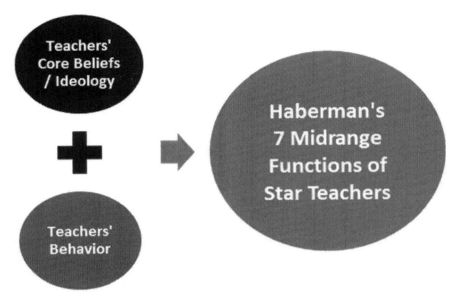

Figure P.1.   Haberman's seven midrange functions (dispositions) of star teachers as a product of teachers' beliefs and behaviors.

of educational carnage because they teach scores of learners every year (often in an uncelebrated career), languishing for decades.

After five decades of research, the Haberman Educational Foundation (HEF) created a Star Teacher Prescreener Questionnaire and Haberman Star Teacher Selection Interview; both used by school districts around the nation in the selection of beginning teachers (HEF, n.d.). The Haberman Star Teacher Selection Interview is grounded in Haberman's seven midrange functions and predicts who will remain in teaching within highly bureaucratic school systems and those who will quit or fail (Baskin & Ross, 1992; Baskin, Ross, & Smith, 1996; Haberman, 1993, 1995, 2010; Hartlep & McCubbins, 2012). The beliefs and behaviors of star teachers embody the following seven midrange functions: (a) persistence to try every strategy to reach every learner, (b) positive values about student learning, (c) the ability to adapt general theories into pedagogical practices, (d) an encouraging approach to at-risk students, (e) professional versus a personal orientation, (f) the ability to avoid burnout, and (g) the tendency to be vulnerable and admit one's shortcomings (for more on this, see Table P.1 and Chapters 1 and 10, this volume).

Star teachers have a way of responding to classroom interactions with their learners that is markedly different from the way a traditional teacher reacts. Haberman (2010) adds,

Table P.1.   Traditional Versus Star Teachers' Responses to Haberman's Seven Midrange Functions/Dispositions

Traditional Teachers Respond in the Following Ways:	Midrange Functions: Beliefs and Behaviors of Star Teachers	Star Teachers Respond in the Following Ways:
S/he teaches in a one-size-fits-all approach to passive learners. If students fail to get the content the first time, then they quickly fall behind or fail.	1. Persistence	S/he has the propensity to work with children who present learning and behavioral problems on a daily basis without giving up on them for the full 180 day work year.
S/he sees protecting ones career or "getting through the material" as their highest priorities.	2. Protects and values student learning	S/he believes that student learning is the teacher's highest priority.
S/he understands educational theory but falls short in adapting these theories into practical lessons for their classrooms.	3. Theory into practice	S/he has the ability to see the implication of generalizations of theory and has the wherewithal to bring theory into practical applications in the classroom.
S/he often comes from a monolingual, Christian, middle-class life where diversity was avoided. These teachers cannot relate to, or teach, learners from diverse backgrounds.	4. Approach to children in poverty or at-risk students	S/he is able to connect with and teach students of all backgrounds and levels.
S/he wears their heart on their sleeve and is easily bruised by the normal behavioral problems or classroom challenges that will arise in underserved classrooms. Their responses are often unprofessional and inappropriate for learners.	5. Professional versus personal orientation to students	S/he expects students to misbehave and attempts to relate to students as an experienced and consummate professional: resisting the urge to "take it personally" in difficult classroom interactions.
S/he is unable to function or thrive in a large depersonalized organization; these teachers often leave the profession by year five or relegate students to impoverished learning experiences.	6. Burnout	S/he is able to function or thrive in a large depersonalized organization.
S/he never acknowledges when s/he is wrong because mistakes are seen as a form of weakness.	7. Fallibility	S/he readily admits when s/he is wrong and creates "teachable moments" from mistakes for students' benefit.

[Stars'] actions reflect their ideology and vice versa. This ideology includes their beliefs about the role of the school serving diverse students in poverty, the nature of learning and the nature of teaching. Because one must have a strong commitment to this undergirding ideology it is not possible to translate what stars do in "ten easy steps" for anyone to follow. To do what stars do, without believing as they do, leads to merely going through the motions of teaching and having little influence on students' learning. For those who accept stars' ideology, these functions can be brought to life; they can become a source of insight and a guide to effective teaching. (p. 131)

The mindset of stars cannot be detached from their classroom practices. For example, a star teacher is more likely to model the midrange function of persistence by supporting students in various ways to learn subject matter. If an individual student struggles with a concept, the star teacher finds multiple teaching strategies to support that leaner's growth in order to help him or her master content. Star teachers will employ every instructional strategy—from peer coaching, demonstrations, personalized one-on-one time—to differentiated instruction; all with the intention to help learners succeed. Alternatively, peers who are quitters/failures are more likely to try a one-size-fits-all approach to teaching diverse learners. If the student does not master the content, the quitter/failure does not take it personally and just blames the student or his or her deficient background. If the student falls behind or is slow to pick up concepts, it is just too bad—the curriculum is moving forward with or without the learner. Quitters/failures have an ideology that is not student centered; this way of thinking prevents them from seeking resources that will help them support student learning.

This ideology can be changed, but only by powerfully sustained life experiences which are reflected upon as a mature adult, not by the superficial and short-term experiences offered to prospective teachers in colleges and universities. A star's ideology is a result of their life experiences and the growth they have experienced as a result of reflecting on their life experiences. Once individuals with the appropriate ideology are selected they can learn to be effective teachers by actually working as responsible teachers of record in poverty schools with the help of on-site mentors.

CLOSING

Upon reflecting on the last half century of preparing teachers on the job, Haberman could not recall a single instance in which a teacher failed who could relate to the children, or a case in which a teacher succeeded who could not relate to learners. Subject-matter content can be learned, but Haberman's seven midrange functions, and their undergirding ideology, cannot. If knowledge of content and pedagogy were the best criteria for predicting teacher effectiveness, then faculty in the math departments of universities, or faculty in the schools of education, could teach effectively for sustained periods in urban middle schools. We recognize such an idea as preposterous because we know that more than technical knowledge of content and pedagogy is required—something more is the relational shrewdness exemplified by the star teacher.

In every underperforming urban school there exists a truly effective teacher who encourages his or her students and produces positive academic results among underserved learners; these teachers operate in isolation in failing districts and schools. The coeditors of *Better Teachers, Better Schools* offer our gratitude to star teachers for your courage and humanity, displayed while teaching underserved learners in your classroom. We applaud your persistence. We hold onto Haberman's optimism and vision for all learners in impoverished urban classrooms; a portrait of effective star teachers like you.

REFERENCES

Alliance for Excellent Education (AEE). (2014). *On the path to equity: Improving the effectiveness of beginning teachers.* Washington, DC: Alliance for Excellent Education.

Anderson, L. M., & Stillman, J. A. (2013). Student teaching's contribution to preservice teacher development: A review of research focused on the preparation of teachers for urban and high-needs contexts. *Review of Educational Research, 83*(1), 3–69.

Baskin, M., & Ross, S. (1992). *Selecting teacher candidates via structured interviews: A validation study of the urban teacher interview.* Memphis, TN: Memphis State University.

Baskin, M. K., Ross, S. M., & Smith, D. L. (1996). Selecting successful teachers: The predictive validity of the urban teacher selection interview. *Teacher Educator, 32*(1), 1–21.

Carter, P. L., & Welner, K. G. (2013). *Closing the opportunity gap: What America must do to give every child an even chance.* New York, NY: Oxford University Press.

Chetty, R., Friedman, J. N., & Rockoff, J. E. (2013). *Measuring the impacts of teachers II: Teacher value-added and student outcomes in adulthood* (No. w19424). Cambridge, MA: National Bureau of Economic Research.

Darling-Hammond, L. (2010). *Evaluating teacher effectiveness: How teacher performance assessments can measure and improve teaching.* Washington, DC: Center for American Progress.

Feng, L. (2010). Hire today, gone tomorrow: New teacher classroom assignments and teacher mobility. *Education Finance and Policy, 5*(3), 278–316.

Goldhaber, D. (2006). *Everyone's doing it, but what does teacher testing tell us about teacher effectiveness?* Seattle, WA: Center on Reinventing Public Education, University of Washington.

Goldhaber, D., Lavery, L., & Theobald, R. (2015). Uneven playing field? Assessing the teacher quality gap between advantaged and disadvantaged students. *Educational Researchers, 44*(5), 293–307.

Guin, K. (2004). Chronic teacher turnover in urban elementary schools. *Education Policy Analysis Archives, 12*(42). Retrieved from http://epaa.asu.edu/epaa/v12n42/

Haberman, M. (1993). Predicting the success of urban teachers: The Milwaukee trials. *Action in Teacher Education, 15*(3), 1–5.

Haberman, M. (1995). Selecting 'star teachers' for children and youth in urban poverty. *The Phi Delta Kappan, 76*(10), 777–782.

Haberman, M. (2010). *Star teachers: The ideology and best practice of effective teachers of diverse children and youth in poverty.* Houston, TX: Haberman Educational Foundation.

Haberman Educational Foundation. (HEF). (n.d.). *The science of teacher selection and interviewing.* Retrieved from http://www.habermanfoundation.org/StarTeacherPreScreener.aspx

Hamre, B. K., Pianta, R. C., Burchinal, M., Field, S., LoCasale-Crouch, J., Downer, J. T., & Scott-Little, C. (2012). A course on effective teacher-child interactions: Effects on teacher beliefs, knowledge, and observed practice. *American Educational Research Journal, 49*(1), 88–123.

Hartlep, N. D., & McCubbins, S. (2012). What makes a star teacher: Examining teacher dispositions, professionalization, and teacher effectiveness using the Haberman Star Teacher Pre-Screener. *Educational Administration and Foundations, Illinois State University.* Retrieved from http://www.habermanfoundation.org/Documents/WhatMakesAStarTeacher.pdf

Hightower, A. M., Delgado, R. C., Lloyd, S. C., Wittenstein, R., Sellers, K., & Swanson, C. B. (2011). *Improving student learning by supporting quality teaching: Key issues, effective strategies.* Bethesda, MD: Editorial Projects in Education.

Howard, T. C. (2015). *Why race and culture matter in schools: Closing the achievement gap in America's classrooms.* New York, NY: Teachers College Press.

Ingersoll, R., Merrill, L., & Stuckey, D. (2014, April). Seven trends: The transformation of the teaching force. *CPRE.* Retrieved from http://repository.upenn.edu/cgi/viewcontent.cgi?article=1003&context=cpre_researchreports

Interstate Teacher Assessment and Support Consortium (InTASC). (2011). *InTASC: Model core teaching standards: A resource for state dialogue.* Washington, DC: Council of Chief State and School Officers.

Kozol, J. (2005). *The shame of the nation: The restoration of apartheid schooling in America.* New York, NY. Three Rivers Press.

Ladson-Billings, G. (2006, October). From the achievement gap to the education debt: Understanding achievement in U.S. schools. *Educational Researcher, 35*(7), 3–12.

National Board for Professional Teaching Standards. (2002). *What teacher should know and be able to do.* Arlington, VA: National Board for Professional Teaching Standards. Retrieved from http://www.nbpts.org/sites/default/files/what_teachers_should_know.pdf

National Council for Accreditation of Teacher Education. (2016). *What makes a teacher effective?* Retrieved from http://www.ncate.org/public/researchreports/teacherpreparationresearch/whatmakesateachereffective/tabid/361/default.aspx

Noguera, P. A. (2003). *City schools and the American dream: Reclaiming the promise of public education.* New York, NY: Teachers College Press.

Putnam, R. D. (2016). *Our kids: The American dream in crisis.* New York, NY: Simon and Schuster.

Reardon, S. F. (2013). The widening income achievement gap. *Educational Leadership, 70*(8), 10–16.

Thornton, H. (2006). Dispositions in action: Do dispositions make a difference in practice? *Teacher Education Quarterly, 33*(2), 53–68.

Villegas, A. M. (2007). Dispositions in teacher education: A look at social justice. *Journal of Teacher Education, 58*(5), 370–380.

Weiner, L., & Jerome, D. (2016). *Urban teaching: The essentials.* New York, NY: Teachers College Press.

CHAPTER 1

SELECTING "STAR" TEACHERS FOR CHILDREN AND YOUTH IN URBAN POVERTY

Martin Haberman

Chapter Objectives

The learner will

1. review the three basic truths about effective teachers of the urban poor;
2. appraise the undergirding ideologies and behaviors that distinguish exemplary urban teachers from quitters and failures; and
3. reflect on the seven midrange functions of star teachers.

No school can be better than its teachers. And the surest and best way to improve the schooling of the approximately 12 million children and youth in poverty is to get better teachers for them. The strategy for doing this is not mysterious and has been evolving for more than 35 years.

The premise of the strategy is simple: selection is more important than training. My calculated hunch is that selection is 80% of the matter. The reason is that the functions, performed by effective urban teachers of students in poverty, are undergirded by a very clear ideology. Such teachers

Better Teachers, Better Schools: What Star Teachers Know, Believe, and Do
pp. 1–11

not only perform functions that quitters and burnouts do not perform, but they also know why they do what they do. They have a coherent vision. Moreover, it is a humane, respectful, caring, and nonviolent form of "gentle teaching" that I have described elsewhere (Haberman, 1994). My point here is that teachers' behaviors and the ideology that undergirds their behaviors cannot be unwrapped. They are of a piece.

Nor can this ideology be readily or easily taught in traditional programs of teacher preparation. Writing a term paper on Piaget's concept of conservation or sharing with other student teachers such problems as why Ray won't sit down will not provide neophytes with the ideological vision of "star teachers." This ideology, while it is open to development, must be selected for. What can be taught are the functional teaching behaviors that are built on the foundation of this belief system. And like the ideology, the teaching behaviors are not typically learned in traditional programs of teacher education but on the job, with the benefit of a teacher/coach, a support network, and some specific workshops.

There are four dimensions of excellence that programs claiming to prepare teachers of children of poverty can and should be held accountable for: (a) the individuals trained should be adults; (b) they should have demonstrated ability to establish rapport with low-income children of diverse ethnic backgrounds; (c) they should be admitted as candidates based on valid interviews that reliably predict their success with children in poverty; (d) and practicing urban teachers who are recognized as effective should be involved in selecting candidates.

My colleagues and I have identified three related truths that grow out of the recognition that selection is the heart of the matter where teachers of the urban poor are concerned: (a) the odds of selecting effective urban teachers for children and youth in poverty are approximately 10 times better if the candidates are over 30 rather than under 25 years of age; (b) there is no problem whatsoever in selecting more teachers of color, or more males, or more Hispanics, or more of any other "minority" constituency if training begins at the postbaccalaureate level; (c) and the selection and training of successful urban teachers is best accomplished in the worst schools and under the poorest conditions of practice.

This last truth requires some comment. States routinely give out teaching licenses that are deemed valid for any school in the state. The most reasonable basis for awarding such licenses would be to prepare teachers in the poorest schools and assume they will be able to deal with the "problems" presented by smaller classes, more and better materials and equipment, and safer neighborhoods if they should ever be "forced" to teach in more advantaged schools. Traditional teacher education makes almost the reverse assumption: create professional development centers (the equivalent of teaching hospitals) and then assume that beginners will be able to function in the impoverished schools to which city school districts typically assign them. "Best practice" should not be thought of as ideal teaching under ideal conditions but as effective practice under the worst of conditions.

IN SEARCH OF "STAR" TEACHERS

By comparing the behaviors and undergirding ideologies of "star" urban teachers with those of quitters and failures, my colleagues and I have identified 14 functions of successful teachers of the urban poor that are neither discrete behaviors nor personality attributes. Instead, these functions are "midrange" in the sense that they represent chunks of teaching behavior that encompass a number of interrelated actions and simultaneously represent beliefs or commitments that predispose these teachers to act.

"Stars" are those teachers who are identified by principals, supervisors, other teachers, parents, and themselves as outstanding. They also have students who learn a great deal as measured by test scores and work samples. Between 5% and 8% of the staff members who now teach in urban impoverished schools are such "star" teachers. The quitters and failures with whom their functioning is compared constitute a much larger group: 30% to 50%, depending on the particular district. In a continuing series of interviews with a population of star urban teachers every year since 1959, we have found that the 14 functions have remained stable. What has changed, in some cases, are the questions needed to elicit interviewees' responses related to these functions.

The structured interview we use has been developed to select beginning teachers who can be prepared successfully on the job. This means that they can function at satisfactory levels while they are learning to teach. The highest success rate for selecting such exceptional neophytes has been achieved by combining both the interview and the opportunity to observe the candidates interacting with and teaching children in the summer prior to their assuming the role of beginning teacher. When the interview is combined with such observation, there is less than a 5% error rate. Use of the interview alone raises the error rate to between 8% and 10%. Compare these figures with the fact that approximately 50% of newcomers to urban schools who were prepared in traditional programs quit or fail in 5 years or less. And these "trained" beginners are only the very small, self-selected group who choose to try teaching in an urban school and not a representative sample of those currently being prepared to teach. It boggles the mind to imagine what the failure rate would be if a truly representative sample of those now graduating from traditional programs of teacher education were hired as first-year teachers in the largest urban school districts.

In the rest of this chapter, I will briefly outline the seven functions that the star teacher interview assesses (and the additional seven for which we have never been able to develop interview questions). In order for a candidate to pass the interview, he or she need not respond at the level of a star teacher. The interview predicts applicants' potential functioning from "average," through "high," to "star." A zero answer on any of the functions constitutes a failure response to the total interview. The interview is couched in behavioral terms; that is, it attempts to determine what the applicant would do in his or her class and why. (Readers should note that merely reading about these functions does not constitute preparation to conduct an interview).

THE SEVEN MIDRANGE FUNCTIONS:
THE DIMENSIONS OF EFFECTIVE TEACHING

Persistence

Many urban teachers honestly believe that most of their students (all in some cases) should not be in their classrooms because they need special help; are not achieving at grade level; are "abnormal" in their interests, attentiveness, or behavior; are emotionally unsuited to school; or are in need of alternative schools, special classes, or teachers trained to work with exceptional individuals. In some urban districts and in individual urban schools many teachers perceive 90% of their students to be not "normal" (Payne, 1984).

Effective urban teachers, on the other hand, believe it is their responsibility to find ways of engaging all their students in learning activities. The continuous generation and maintenance of student interest and involvement is how star teachers explain their jobs to themselves and to others. They manifest this persistence in several ways. They accept responsibility for making the classroom an interesting, engaging place and for involving the children in all forms of learning. They persist in trying to meet the individual needs of the problem student, the talented, the handicapped, and the frequently neglected student who falls in the gray area. Their persistence is reflected in an endless search for what works best with each student. Indeed, they define their jobs as asking themselves constantly, "How might this activity have been better for the class or for a particular individual?"

The persistence of star teachers demonstrates several aspects of their ideology: teaching can never be "good enough," since everyone could always have learned more in any activity; teaching inevitably involves dealing with problems and problem students, and such students will be in every class, every day; and better materials and strategies can always be found. The basic stance of these teachers is never to give up trying to find better ways of doing things. The quip attributed to Thomas Edison, "The difference between carbon and diamonds is that diamonds stayed on the job longer," might describe these teachers as well.

Protecting Learners and Learning

Star teachers are typically involved in some life activity that provides them with a sense of well-being and from which they continually learn. It might be philately, Russian opera, a Save the Wolves Club, composing music with computers, travel, or some other avocation from which they derive meaning as well as pleasure. Inevitably, they bring these activities and interests into their classrooms and use them as ways of involving their students in learning. It is quite common to find teachers' special interests used as foci that generate great enthusiasm for learning among the students. The grandiose explanation for this phenomenon is that people who continually experience learning have the prerequisites to generate the desire to learn in others. A more practical explanation would be that we teach best what we care most about.

In any event, star teachers frequently involve their students in learning that transcends curriculum, textbooks, and achievement tests. Their commitment to turning students on to learning frequently brings them into noncompliance with the extremely thick bureaucracies of urban schools. Stars do not view themselves as change agents per se, but they do seek ways to give themselves and their students greater latitude within the traditional curriculum.

Consider the following episode: The teacher has succeeded in truly involving the class in a learning activity. It might be an environmental issue (What happens to our garbage?); a biological study (How does a lie detector work?); or the production of a class play dealing with violence in the neighborhood. Imagine further that the intense student interest has generated some noise, the use of unusual equipment, or a need for extra cleaning of the classroom. The principal learns of the activity and requests that it be discontinued. The principal also instructs the teacher to stick with the approved texts and to follow the regular curriculum. At this point the lines are clearly drawn: continuing a genuine learning activity in which the students are thriving versus complying with the directive of a superior and following a school policy.

The way star teachers seek to work through such a problem is in direct opposition to the reaction of quitters and failures. Star teachers see protecting and enhancing students' involvement in learning activities as their highest priority; quitters cannot conceive of the possibility that they would diverge from the standard curriculum or that they would question a school administrator or a school policy.

To the uninitiated, such struggles over red tape may seem atypical. Experienced star teachers, however, find themselves involved in a continuous, day-to-day struggle to redefine and broaden the boundaries within which they work. One reason they so often find themselves at odds with the bureaucracy of urban schools is that they persist in searching for ways to engage their students actively in learning. Indeed, their view that this is their primary function stands in stark contrast to the views of teachers who see their primary function as covering the curriculum.

Star teachers try to resolve their struggles with bureaucracy patiently, courteously, and professionally. They seek to negotiate with authority. Quitters and failures perceive the most professional response to be unquestioning compliance.

Application of Generalizations

Some teachers have 30 years of experience, while others have one year of experience 30 times over. One basis for professional growth is the ability to generate practical, specific applications of the theories and philosophies. Conversely, successful teachers can also reflect on their many discrete classroom activities and see what they add up to. If you ask stars to give examples of some principle they believe in (e.g., "What would an observer see in your classroom that would lead him/her to believe that you believe all children can learn?"), they are able to cite clear, observable examples. Conversely, if a star is asked to offer a principle or make a generalization that accounts for a series of behaviors in which he or she engages, the star is equally able to move from the specific to the general.

The importance of this dimension is that teachers must be able to improve and develop. In order for this to happen, they must be able to take principles and concepts from a variety of sources (i.e., courses, workshops, books, and research) and translate them into practice. At the same time, stars can explain what their day-to-day work adds up to; they have a grasp not only of the learning principles that undergird their work but also of the long-range knowledge goals that they are helping their students achieve.

At the other extreme are teachers who are "concretized." They do not comprehend the difference between information and knowledge; neither do they see any connection between their daily lessons and the reasons why children and youth are required to go to school for 13 years. Indeed, quitters and failures frequently respond to the question, "Would you give an example of a principle in which you believe that guides your teaching?" with, "I don't like to generalize" or "It's wrong to make generalizations."

The ability to derive meaning from one's teaching is also a function of this ability to move between the general and the specific. Without this ability to see the relationship between important ideas and day-to-day practice, teaching degenerates into merely "keeping school."

Approach to "At-Risk" Students

Of all the factors that separate stars from quitters and failures, this one is the most powerful in predicting their future effectiveness with urban children of poverty. When asked to account for the large numbers of at-risk students or to suggest what might be done about cutting down on the number of at-risk students, most teachers are well-versed in the popular litany of causes. The most common causes cited are poverty, violence, handicapping conditions, racism, unemployment, poor housing, lack of health care, gangs, drugs, and dysfunctional families. But while the quitters and failures stop with these, the stars also cite irrelevant school curricula, poor teaching, and overly bureaucratic school systems as additional causes.

Since quitters and failures essentially blame the victims, the families, and the neighborhoods, they do not come up with any measures that schools and teachers can or should take to improve the situation. Indeed, they say such things as "You can't expect schools to be all things to all people" or "Teachers can't be social workers, nurses, and policemen." Stars also see all the societal conditions that contribute to students' problems with school. But they are able to suggest that more relevant curricula and more effective teaching strategies are things that schools and teachers could try and should be held accountable for. Star teachers believe that, regardless of the life conditions their students face, they as teachers bear a primary responsibility for sparking their students' desire to learn.

Professional Versus Personal Orientation to Students

Stars expect to find some youngsters in their classrooms that they may not necessarily love; they also expect to be able to teach them. Stars expect that some of their students will not necessarily love them, but they expect these students to be able to learn from them. They use such terms as *caring*, *respect*, and *concern*, and they enjoy the love and affection of students when it occurs naturally. But they do not regard it as a prerequisite for learning.

Quitters and failures, on the other hand, cannot and do not discriminate between the love of parents for their children and the love of teachers for their students. They regard such love as a prerequisite for any learning to occur. They also believe that the children should feel a similar sort of love for their teachers. Consequently, it is not uncommon for quitters and failures to become disillusioned about their work in impoverished schools. Once they realize that the children do not love them or that they cannot love "these" children, they find themselves unable to function in the role of teacher. For many quitters and failures, this love between students and teachers was a major reason for seeking to become teachers.

Star teachers have extremely strong, positive feelings toward their students, which in many cases might be deemed a form of love. But these feelings are not the primary reasons that stars are teachers, nor are these feelings the basis of their relationships with their students. Indeed, when their students misbehave, star teachers do not take it as a personal attack. Neither do they maintain class order or inspire effort by seeking to instill guilt. Genuine respect is the best way to describe the feelings star teachers have for their students.

Burnout: Its Causes and Cures

Star teachers in large urban school systems are well aware that they work in mindless bureaucracies. They recognize that even good teachers will eventually bum out if they are subjected to constant stress, so they learn how to protect themselves from an interfering bureaucracy. As they gain experience, they learn the minimum things they must do to function in these systems without having the system punish them. Ultimately, they learn how to gain the widest discretion for themselves and their students without incurring the wrath of the system. Finally, they set up networks of a few like-minded teachers or they teach in teams or they simply find kindred spirits. They use these support systems as sources of emotional sustenance.

Without such organizational skills and lacking the awareness that they even need such skills, failures and quitters are literally beaten down by the system. The paperwork, the conflicting rules and policies, the number of meetings, the interruptions, the inadequate materials, the lack of time, large classes, and an obsessive concern with test scores are just some of the demands that drive the quitters out of the profession. Moreover, quitters and failures are insensitive to many of the conflicting demands that every large, impersonal organization makes. And worst of all, they don't believe a good teacher "should" ever bum out. They believe that a really good person who really wants to be a teacher should never be ground down by any bureaucracy. This set of perceptions leads them to experience feelings of inadequacy and guilt when they do bum out. And unlike stars, who use their support networks to offset the expected pressures, quitters and failures respond to the pressures by feeling that they probably should never have become teachers.

Fallibility

Children and young people cannot learn in a classroom where mistakes are not allowed. One effective way to ensure that we find teachers who can accept the mistakes of students is to select those who can accept their own mistakes. When teachers are asked, "Do you ever make mistakes?" they answer, "Of course, I'm only human!" or "Everyone makes mistakes." The difference between stars and quitters is in the nature of the mistakes that they recognize and own up to. Stars acknowledge serious problems and ones having to do with human relations; quitters and failures confess to spelling and arithmetic errors.

FUNCTIONS BEYOND THE INTERVIEW

Thus far I have outlined seven teaching functions for which we have been able to create and validate interview questions. While the actual questions we use in the interview cannot be shared, I have described above the goals of the questions. It is noteworthy that there are seven additional functions for which we have never been able to develop interview questions but which are equally powerful in discriminating between stars and quitters. These functions and brief explanations follow:

- Organizational ability: the predisposition and ability to engage in planning and gathering materials.
- Physical/emotional stamina: the ability to persist in situations characterized by violence, death, and other crises.
- Teaching style: the predisposition to engage in coaching rather than directive teaching.
- Explanations of success: the predisposition to emphasize students' effort rather than ability.

- Basis of rapport: the approach to student involvement. Whose classroom is it? Whose work is to be protected?
- Readiness: the approach to prerequisite knowledge. Who should be in this classroom?

For children in poverty, schooling is a matter of life and death. They have no other realistic options for "making it" in American society. They lack the family resources, networks, and out-of-school experiences that could compensate for what they are not offered in schools. Without school success, they are doomed to lives of continued poverty and consigned to conditions that characterize a desperate existence: violence, inadequate health care, a lack of life options, and hopelessness. The typical high school graduate has had approximately 54 teachers. When I ask successful graduates from inner-city schools, "How many of your teachers have led you to believe that you were particularly good at anything?" the modal response is none. If graduates report this perception, I wonder what those who have dropped out would say?

I recognize that getting better teachers is not a reconstructive change strategy. Indeed, I may well deserve the criticism that I am offering a Band-Aid solution by finding great people who are merely helping to shore up and preserve bad systems. As I listened to the great change experts of the 1950s, I bet myself that they would not succeed, and I set myself the modest task of doing whatever I could to save young people in schools as they are currently constituted by getting them a few better teachers. After 35 years the movers and shakers seem further behind than ever. School systems serving poor children have become more rigid, less financially stable, more violent, and further behind their advantaged counterparts.

During the same period the school districts using my selection and training methods have become a national network. We now know how to recruit and select teachers who can succeed with children in poverty. The number of such teachers in every urban school system will continue to grow. So too will the impact these star teachers are making on the lives of their students.

CONCLUDING THOUGHTS

Mark Twain once quipped, "To do good things is noble. To advise others to do good things is even nobler—and a lot easier." I fail to understand why talking about the reconstruction of urban schools in America is noble work, while what star teachers and their students actually accomplish in these schools is merely a palliative. In my own admittedly naïve view, it seems that the inadequate nostrums of policy analysts and change agents are being given more attention than the effective behaviors of people who are busy making schools work better. A society that values ineffectual physicists over effective plumbers will find itself hip-deep in insoluble problems.

ACKNOWLEDGMENT

This chapter was originally published in 2005 in *Phi Delta Kappan*, volume 76, number 10, pages 777–281. Reprinted with permission of Phi Delta Kappa International, www.pdkintl.org. All rights reserved.

CHAPTER QUESTIONS

1. What is your philosophy on making mistakes with learners in the classroom? In other words, are mistakes a sign of weakness or strength? Explain. Describe a situation in your classroom in which you readily admitted a mistake or lack of professional judgment to your students. How did your students react?
2. Stars are able to move from the specific to the general and the reverse is true as well. Share an instructional theory that is unique to your grade level and subject matter. How have you, or a respected peer, brought this theory to life in classroom practices?
3. Obtain a piece of blank paper with three columns and eight rows. In the top row and far left column, write the word "functions," then itemize each function. Next, write the word "yes" in the middle column and "no" in the far right column. Based on the description of each function, mark each function yes or no for which you do or do not possess. How can you improve in the functions that are lacking?

REFERENCES

Haberman, M. (1994, Spring). Gentle teaching in a violent society. *Educational Horizons, 72*(3), 131–136.
Payne, C. M. (1984). *Getting what we ask for: The ambiguity of success and failure in urban education.* Westport, CT: Greenwood Press.

CHAPTER 2

GENTLE TEACHING IN A VIOLENT SOCIETY

A Postscript for the 21st Century

Martin Haberman With Valerie Hill-Jackson

Chapter Objectives

The learner will

1. examine the impact of violence on today's urban learners and teachers;
2. identify the five forces which influence children growing up in poverty;
3. analyze the star teacher's approach to gentle teaching in a violent society; and
4. explore a mechanism to allow teachers to face themselves through a five-step self-analysis of their prejudices.

Students need safe environments in which to thrive and succeed in schools. This argument is especially cogent when faced with the reality that American children are more susceptible to exposure to violence than

Better Teachers, Better Schools: What Star Teachers Know, Believe, and Do
pp. 13–29

adults (Finkelhor, 2008). Nearly 900,000 nonfatal victimizations (theft and violent crimes) are committed every year in school, which includes 363,700 thefts and 486, 400 violent assaults; crime victimization rates hover around 33 for every 1,000 students at school and 24 per 1,000 students away from school; and there are 1.3 million incidences of alcohol, drugs, weapon possession, or violence occurring on school property annually (Robers, Zhang, Morgan, & Musu-Gillette, 2015).

While most schools in America, generally, are islands of safety for learners as compared to their home communities, urban students are less safe in school. In 2016, twenty-two hundred people were shot in the city of Chicago, and 21 of them were school children age 13 or younger (Sobol, Nickeas, & Chachkevitch, 2016). During 2014, in a relatively small city such as Milwaukee, Wisconsin, 58 school-aged children were murdered and 70 were involved in nonfatal shootings. New York City Public Schools fund the tenth-largest police force in the United States (Mukherjee, 2007). Miami Dade Public Schools retains its own school police force and has budgeted millions of dollars annually for security (Miami-Dade County Public Schools, 2015). The society is violent, the urban neighborhoods are violent, and the schools are violent. In urban communities throughout the United States, 18% of inner-city youth report a gang presence compared to 11% of their suburban peers (NCES, 2016), while one in five young children aged 2 to 5 have witnessed some form of family or community violence in their lifetime (Finkelhor, 2009, as cited in David, LeBlanc, & Self-Brown, 2015, p. 303). The exposure of inner-city youth to violence in schools, at home, and in their communities is termed *co-victimization* (Warner & Weist, 1996) or *poly-victimization* (Finkelhor, Ormrod, & Turner, 2009); leading to myriad issues such as depression (Ofonedu, Percy, Harris-Britt, & Belcher, 2013) or posttraumatic stress disorder (Nooner et al., 2012; Post et al., 2014). Chillingly, Figure 2.1 outlines the types of violent acts perpetrated against adolescents age 12 and older. The National Survey of Children's Exposure to Violence confirms that

> most of our society's children are exposed to violence in their daily lives. More than 60% of the children surveyed were exposed to violence within the past year, either directly or indirectly (i.e., as a witness to a violent act; by learning of a violent act against a family member, neighbor, or close friend; or from a threat against their home or school). Nearly one-half of the children and adolescents surveyed (46.3%) were assaulted at least once in the past year, and more than 1 in 10 (10.2%) were injured in an assault; 1 in 4 (24.6%) were victims of robbery, vandalism, or theft; 1 in 10 (10.2%) suffered from child maltreatment (including physical and emotional abuse, neglect, or a family abduction); and 1 in 16 (6.1%) were victimized sexually. More than 1 in 4 (25.3%) witnessed a violent act and nearly 1 in 10 (9.8%)

saw one family member assault another. Multiple victimizations were common: more than one-third (38.7%) experienced two or more direct victimizations in the previous year, more than 1 in 10 (10.9%) experienced five or more direct victimizations in the previous year, and more than 1 in 75 (1.4%) experienced 10 or more direct victimizations in the previous year.... Nearly seven in eight children (86.6%) who reported being exposed to violence during their lifetimes also reported being exposed to violence within the past year, which indicated that these children were at ongoing risk of violent victimization. The reports of lifetime exposure also indicate how certain types of exposure change and accumulate as a child grows up. (cited in Finkelhor, Turner, Ormrod, Hamby, & Kracke 2009, pp. 1–2)

These statistics should be disturbing for educators since learners who are assaulted or offended at school are predisposed to absenteeism (Ringwalt et al., 2003), lowered academic performance and increased drop-out rates (MacMillan & Hagan, 2004), alterations in the brain's structure (Carion & Wong, 2012; Keding & Herringa, 2015; Lim, Radua & Rubia, 2014), as well as aggressive behaviors (Nansel, Overpeck, Haynie, Ruan, & Scheidt, 2003).

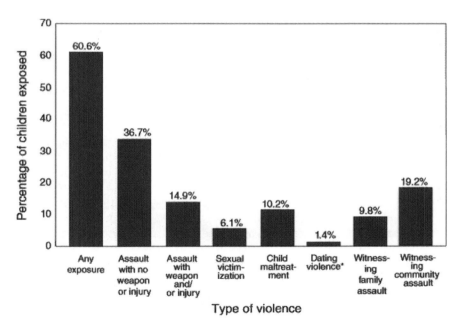

Source: Figure adapted from Finkelhor et al. (2009).

Figure 2.1.   Percentage of children exposed to different types of violence (n = 4,549).

Teachers are not immune to injury or harm in schools. According to the American Psychological Association (APA, 2016), the violence perpetuated against K–12 teachers is a national silent crisis. Across the nation, 80% of teachers in a national survey admitted to being victimized or threatened in the current or prior school year (McMahon et al., 2014). In school districts such as Rochester, New York, teachers bargain for security ahead of salary (Chodak, 2016).

People who want to teach in urban schools need to acknowledge the reality of the situation they will enter. Beginning and experienced teachers must recognize that preventing violence is an integral part of their legitimate work. The more effective they are at empowering youngsters, the less violence they will engender; the less effective they are, the more violence they will cause. Beneath the surface and not very far beneath the surface of all urban teaching is the potential for unleashing uncontrollable violence. Only those who really understand the constant threat and horrific consequences of school violence will be sufficiently on guard to do the countless things that will prevent it. Violence is already smoldering in the children, and only those vigilant teachers who see the deep frustration and anger children carry into the school building will be sufficiently sensitive to avoid setting off these negative forces in the school environment.

FIVE FORCES INFLUENCING YOUNGSTERS
GROWING UP IN POVERTY

Five forces influence youngsters growing up in poverty. First, a lack of trust in adults naturally makes young children suspicious of adults' motives and actions. Appearing to be shy or withdrawing from adults becomes a perfectly normal response. (Not expecting or seeking safety from adults or the solution to one's problems from adults might be another reasonable response.) For example, inner-city youth of color in the post-Ferguson era are becoming increasingly distrustful of authoritative figures in their neighborhoods and schools. The fact that unarmed young men of color disproportionately encounter police through unconstitutional stop-and-frisk incidents (Johnson, 2015; Meares, 2015) or murdered at the hands of law enforcement (Watkins, Patton, & Miller, 2016) feeds the cynicism of inner-city youths regarding their safety and protection by police and other authority figures in their lives.

The second force affecting youth development is the violence typical of urban life today. If those around us are potentially dangerous or life threatening, then it is normal to avoid interacting with them whenever possible. According to Dill and Ozer (2015) in *"I'm Not Just Runnin' the Streets": Exposure to Neighborhood Violence and Violence Management Strategies*

Among Urban Youth of Color, a frame of violence management strategies becomes a way of life for kids of color. These urban youth embrace innovative adaptive solutions to avoid neighborhoods marked by high rates of crime. While these urban savants find ways to survive in the city, this constant vigilance to avoid violence can be mentally exhausting and pushes the limits of one's ability to cope long term (Nooner et al., 2012).

The perception of "no hope" is the third force that characterizes urban life for older children and adults in poverty. It frequently is mistaken as a lack of initiative. If one sees no viable options, it seems useless to expend effort. The urban context engenders an onslaught of physical and psychological predicaments for urban learners (Kappel & Daley, 2004), thereby creating the perfect environment for hopelessness and despair (Landis, Gaylord-Harden, Malinowski, Grant, Carleton, & Ford, 2007) to spiral into depression (Ofonedu et al., 2013).

The fourth force affecting development is the impact of mindless bureaucracies. It becomes natural, normal—even desirable—to give the bureaucracy what it wants rather than try to respond to it in sensible or honest ways. Only by responding to the bureaucracy on its own terms can any benefits be derived. This attitude teaches children who grow up under such conditions to initiate and reveal as little as possible and give only what is being asked of them as their normal response.

The fifth major influence relates to the culture of authoritarianism; one's power becomes one's self-definition. The giving and taking of orders becomes the normal way of life. Stars are not authority figures in their classroom as all students are respected and share power. The rules for discipline are simple and only needed as management issues arise, but authoritative policies are not a priority in their rooms.

> Stars' ability to relate to children puts them on the same side as the students rather than making them adversaries. The inability of quitter/failures to relate to their students makes any management system they try ineffective and explains why discipline and classroom control remains their top concern regardless of how long they teach. (Haberman, 2010, p. 191)

These ideas parallel authoritative school climate theory, which demonstrates a positive correlation between students' perception of their supportive teachers to lowered drop-out rates and increased achievement (Jia, Konold, & Cornell, 2016).

Taking all these factors together, the outstanding attribute one can normally be expected to develop as a result of growing up and living in poverty is frustration. Feelings of deep frustration are a major characteristic of both adults and children who grow up and live the experience of urban poverty. And the result of this abiding frustration is some form of aggression. For many it is expressed as violence toward others. For others it takes the form of passive resistance. And for some it is turned inward, expressed in the multiple ways poor people demonstrate a reckless abandon for their own bodies, including suicide.

The world in which poor children frequently begin school is remarkably positive given their life experiences. Not being certain or trusting of adults, surrounded by family and friends being "done to," living in violence, and having learned how to give and take orders; yet they still come to school eagerly. It is up to schools and teachers, however, to demonstrate more than a continuation of mindless bureaucracy and overly directive, threatening adults.

STAR TEACHERS' IDEOLOGY REGARDING VIOLENCE

The ideology of star teachers regarding violence and what they can do about it is both realistic and hopeful. Their first goal is to not make matters worse. Their second goal is creating a school experience in which students succeed and relate to one another in ways not determined by the threat of force and coercion. Stars work toward this goal by various forms of gentle teaching. Stars understand that the key to dealing with violence is to know your students and respect them. As with the other functions performed by star teachers, this is a combination of teacher behaviors undergirded by their teacher's ideology. The qualities that bring a teacher function to life and make it effective are the unseen teacher beliefs beneath his or her behavior. If, for example, the teacher's real goal is to manipulate and control students, it will be sensed, understood, and communicated to the students. If, on the other hand, it is the teacher's intention to empower the students to control their own behavior, this too will be communicated by the teacher's actions. Teacher acts never impact on students independently of the teacher's real intentions. Students will always know whether the teacher's goal is to control or empower them.

Teachers in schools serving children in poverty have no choice other than gentle teaching. Beyond kindergarten and the first two grades, teachers can no longer physically control their students with external sanctions or fear. For teachers to pretend they have means to force students to learn or even comply is a dangerous myth that can make poor schools as coercive and violent as the neighborhoods outside the school. Children growing up in neighborhoods where they are socialized to violence, physical abuse, and even death will not be brought readily into submission by such punishments as a "time-out room," suspension, or even expulsion. If the harshest punishments available to teachers and schools can be ignored or even laughed at by the students, why do school officials and teachers continue to pretend they can coerce, force, insist upon, demand, require, or see to it that the children can be made to comply and learn? The only answers I can come up with are that (a) most educators do not know viable alternatives to coercive teaching; (b) those who prepared them to teach could not or did not teach them alternatives; (c) or most people who choose to become teachers were themselves socialized by power relationships and did not have school experiences derived from their intrinsic needs and interests.

If a teacher, recalling his or her own childhood and schooling, remembers a teacher's disapproval, a failing grade, or a father's spanking as a force that "inspired" learning by fear, it is natural to expect this teacher to be shocked when he or she discovers that today's poor students cannot be made to comply, shape up, and do what they are told by the threat of a teacher's scolding, a failing grade, a spanking, or even a suspension. The fears that such threats can instill today are almost nonexistent to a child in poverty who lives daily with threats of death, violence, and abuse. Some teachers give up when they see they do not have powerful negative rewards (punishments) that can force children's compliance. Stars realize very quickly they can succeed only by getting off the power theme and that ultimately each child is in control of how much and what he or she learns.

Some teachers seek ways to "make" children learn. "Make" is the critical word here. Stars define their jobs as making them want to learn. How is this related to violence? In a life engulfed by violence, urban schools cannot make children or youth comply. They can only select and prepare teachers who will empower students to control their own learning.

There can be no debate about this point. Teachers who start out intending to dominate poor children or youth are doomed to failure. Teachers who seek to empower students may become effective if they believe in and can implement the functions of star teachers. Examples of gentle strategies include the following behaviors:

- Put students ahead of subject matter. Use students' interests. Generate students' interests.
- Never go through the meaningless motion of "covering" material apart from students' involvement and learning.
- Never use shame or humiliation.
- Never scream or harangue.
- Never get caught in escalating punishments to force compliance.
- Listen, hear, remember, and use students' ideas.
- Model cooperation with all other adults in the building.
- Respect students' expressions of ideas.
- Demonstrate empathy for students' expressions of feelings.

- Identify student pain, sickness, and abuse, and follow up with people who can help them.
- Redefine the concept of a hero. Show how people who work things out are great.
- Teach students peer mediation. Do not expect students to learn from failing; repeated failure leads only to more frustration and giving up.
- Devise activities at which students can succeed; success engenders further effort.
- Be a source of constant encouragement by finding good parts of all students' work.
- Defuse, sidestep, redirect all challenges to your authority. Never confront anyone, particularly in public.
- Use cooperative learning frequently.
- Create an extended family in the classroom.
- Use particular subject matters as the way to have "fights": science "fights" about rival explanations, math "fights" about different solutions, social studies "fights" about what really happened.
- Never ask students for private information publicly.
- Don't try to control by calling on children who are not paying attention and embarrassing them.
- Demonstrate respect for parents in the presence of their children.

The list of do's and don'ts can be shortened by simply remembering that everyone needs to be treated with respect and courtesy. Will all these behaviors ensure that violence will be kept out of the school? No. The effect of these and other gentle, respectful behaviors is that schools will cut down on the degree to which they contribute to problems of violence and not exacerbate the violent culture children and youth bring from society into the school.

Star teachers see their jobs as helping to create safe havens where, for a good part of every day, the madness of violence will not intrude and their children will experience freedom from fear. Some other teachers do not subscribe to this aspect of their job at all—they simply believe that because violence should not occur, it should not be in school and therefore should not be part of the teacher's day-to-day work. Stars look at the world as it is, and traditional teachers see it in terms of some idealized fantasy—the two groups come to perform entirely different in their teaching jobs. Stars engage in gentle teaching aimed at making learning intrinsic and students accountable, while the others implement top-down management models the youngsters are bound to resist and conquer by noncompliance.

Only those who have the self-confidence and strength to function in peaceful ways in volatile and potentially violent situations need apply. Many frail, elderly, female middle school teachers succeed every day while macho, male, ex-football heroes are driven out. Teacher strength is an inner quality demonstrated by an ability to share authority with children and youth whom most people are unwilling to trust.

WHEN TEACHERS FACE THEMSELVES

To some degree, all of us are socialized to regard our culture group as superior to others. Our preferential group may be based on politics, religion, language, sex, class, or all of the above. To grow up in American society as well as others is to be carefully taught prejudices in favor of some kinds of people and against others. Many teachers are likely to overlay these notions of better or worse groups with factors such as age, lack of apparent handicaps, or appearance. Rios (2011) explains that the phenomenon by which a person's daily actions and mannerisms become universally perceived as deviant, threatening, or deviant is known as *hypercriminalization*. Many students of color are unconsciously stereotyped by educators (Tilestone, 2010) because they have been acculturated to believe, by society and the media, that young people of color are dangerous (Muncie, 2014). For many teachers who are not aware of their biases, issues of violence are collapsed into discourses on race and cement the image for students of color as juvenile delinquents who should be feared. Teachers, similar to other members of society, naturally recoil when a young Brown or Black male enters an elevator with them or walks by on a sparse city street. This reflex may cause some insensitive educators to see students of color as perpetuators of school and classroom aggression (Moore, Robinson, & Adedoyin, 2016), fueling school suspension rates (Skiba, Michael, Nardo, & Peterson, 2002).

When prospective and in-service teachers are ready to come to terms with the biases that they have, they should employ a five-step self-analysis that will help them identify and overcome their prejudices (see Figure 2.2). The first step for teachers is a thorough self-analysis of the content of their prejudices. Which are the "superior" people and what are their attitudes? Which are the "inferior" people and what are their attributes? This analysis will take a long period of soul searching. For those who go into denial ("I'm not a prejudiced person"), there's always the possibility they may never get beyond this first step. If so, they should not be allowed near children or youth. The literature on teacher beliefs demonstrates

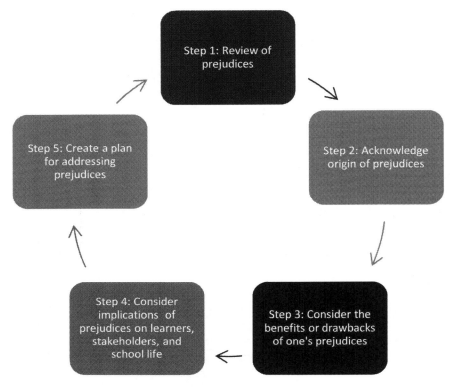

Figure 2.2.   Teachers' five-step self-analysis of recognizing and overcoming prejudices.

that many teachers are White, female, suburban/rural, monolingual, and
Christian and are hesitant to work in urban schools and more inclined to
teach students whose backgrounds are similar to their own (Hill-Jackson,
Sewell, & Waters, 2007).

The second step is to seek answers to the question of source: How did I
learn or come to believe these things? Who taught them to me? When?
Under what conditions? How much a part of my daily life are these
beliefs? This second phase will be illuminating as one considers his or her
biography and the significant others who have shaped his or her perceptions.

Step three of the self-analysis becomes even more interesting. In what
ways do I benefit or suffer from my prejudices? For example, as a White
male I may benefit from lower health insurance rates at the expense of

others. I may also suffer from a loss of many valuable interactions by cutting myself off from individuals I perceive as unworthy of friendship. This phase is an especially critical step, because it reveals the myriad ways in which our daily living is affected by our prejudices.

Step four is to consider how our prejudices may be affecting the many issues surrounding what we believe about schools, children, and how they learn best. Do we believe in a hierarchy of native intelligence related to race? Are females capable of learning math and science? Why are almost all superintendents male? Should a deaf person be licensed to teach? Can high school dropouts who are parents really serve as role models? Weiner and Jerome (2016) offer a powerfully reflective story by an educator who confesses her feelings about a student who carried a knife in school:

> I was more than a little frightened about how Danny, who attended class irregularly, might have used the knife on me or a classmate. As I eavesdropped on a conversation between two colleagues, one of whom had taught Danny in previous years, I heard the situation cast differently. Danny, who was large for his 15 years, took the subway to his full-time job in a distant, dangerous section of the Bronx every day after school. He worked from 3:00 to 11:00 p.m. 6 days a week, to support his siblings and infirmed mother. Because he had to be at work promptly at 3:00 p.m. for the shift change, on school days he had no time to go home to pick up the knife, which he needed for protection coming home late at night. A teacher who spotted the knife when it fell out of Danny's pocket, as Danny bent over in the hallway to pick up a dropped book, notified a security guard. Danny was suspended automatically ... We had not developed much of a relationship, because he was seldom in class, but the information I had learned about his full-time job made me look on him differently. (p. 87)

In the excerpt above, the teacher later established a relationship with Danny and her feelings about him were changed as she understood his personal story and management strategies for dealing with violence in his urban surroundings. Educators must understand the pitfalls of school policies like Zero Tolerance (Mills, 2013) as well as the Gun-Free Zones Act and Comprehensive Crime Control Act (Abusivekids.com, n.d.). We contribute to the risk of violence to school-aged urban learners when a suspension brought about by these antiviolence policies is tantamount to exposing inner-city youth to economic fragility or adolescents left home with no caring adults looking out for their safety and welfare (Brown, 2004).

Step five is the phase in which we lay out a plan explicating what we plan to do about our prejudices. How do we propose to check them, unlearn them, counteract them, and get beyond them? Brown (2004) explains that a caring and gentle teacher attitude is the most prevailing solution to being proactively attuned to the needs of urban learners:

> Most significant perhaps to each child or adolescent in urban schools is the willingness and ability of an educator to genuinely touch each student's social and emotional persona. Urban students may experience a greater need than suburban students for developing close relationships with teachers (Brown, 2001). This need is based on possible feelings of alienation, struggles with identity development, and what Dryfoos (1998) reported concerning adolescents at risk who "lack nurturance, attention, supervision, understanding, and caring," (p. 37) and may have inadequate communication processes with adults in their homes. (p. 269)

Additional research is needed to help educators understand challenging behavior and violence in classrooms, improve interpersonal peer conflict, and implement restorative justice programs to deter violence (Brown, 2004).

These five steps are, of course, not taught in traditional teacher education programs; neither are they required by state bureaus of teacher licensure. Indeed, it is now possible to write to any of the 50 state departments of education stating, "I don't believe Black children can ever be taught as much as White children," and still receive a teacher's license, provided one has completed the required coursework and passed a basic skills test.

For beginning teachers to succeed with children in poverty from diverse cultural backgrounds, they must successfully complete the five steps above. Middle-class suburban children also need teachers who have faced themselves and their own biases, but in the multicultural, urban schools the teacher must pass the most severe test. In urban schools, interacting successfully with children or youth from all groups is not an academic textbook exercise but a face-to-face interaction. Although the effects of a prejudiced teacher on children are detrimental in all schools and to be avoided, a culturally incompetent teacher who might survive in a small town or suburb will not last a day in an urban situation, except as a failure or burnout.

As if this level of self-understanding were not sufficiently difficult to attain, there are still other self-tests beginners need to administer. These involve the beginning teacher asking what he or she believes about cultural diversity and its role in teaching, learning, and school curriculum.

ONLY DECENT PEOPLE CAN BE PREPARED TO TEACH

The question is what "decent" means. As the first author has interacted with star teachers and tried to understand their ideology, it is clear to him that they live what they believe. It is not possible to list their beliefs and commitments apart from their behaviors. Just as the functions they perform as teachers cannot be understood apart from their undergirding ideology, the converse is also true.

The problem is that most people who select future teachers, either to train or to hire, do not use the definition of "decent" that is represented by star teachers: they simply use their own views of the world. When the first author reflected on what star teachers have told him, their basic decency is reflected by, but not limited to, the following attributes.

- They tend to be nonjudgmental. As they interact with children and adults in schools, their first thought is not to decide the goodness or badness of things but to understand events and communications.
- They are not moralistic. They don't believe that preaching is teaching.
- They are not easily shocked even by horrific events. They tend to ask themselves, "What can I do about this?" and if they think they can help, they do; otherwise they get on with their work and their lives.
- They not only listen, they hear. They not only hear, they seek to understand. They regard listening to children, parents, or anyone involved in the school community as a potential source of useful information.
- They recognize they have feelings of hate, prejudice, and bias and strive to overcome them.
- Teachers have a clear sense of their own ethnic and cultural identities.
- Teachers are culturally competent; they include diverse cultural perspectives in their classroom programs.
- They do not see themselves as saviors who have come to rescue their schools. They don't really expect their schools to change much.
- They do not see themselves as being alone. They network.
- They see themselves as "winning" even though they know their total influence on their students is much less than that of the total society, neighborhood, and gang.
- They visit parents in their homes or in neighborhood places away from school.
- They enjoy their interactions with children and youth so much they are willing to put up with irrational demands of the school system.

- They think their primary impact on their students is that they've made them more humane or less frustrated, or raised their self-esteem.
- They derive all types of satisfactions and meet all kinds of needs by teaching children or youth in poverty. The one exception is power. They meet no power needs whatever by functioning as teachers.

This is not a summary of what makes stars "decent"; these are simply a few manifestations of their decency. It seems strange that while so many reasonable people understand that it takes decent people for teacher education to "take," we continue to select and prepare people for this sensitive occupation by examining only their grades and test scores. Violence has catastrophic effects on the learner's academic performance, psyche, and life changes, and their life chances are dependent upon caring educators responding well to their needs. Might the injurious effects of violence on school-aged children be extended to the process of preparing, licensing, and hiring sensitive and gentle teachers?

CHAPTER QUESTIONS

1. What are the statistics on violence in your school district? What are the numbers on discipline and violence specific to your school and grade level? What is the impact on your classroom in terms of relationships and instruction? How have the district or school level statistics on violence affected you or your peers' decision to remain in the profession? How does your school district or school fight back against school violence? Do the students and staff feel safe? Why or why not?

2. The authors share five forces that affect learners in poverty. Share your experience of recognizing two of the five forces among your learners and ways you used instruction or counseling to combat these forces.

3. If you were principal for a day, what initiative might you implement or how would you improve current antiviolence initiatives in your school?

4. Complete the five-step self-analysis for identifying and addressing one's prejudices; be specific and map out a one page summary.

5. Consider the attributes of star teachers identified by the bullet points above. Assess whether or not you have these attributes; mark each bullet with a + or a -. Based on your findings, are you a sensitive or insensitive teacher? Also discuss in a group of three to

four peers whether or not these attributes are achievable for teachers who serve in schools with a proclivity for high rates of violence.

ACKNOWLEDGMENT

This chapter, one of the most requested articles in the recent decades of *Educational Horizons*, was originally published as "Gentle Teaching in a Violent Society" in Spring 1994, volume 72, number 3, pages 131–136. Reprinted with permission of Phi Delta Kappa International, www.pdkintl.org. All rights reserved.

REFERENCES

Abusivekids.com. (n.d.). *The laws against school violence.* Retrieved from http://www.abusivekids.com/the-laws-against-school-violence.html

American Psychological Association (APA). (2016). *A silent national crisis: Violence against teachers, all educators are at risk.* Washington, DC: American Psychological Association. Retrieved from http://www.apa.org/education/k12/teacher-victimization.pdf

Brown, D. F. (2004). Urban teachers' professed classroom management strategies reflections of culturally responsive teaching. *Urban Education, 39*(3), 266–289.

Carrion, V. G., & Wong, S. S. (2012). Can traumatic stress alter the brain? Understanding the implications of early trauma on brain development and learning. *Journal of Adolescent Health, 51*(2), S23–S28.

Chodak, A. (2016, March 17). Teacher safety addressed in new RCSD contract. *Rochester First.com.* Retrieved from http://www.rochesterfirst.com/news/local-news/teacher-safety-addressed-in-new-rcsd-contract

David, K. B., LeBlanc, M. M., & Self-Brown, S. (2015). Violence exposure in young children: Child-oriented routines as a protective factor for school readiness. *Journal of Family Violence, 30*(3), 303–314.

Dill, L. J., & Ozer, E. J. (2015, September). "I'm not just runnin' the streets": Exposure to neighborhood violence and violence management strategies among urban youth of color. *Journal of Adolescent Research, 55*(1/2), 128–135. doi:0743558415605382

Finkelhor, D. (2008). *Childhood victimization: Violence, crime, and abuse in the lives of young people.* New York, NY: Oxford University Press.

Finkelhor, D., Ormrod, R. K., & Turner, H. A. (2009). Lifetime assessment of poly-victimization in a national sample of children and youth. *Child Abuse & Neglect, 33*(7), 403–411.

Finkelhor, D., Turner, H., Ormrod, R., Hamby, S. & Kracke, K. (2009). Children's exposure to violence: A comprehensive national survey. *National Survey of Children's Exposure to Violence.* Retrieved from https://www.ncjrs.gov/pdffiles1/ojjdp/227744.pdf

Haberman, H. (2010). *Star teachers: The ideology and best practice of effective teachers of diverse children and youth in poverty* (1st ed). Houston, TX: Haberman Educational Foundation.

Hill-Jackson, V., Sewell, K. L., & Waters, C. (2007). Having our say about multicultural education: Five dispositions of advocates and resisters in the multicultural classroom. *Kappa Delta Pi Record, 43*(4), 174–180.

Jia, Y., Konold, T. R., & Cornell, D. (2016). Authoritative school climate and high school dropout rates. *School Psychology Quarterly, 31*(2), 289.

Johnson, R. N. (2015). How students became criminals: The similarities between "stop and frisk" and school searches and the effect on delinquency rates. *Boston University Public Interest Law Journal, 24*(1), 1–25. Retrieved from http://www.bu.edu/pilj/files/2016/03/Winter-2015-Rachel-N.-Johnson.pdf

Kappel, P. L., & Daley, B. J. (2004, March 16). Transformative learning and the urban context. *New Directions for Adult and Continuing Education, 2004*(101), 83–94.

Keding, T. J., & Herringa, R. J. (2015). Abnormal structure of fear circuitry in pediatric post-traumatic stress disorder. *Neuropsychopharmacology, 40*(3), 537–545.

Landis, D., Gaylord-Harden, N. K., Malinowski, S. L., Grant, K. E., Carleton, R. A., & Ford, R. E. (2007). Urban adolescent stress and hopelessness. *Journal of Adolescence, 30*(6), 1051–1070.

Lim, L., Radua, J., & Rubia, K. (2014). Gray matter abnormalities in childhood maltreatment: A voxel-wise meta-analysis. *American Journal of Psychiatry, 171*(8), 854–863.

MacMillan, R., Y., & Hagan, J. (2004, June). Violence in the transition to adulthood: Adolescent victimization, education, and socioeconomic attainment in later life. *Journal of Research on Adolescence, 14*(1), 127–158.

McMahon, S. D., Martinez, A., Espelage, D., Rose, C., Reddy, L. A., Lane, K., ... Brown, V. (2014, June 29). Violence directed against teachers: Results from a national survey. *Psychology in the Schools, 51*(7), 753–766.

Meares, T. L. (2015). Programming errors: Understanding the constitutionality of stop-and-frisk as a program, not an incident. *The University of Chicago Law Review, 82*(1), 159–179.

Miami-Dade County Public Schools. (2015). Executive summary tentative budget: For fiscal year ending June 30, 2016. *Miami-Dade County Public Schools.* Retrieved from http://financialaffairs.dadeschools.net/ES15-16/ES15_16.pdf

Mills, C. (2013). *Zero tolerance: What happens when rules are broken and the lines between good and bad aren't quite what you thought?* Harrisonburg, VA: R.R. Donnelley & Sons.

Moore, S. E., Robinson, M. A., & Adedoyin, A. C. (2016). Introduction to the special issue on police shooting of unarmed African American males: Implications for the individual, the family, and the community. *Journal of Human Behavior in the Social Environment, 26*(3/4), 247–250.

Mukherjee, E. (2007). *Criminalizing the classroom: The over-policing of New York City Schools.* New York, NY: New York Civil Liberties Union. Retrieved from http://www.nyclu.org/pdfs/criminalizing_the_classroom_report.pdf

Muncie, J. (2014). *Youth and crime.* Los Angeles, CA: SAGE.

Nansel, T. R., Overpeck, M. D., Haynie, D. L., Ruan, W. J., & Scheidt, P. C. (2003). Relationships between bullying and violence among U.S. youth. *Archives of Pediatric and Adolescent Medicine*, *157*, 348–353.

Nooner, K., Linares, L. O., Batinjane, J., Kramer, R. A., Silva, R., & Cloitre, M. (2012). Factors related to posttraumatic stress disorder in adolescence. *Trauma, Violence, & Abuse*, *13*, 153–166. doi:10.1177/1524838012447698

Ofonedu, M. E., Percy, W. H., Harris-Britt, A., & Belcher, H. M. (2013). Depression in inner-city African American youth: A phenomenological study. *Journal of Child and Family Studies*, *22*(1), 96–106.

Post, M., Hanten, G., Li, X., Schmidt, A. T., Avci, G., Wilde, E. A., & McCauley, S. R. (2014). Dimensions of trauma and specific symptoms of complex posttraumatic stress disorder in inner-city youth: A preliminary study. *Violence and Victims*, *29*(2), 262–279.

Quirmbach, C. (2014, December 26). Number of children killed or wounded by guns has risen over past year. *Wisconsin Public Radio News*. Retrieved from http://www.wpr.org/number-children-killed-or-wounded-guns-has-risen-over-past-year

Rios, V. M. (2011). *Punished: Policing the lives of Black and Latino boys*. New York, NY: New York University Press.

Ringwalt, C. L., Ennett, S., Johnson, R., Rohrbach, L. A., Simons-Rudolph, A., Vincus, A. & Thorne, J. (2003). Factors associated with fidelity to substance use prevention curriculum guides in the nation's middle schools. *Health Education & Behavior*, *30*, 375–391.

Robers, S., Zhang, A., Morgan, R. E., & Musu-Gillette, L. (2015). *Indicators of school crime and safety*: 2014 (NCES 2015-072/NCJ 248036). Washington, DC: National Center for Education Statistics, U.S. Department of Education, and Bureau of Justice Statistics, Office of Justice Programs, U.S. Department of Justice. Retrieved from http://nces.ed.gov/pubsearch/pubinfo.asp?pubid=2015072

Skiba, R. J., Michael, R. S., Nardo, A. C., & Peterson, R. L. (2002). The color of discipline: Sources of racial and gender disproportionality in school punishment. *The Urban Review*, *34*(4), 317–342.

Sobol, R. R., Nickeas, P., & Chachkevitch. (2016, July 20). More than 2,200 shot in Chicago this year, 21 of them kids 13 and under. *Chicago Tribune*. Retrieved from http://www.chicagotribune.com/news/local/breaking/ct-south-west-side-shootings-injure-four-including-girl-6-20160719-story.html

Tileston, D. W. (2010). *What every teacher should know about diverse learners*. Thousands Oak, CA: Corwin Press.

Warner, B. S., & Weist, M. D. (1996). Urban youth as witnesses to violence: Beginning assessment and treatment efforts. *Journal of Youth and Adolescent*, *25*(3), 361–377.

Watkins, D. C., Patton, D. U., & Miller, R. J. (2016). Introduction to the special issue on the intersections of race, gender, and class in the wake of a national crisis the state of Black boys and men post-Ferguson. *The Journal of Men's Studies*, *24*(2), 119–129.

Weiner, L., & Jerome, D. (2016). *Urban teaching: The essentials* (3rd ed.). New York, NY: Teachers College Press.

CHAPTER 3

TEACHER BURNOUT IN BLACK AND WHITE

Martin Haberman

Chapter Objectives

The learner will

1. comprehend the definitions for stress and burnout;
2. identify the sources of stress and burnout for teachers;
3. inspect the rationale for why quitters leave urban or diverse school districts; and
4. discern between teacher stress and burnout in educators of color and their White counterparts.

DEFINING TEACHER STRESS AND BURNOUT

Scholars define teacher burnout as a condition caused by depersonalization, exhaustion, and a diminished sense of accomplishment (Fernet, Guay, Senécal, & Austin, 2012; Schwab, Jackson, & Schuler, 1986). A psychological model of how stress leads to burnout describes it as a syndrome resulting from teachers' inability to protect themselves against threats to

Better Teachers, Better Schools: What Star Teachers Know, Believe, and Do
pp. 31–55

their self-esteem and well-being (Hultell, Melin, & Gustavsson, 2013; Kyriacou & Sutcliffe, 1978). In this model, teachers' coping mechanisms are activated to deal with demands. When those coping mechanisms fail to stem the demands then stress increases and threatens the teachers' mental and physical well-being, ultimately leading to teachers quitting or burning out. Because many of the conditions which determine teacher effectiveness lie outside of their control and because a high level of continual alertness is required, teaching is a high-stress job. A behavioral definition of burnout is a condition in which teachers remain as paid employees but stop functioning as professionals.

The coping skills needed to remain in the classroom require active problem-solving abilities. The case of special-education teachers is both the area of greatest shortage and most leavers, reporting an attrition rate of 43% for fully trained teachers beginning in 1993.Those with low coping skills were most at risk of burnout or leaving. Brownell, Smith, McNellis, and Lenk (1995) identified new special-education teachers' basic problem as an inability to provide instruction resulting from their inability to handle discipline coupled with the fact that their most common coping mechanisms were limited to trying to suppress problems or crying. The National Center for Education Statistics (NCES, 1996) found a correlation between teachers' commitment and children with special needs. Those who leave have an unselfish regard as well but lack the depth of conviction found in teachers who stay. Special education teachers who stay express an altruistic purpose and deep personal obligation to serve their students (Jones, Youngs, & Frank, 2013; NCES, 1996).

Burnouts go through the motions of teaching with no emotional commitment to the task and no sense of efficacy. They have come to believe that what they can do will make no significant difference in the lives of their students and see no reason to continue caring or expending any serious effort. Burnouts remain in teaching as "strong insensitives" who are able to cope with the debilitating problems faced by their students and the negative conditions of work in dysfunctional bureaucracies because they no longer take their failures as a sign of any personal inadequacies. They have become detached job-holders who feel neither responsible nor accountable for students' behavior, learning, or anything else. Their only goal is to do the minimum required to remain employed (Haberman, 1995). While "work appears as a major source of stress for working people, teachers appear to experience more stress through work than non-teachers" (Cox & Brockley, 1984, p. 86), the demands on educators have not eased (Gold & Roth, 2013). In-depth studies have established a clear linkage between prolonged stress and burnout (Blasé, 1986; Wang et al., 2015).

Idealists are the other extreme from the strong insensitive and significantly more likely to leave teaching (Cherniss, 2016; Miech & Elder, 1996). The explanation for the departure of idealists is that because they are deeply committed to serving children they are more easily frustrated by the working conditions in dysfunctional school bureaucracies which prevent them from doing what they deem best in the teaching of their students. In 1963 the Milwaukee Intern Program became the model for the National Teacher Corps. In the 10 years (1963–1972) of the Corps' existence, approximately 100,000 college graduates with high GPAs were prepared nationally for urban teaching. These were idealistic young, White college graduates who set out to "find" themselves by "saving" diverse children in poverty. When they actually encountered the realities of how teachers have to struggle against their school bureaucracies in order to serve children, over 95% of them quit in 5 years or less (Corwin, 1973; Goldring, Tai, & Riddles, 2014). Since this was the largest, longest study ever done in teacher education, the notion that altruism can be the motivation of teachers serving diverse children in poverty should be problematic.

The average length of a teaching career in the United States is now down to 11 years (Ingersoll, Merrill, & Stuckey, 2014; NCES, 2014; Stephens, 2001). One quarter of all beginning teachers leave teaching within 4 years (Benner, 2000). The length of an urban teaching career is even less since 50% of beginners leave in 5 years or less (Day & Hong, 2016; Rowan, Correnti, & Miller, 2002). But teachers who leave have less of a negative impact on schools and students than those who burn out but remain in teaching. It has long been established that burnouts who remain use significantly less task-oriented behavior (i.e., less hands-on, active learning) and provide less positive reinforcement for their students (Hakanen, Bakker, & Schaufeli, 2006; Koon, 1971). The research supports the contention that stress affects teachers' effectiveness with students (Blasé, 1982, Young, 1978). When teachers feel good about their work student achievement rises (Black, 2001; Collie, Shapka, & Perry, 2012). The National Education Association (NEA) has conducted studies spanning 65 years, indicating that teachers experience health problems, absenteeism, and performance let-down as a result of their working conditions (NEA, 1938, 1951, 1967). Since stress causes physical and emotional problems which lead to lower teacher effort and greater teacher absenteeism, the connection between teacher stress and student learning is a significant relationship (Ehrenberg, Ehrenberg, Ehrenberg, & Rees, 1989).

The persistent and pervasive nature of teacher stress studies makes it clear that teaching has become a high-stress occupation. Numerous studies of American teachers, particularly those in urban schools, have documented the high level of stress and burnout among teachers (Cunningham, 1983; Love, 2015). In May, 2000 the National Association of Head Teachers in Great Britain found that 40% of teachers had visited doctors for stress-related problems the previous year; 20% admitted to drinking too much; 15% admitted to being alcoholics; and 25% reported stress-related problems such as hypertension, insomnia, depression, and gastrointestinal disorders. It was also found that 37% of teacher vacancies were due to ill health (Jarvis, 2002). As early as 1933, surveys of American teachers found that 17% of them were usually nervous and that 11% of them had suffered nervous breakdowns (Hicks, 1933). Some stress is inevitable and may be beneficial. This is especially true in teaching where teacher effort and enthusiasm has a positive impact on student learning. At some point however, and this varies for individuals, too much stress is a predictor of poor teacher performance, absenteeism, and teacher turnover (West & West, 1989). The inexorable link between teacher stress and burnout leads researchers to examine the causes of teacher stress. Based on a review of the research, it can be reasonably concluded that teacher stress is a real phenomenon that can reliably be connected to both intrinsic causes which interact with teacher attributes and personal predispositions as well as to external causes which exist in the actual working conditions teachers face. Both intrinsic and extrinsic job stressors affect K–12 teachers who experience physical illness and psychological strain on the job (Evans, Ramsey, Johnson, & Evans, 1985).

OUTSIDE FACTORS AFFECTING STRESS AND BURNOUT

Historically, studies have focused on external causes which are assumed to exist independent of teacher perceptions, these include ambiguous role expectations (Kyriacou & Sutcliffe, 1977); unreasonable time demands (Lortie, 1975); large classes (Coates & Thoresen, 1976); poor staff relations (Young, 1978); inadequate buildings and facilities (Rudd & Wiseman, 1962); salary considerations (Buckley, Schneider, & Yi, 2004; Gritz & Theobold, 1996; Tye & O'Brien, 2002); lack of resources, isolation, and fear of violence (Brissie, Hoover-Dempsey, & Bassler, 1988); and disruptive students (Dunham, 1977; Friedman, 1995). The need for administrative support is also frequently cited as a critical condition of work (Tapper, 1995). Lack of administrative support is a category that includes but is not limited to the following teacher perceptions: principals (a) are "not supportive" if they do not handle discipline to the teachers' liking; (b) do not understand the instructional program the teachers are trying to offer; (c) do not provide the time and resources the teachers believe necessary; (d) do not value teachers' opinions or involve them sufficiently in decision making; (e) do not support them in disputes with parents; or (f) fail to listen to their problems and suggestions.

Low salary as a cause of stress is frequently expressed by teachers as resulting from preparing their students for colleges they cannot afford to send their own children to or from being forced to moonlight. Teachers who moonlight work 10 or more hours per week and believe that extra jobs take a toll on their energy and morale (Henderson & Henderson, 1997). Safety concerns are cited as a cause of stress and low morale by over 62% of teachers in middle and high schools. So too is the need for teachers to annually spend almost $600 of their own money for supplies and equipment they regard as necessary (Lumsden, 1988).

Many factors related to the quality of school buildings affect teacher stress. A synthesis of 53 studies pertaining to school facilities concludes that daylight fosters student achievement (Lemasters, 1999). The positive psychological and physiological effects of daylight have heightened interest in increasing daylight in classrooms (Benya, 2001). Yet 20% of the teachers in Washington, DC, report that they cannot see out of their windows (Corcoran, Walker, & White, 1988). Teachers believe that thermal comfort affects not only the quality of their teaching and student achievement but their morale (Lackney, 1999). Some of the best teachers in the country indicated that when they could control the temperatures in their rooms, their effectiveness increased (Lowe, 1990). Studies of poor indoor air quality have contributed to the development of the concept of "sick building syndrome," which affects both students and teachers. Asthma studies show that both students and teachers lose considerable school time. Two thirds of the teachers in Washington, DC, reported poor air quality as a concern. In a Chicago study that paralleled the DC study, over one quarter of teachers reported asthma and respiratory problems as their most frequent health problem. Another 16% reported health problems linked to poor air quality (Buckley et al., 2004). Noise seems to cause more discomfort and lowered efficiency for teachers than for students (Lucas, 1981). Almost 70% of Washington DC, teachers report that their classrooms and hallways are so noisy they cannot teach. Until the studies by Buckley and associates (2004), there was not a clear link between school facilities and teacher burnout and turnover. They used their data to contend that the benefits of improving physical facilities may even outweigh those derived from pay increases. They argue that since improving facilities is a one-time expense, while salary increases are continuous, that capital improvements may turn out to be as cost effective in the United States as they have proven to be in developing countries (Oliveira & Farrell, 1993).

Several studies seek to weigh or rank the relative importance of the conditions of work causing stress and finally burnout. For example, one study concludes that teachers might be willing to take lower salaries for smaller classes (Hanushek & Lugue, 2000). Others compare the impact of salary with other conditions of work (Murnane & Olsen, 1989). A few studies combine the effects of several conditions of work with demographic factors. The school's management of students' misbehavior and the burden of nonteaching duties affects more-experienced teachers less than new teachers. Experienced teachers are more concerned with maintaining their autonomy and discretion than less-experienced teachers (Macdonald, 1999).

In reviews of teachers' job satisfaction, there have been different effects of different climates on teacher stress. Traditional, rigid bureaucratically administered schools result in low teacher commitment and job satisfaction. Flexible schools that use collaborative problem- solving strategies and promote greater teacher affiliation with the school raise teacher morale. In the more flexible schools, teachers believe they can contribute to positive school change and that their ideas will be sought after and used (Macmillan, 1999).

It is clear that none of these conditions, especially difficult students, can be entirely separated from teachers' perceptions and interaction with these conditions; for example, a class that is deemed too large to work with by one teacher can be managed by another; time demands that one teacher finds impossible to meet are met by another; and, students considered disruptive by some teachers are engaged and hard working in the classrooms of other teachers. There are no conditions of work that exist independently of the teacher's values, perceptions, and personal attributes. Rather than arbitrary distinctions between internal and external causes of burnout, the more useful studies focus on the number of teachers who regard a particular condition of work as negative and the degree to which the particular condition impinges on their performance.

Depersonalization can be defined as a school climate in which teachers perceive that their individual voices have no impact and that even their existence is unnoticed. For example, with automated telephoning for substitutes it is not uncommon for no adult in a school building to know, or particularly care, that a teacher is absent on a given day.

Teachers' feelings of job satisfaction and years of experience were statistically significant predictors of less stress (Konert, 1997). In a study of elementary school teachers, lack of social support, classroom climate, work overload, and lack of participation in decision-making were identified as significantly related to teacher burnout. This study also compared year-round and traditional school calendars and found no differential effects on teacher burnout (Walker, 1998). Differential effects are related to school size; stress appears to be more prevalent in larger school systems than in smaller ones (Green-Reese, Johnson, & Campbell, 1991).

Several recent studies argue that the focus on greater teacher account-ability and high-stakes student testing has forced teachers to follow a "drill and kill" curriculum. This constant and increasing pressure on teachers has made testing and accountability a primary cause of teacher stress (Darling-Hammond & Sykes, 2003). Teachers report stress from teaching in schools that have been designated as failing (Figlio, 2001). It must be noted however, that as teachers become more effective, they are less stressed by testing. In studies of star teachers serving Latino children in Houston, Texas, and African American children in Buffalo, New York, teachers identified as effective with diverse children in poverty did not focus or limit their teaching to preparing their students for tests. These star teachers were able to follow best practice rather than drill and kill and still have children whose test scores improved markedly (Haberman, 1999a). While the accountability movement has certainly made teachers more directly accountable for raising test scores and become a major cause of stress, any reading of the total literature must inevitably conclude that the preponderance of studies still point to lack of discipline and classroom management as the primary cause of teacher stress and burn-out.

In addition to problems which exist in schools, several demographic characteristics are also related to burnout: teachers' age, level of educa-tion, and years married have significant mediating effects on burnout. In one study, religiousness was identified as having a mediating effect on burnout while lack of religiousness was identified as the most significant predictor of burnout (Gonzalez, 1997). Female teachers tend to be more satisfied with their jobs than males; elementary teachers report less stress than secondary teachers; and younger, less-experienced teachers report feelings of greater alienation, powerlessness, and greater stress (Black, 2001). In other words, it is possible to predict that, other things being equal, female, elementary, older, more-educated, more-religious teachers who have been married for longer periods will experience less burnout. The caveat is that experience is a mediating factor until about the 10th year and then becomes a predictor of burnout. These findings also sup-port the contention that the conditions of work in schools do not exist independently but must be strained through the perceptions and value systems of the teachers before they become either causes of teacher burn-out or simply conditions that teachers can cope with or ignore.

The costs to the school systems of teacher turnover have been escalat-ing on an unbroken upward trend line for the last 30 years. In earlier studies, teacher stress and burnout were computed in terms of the cost of simply hiring substitute teachers (Bruno, 1983). More recently, the costs of teacher attrition has been expanded to include the costs of recruiting, hiring and processing new teachers. The current estimate is that teacher stress and turnover now costs school districts 2.6 billion dollars annually. The researchers make a case that this is an underestimate (AEE, 2004). A legitimate claim can be made that these are public funds intended for children and youth in urban school districts which claim to be under-funded and that redirecting 2.6 billion dollars annually to a continuous process of hiring quitters and failures is a misappropriation of funds.

Stress Among Teachers in Rural and Urban Contexts

In comparing stress on rural and urban teachers, it was found that rural teachers perceive too much parental contact as a source of stress while urban teachers regard the lack of parental involvement as stressful. The major difference between the groups was that rural teachers feel greater stress from time demands and the conditions of work, while urban teachers attributed greater stress to student discipline and behavior problems (Abel & Sewell, 1999). In 1995 the Metropolitan Life Survey of 1,011 teachers examined changes in the views and perceptions of teachers from a previous, similar survey conducted in 1984. In this 10-year period, rural teachers perceived improvements in their work environments and expressed positive views regarding their professional recognition and social support while urban teachers perceived the opposite. Urban teachers' perceptions were that their working conditions had deteriorated. They also expressed less positive views regarding their professional recognition and more negative views of their school systems' policies, including curricula and academic standards (Leitman, Binns, & Duffett, 1995).

The Abel and Sewell (1999) study is important because it supports substantial previous literature on teacher stress in rural versus urban schools. This study concludes that urban teachers have greater stress and that there is a clear relationship between their stress and burnout as a result of having difficult classes, problem students, poor classroom climate, poor working conditions, shortage of resources, lack of recognition, and inordinate demands on time leading to burnout.

In urban schools, teachers also use "lack of administrative support" as jargon to signify their belief that the principal has engaged in "dumping," or has "dumped" on them. This means that they believe the principal has assigned too many students with discipline problems, with special needs, those lacking in basic skills, or even too many male students to their classrooms. Other external stress factors commonly cited include the low status of the profession and the inadequacy of training programs which foster unreal expectations (Rudd & Wiseman, 1962).

One indicator of how teachers feel about the conditions of work in urban schools is where the teachers send their own children. In a study of

50 urban school districts, more teachers (29.4%) than the general public (23.4%) sent their children to nonpublic schools. In 29 of the 50 cities, the number of teachers choosing private schools for their own children was greater than for the general public. The disparity was greatest in Rochester, New York, where 37.5% of the teachers and only 14.6% of the general public chose private over public schools (Doyle, Diepold, & DeSchryver, 2004).

In a study of teachers in urban secondary schools, students' lack of discipline and motivation was the primary source of teacher stress and the most significant predictor of burnout (Gonzalez, 1997). In a comparable study of urban middle-school teachers, three conditions of work were identified as significant predictors of stress: higher levels of emotional exhaustion, a depersonalized school climate, and lower levels of perceived accomplishment. These results were equally true for both male and female teachers (Konert, 1997).

URBAN TEACHERS WHO LEAVE

Studies of quitters and leavers identify stress factors as the explanation of why teachers leave a particular school system or teaching entirely. A typical list of why teachers say they leave is very similar to the factors identified in the stress literature and includes overwhelming workload, discipline problems, low pay, little respect, lack of administrative support and the clerical workload. Not surprisingly, the most commonly cited reasons refer to the difficulty of managing children and poor working conditions. The difficult working conditions in many urban schools do discourage beginning (and experienced), teachers but such complaints also raise questions about the validity of these responses, the maturity of the teacher-leavers making these responses, and the quality of the teacher preparation offered those who give these reasons for leaving. The reason for concern over the authenticity of the reasons offered for leaving urban schools is that the negative conditions of work are well known even to the general public and must surely have been known to the teachers accepting positions. Indeed, interviews of high school students indicate quite clearly that even young adolescents are well aware of the negative conditions under which their teachers work (Florida State Department of Education, 1985). Quitters and leavers who offer these reasons for terminating their employment and those who accept and analyze these responses as the complete explanations make the findings of studies on why teachers quit or fail highly problematic.

While poor working conditions most certainly do contribute to teachers leaving, in-depth interviews of quitters and failures from schools serving diverse children in urban poverty over the past 45 years reported by the author reveal other additional explanations for leaving than those gleaned from superficial questionnaires, surveys, and brief exit interviews. Based on actual classroom observations of failing teachers in the Metropolitan Multicultural Teacher Education Program between 1992 and 2003, there are more basic reasons for leaving than those gained from typical exit interviews (Haberman & Post, 1998). The attitude of quitters and leavers which may have at first appeared to indicate a simple, straightforward lack of skills on the part of a neophyte still learning to maintain discipline, can now be recognized as actually representing much deeper issues. Rather than a simple matter which can be corrected by providing more training to caring beginning teachers who understandably just need some tips on classroom management and more experience, an irreconcilable chasm between these teachers and their students is uncovered.

Teacher attrition increases as the number of minority students increases (Rollefson, 1990). According to the Goldring et al., (2014) and Ronfeldt, Loeb, and Wyckoff (2013), schools with 50% or more minority students experience twice the turnover rate as schools with lower minority populations. In a study of 375,000 primary teachers over a 3-year period, researchers found that the greatest tendency of leavers was to switch to schools with fewer minority students, higher test scores, and smaller percentages of low-income students (Hanushek, Kain, & Rifkin, 2002). The same results are obtained when questions are posed in positive terms: that is, when is teacher satisfaction greatest? "Teachers report greatest satisfaction working in schools with students who have high test scores, high graduation rates and where 81% or more of the students are working on grade level" (SCTQ, 2003, p.1). These are also schools serving predominantly White students who are not from low-income families.

Quitters and leavers cannot connect with, establish rapport, or reach diverse children in urban poverty because, bottom line, they do not respect and care enough about the children to want to be their teachers. Such attitudes and perceptions are readily sensed by students who respond in kind by not wanting "those" people as their teachers. Contrary to the popular debates on what teachers need to know to be effective, teachers in urban schools do not quit because they lack subject matter or pedagogy astuteness. If this contention is true, quitters and leavers know how to divide fractions and they know how to write lesson plans. They leave because they cannot connect with the students and it is a continuous, draining hassle for them to keep students on task. In a very short period, leavers are emotionally and physically exhausted from struggling against resisting students for 6 hours every day (Chang, 1999; Klassen & Chui, 2010; Split, Koomen, & Thijs, 2011). Haberman and Post's (1998) classroom observations of failing teachers report never finding an exception to this condition; that is, if there is a disconnect between the teachers and their students then no mentoring, coaching, workshop, class on discipline and classroom management, or class offering more subject-matter content can provide the teacher with the ability to control children s/he does not genuinely respect and care about. This disconnect is most likely to occur between teachers and diverse students in urban poverty. In truth, the graduates of traditional programs of teacher education are "fully qualified" only if we limit the definition of this term to mean they can pass written tests of subject matter and pedagogy. Unfortunately, while knowledge of subject matter and pedagogy are absolutely necessary, they are not sufficient conditions for being effective in urban schools. Knowing what and how to teach only becomes relevant after the teacher has connected and established a positive relationship with the students.

Many who give advice on how to solve the teacher shortage in urban schools frequently assert that "these" children need to be taught by "the best and the brightest." Unfortunately, the typical criteria used to define the best and the brightest identify teachers who are precisely those most likely to quit and fail in urban schools. The majority of early leavers are individuals with higher IQs, GPAs, and standardized test scores than those who stay; more have also had academic majors (Darling-Hammond & Sclan, 1996). Teachers who earn advanced degrees within the prior 2 years leave at the highest rates (Boe, Bobbit, Cook, Whitener, & Leeber, 1997). Those who see teaching as primarily an intellectual activity are eight times more likely to leave the classroom (Quartz, Thomas, Hasan, Kim, & Barraza-Lawrence, 2001). The fact that the shibboleth "the best and brightest" still survives is testimony to the fact that many prefer to maintain their pet beliefs about teacher education in spite of the facts. In effect, the criteria typically used to identify the best and brightest are powerful, valid identifiers of failures and quitters in urban schools.

There is a degree of unreality in the expectations of beginning teachers that leads them to believe that while there will be stressful problems that they personally should be able to avoid them. Beginning teachers want to serve in educational settings where parents are involved, with a supportive principal, and small classes with compliant learners (Farkas, Johnson, & Foleno, 2004). The available positions however are extremely unlikely to be in schools where these are the typical conditions of work. This disconnect, between new teacher education graduates and the needs of the schools serving diverse children in urban poverty, is demonstrated by the number of "fully qualified" graduates who take jobs and by how long they last. Only 58% of the newly certified graduates even take teaching jobs (Yasin, 1999) and of those who teach in the 120 largest urban districts, 50% leave in five years or less. In some states (e.g., New York) only 27% of the "fully qualified" even take jobs (Yasin, 1999). The disconnect between preparation and practice appears to be a systemic breakdown.

TEACHER ETHNICITY, BURNOUT, AND ATTRITION

Of the more than 53 million children in public schools, about 30% are living in poverty. Seven million of them are concentrated in the 120 largest schools districts. The numbers who are members of linguistic or racial/ethnic minority groups is 35% and will reach 40% by the end of this decade. Of the nearly three million teachers, counselors, and administrators, approximately 5% are African Americans, down from 12% in the 1960s (Wilson & Butty, 1999). "Improvements in the recruitment of Hispanic American, Asian American and Native American teachers have been offset by this decline in the recruitment of African American teachers" (Darling-Hammond, 1999, p. 289).

In a summary of the research literature from Texas, Lopez (1995) found that (a) neither written competency exams nor certification predicted teacher quality in the classroom; (b) there were no differences in the classroom performances of teachers with bachelor's or master's degrees; (c) teachers' classroom experience is the most important source of teacher capacity; and (d) it takes 6–7 years of experience for teachers to fully develop the requisite skills and knowledge. The most important finding of this research review was that "Hispanic and African American teachers are able to maximize student performance for classrooms where the teacher's ethnicity is dominant among the classroom student population" (Lopez, 1995, p. 1). If 50% of new teachers leave in 5 years or less then students will not have many teachers who complete the 6 or 7 years of experience needed to reach the level of full skill development. Further, if over 80% of teacher candidates in traditional university-based programs of teacher education are White, the finding that Hispanic and African American teachers maximize students' performance cannot be implemented. The question is whether these data are confined to the State of Texas or represent the situation nationally. The likelihood is that they are representative of the 120 major urban school districts.

In a summary of the research literature in California, Keleher, Piana, and Fata (1999) projected a student population of 6.2 million children, 70% of whom will be students of color by the year 2007. There was a need for almost 30,000 teachers per year in that state's 1,055 school districts. Yet the recruitment of teacher candidates of color is simply not happening (Keleher et al., 1999). In 1999 the number of teacher candidates in California passing the Professional Assessments for Beginning Teachers (Praxis Exam) was 49.3% for Whites, 31.6% for Asian Americans, 27.5%

for Mexican Americans, 25.7% for other Latinos, and 18% for African American. If California is representative of the nation, there is both a shrinking pool of teacher candidates of color and a smaller pool that pass the required state exams for licensure. A few states are trying to fight this trend with financial aid and tutoring programs for minorities in university-based programs. The most powerful recruitment of minorities however continues to occur in on-the-job training programs where adult minorities can be paid while they learn on the job (Keleher et al., 1999).

A 10-year study of 315,442 graduates of public universities in Florida tracked the top ten discipline choices producing African American graduates. Over the decade studied, health science and computer science majors increased and education majors decreased as a percentage of graduates. For African American, White, and Hispanic males business, engineering, and social science remained the top three disciplines. For females, business and education remained the most frequently chosen. This study supports the literature (NCES, 1997) that minorities choose majors in fields that are higher paying and which enable them to recover the costs of their college educations. The study also corroborates the literature that states that in their motivation for choosing majors "the differences between men and women are greater than the differences among race and ethnic groups" (Pitter, Whitfield, Gjazwan, & Posey, 2003).

The question of how to recruit more teachers of color has stymied traditional university-based teacher preparation. With the advent of alternative routes, more minorities are entering teaching, but the problem has not been "solved" if the goal is to have a teaching force representative of the children being taught. This leads to further analysis of the literature on motivation for entering teaching and why Whites or individuals of color choose to become teachers.

The few studies of when African Americans decide to become teachers indicate that approximately 25% decide when they are in elementary school and about half when they are in college. The source of their motivation is relatives, primarily mothers and children. Those who discourage them most are college peers (King, 1993a). Difficult working conditions and the lure of other occupations seemed to influence males more than females. One study of a talented cohort of African American teachers concluded that to attract others like themselves would require providing a great deal more encouragement than is currently typical in the recruiting process (King, 1993a).

Among White populations, teaching diverse children in urban schools has declined in status so that while White women still predominate, they represent lower socioeconomic levels and lower educational achievements than in the past (King, 1993b; Lanier & Little, 1986). These data are supported by the fact that many White teacher candidates are the first-generation college graduates in their families and that with the opening up of higher-status professions to women over the last 40 years (medicine, law, business, engineering, architecture, and others), women students from higher socioeconomic levels and those with stronger educational achievements have not entered teaching, particularly teaching of diverse children in poverty. Among people of color however teaching retains some degree of status. In a study of motivation for teaching among 124 African American college students, it was found that the historical respect given teachers remains. Respondents indicated that family members encouraged them to become teachers. The salary and benefits of the job itself also was a motivating factor. Among African Americans and Hispanics, there is a higher proportion of low income individuals than Whites who perceive a salary range of $30,000–$60,000 per year as a good salary and fringe benefits which now typically exceed 50% as high. The important difference in motivation however was not between ethnic or racial groups but between males and females. This is also true for African Americans. In addition to the typical reasons offered for considering teaching, African American males who do decide to enter teaching perceive themselves as role models, while females claim to be motivated by their love of children (Bauman, 2002).

A review of the literature explaining the shortage of African American teachers makes four basic arguments: first, that elementary and secondary education is inferior for people of color and therefore produces fewer graduates and fewer graduates with the basic skills requisite for higher education; second, that there is declining enrollment in the historically Black colleges that are more supportive and can get their students through college; third, that there are now wider opportunities for African American college graduates to enter higher-status, higher-paying careers than teaching; and finally, that the widespread and growing use of competency and other forms of testing for licensure discriminates against minorities (King, 1993a). There is widespread agreement, supported by data, that three of these arguments are valid. The fourth contention, that testing by states and universities is unfairly keeping minorities out of teaching, is still debated on the methodological grounds used in these studies and by the argument that the commonly used tests have been standardized with diverse populations and are race neutral and valid (Cizek, 1995).

The empirical studies explaining the causes of why teachers either burnout and stay, or leave teaching entirely do not identify different causes for Whites, African Americans, and teachers of other ethnic groups. There is a substantial and growing literature of case studies, exploratory studies, and qualitative studies which do seek to provide insight into the causes of burnout and leaving among the various ethnic groups. Typically, such studies make the following argument: First, that schools represent European American culture, even urban schools serving predominantly diverse children in poverty; that this "cultural imperialism" is accomplished by means of the curriculum content as well as by the policies and procedures by which schools are organized and function; that this school culture is antithetic to both minority children and their teachers, causing lower levels of achievement, higher frequency of suspensions and dropouts, and greater stress among minority teachers. Second, that in these schools dominated by European American culture, African American teachers, especially male teachers, are made spokespersons and are required to represent the "Black" perspective. Being put in the position of cultural representative or spokesperson is identified as a source of stress. The argument is that forcing members of minority groups to serve as spokespersons supports the dominant culture group's stereotypes and maintains a fictitious view of African Americans. The third part of the argument is that the testing and evaluation used in schools is unfair to students of color and causes greater stress among teachers, particularly among teachers of color who are perceived as representative of their group. The final part of the argument is that there is not a critical mass of African American teachers who understand these dynamics and who can serve as an advocacy group with sufficient voice to transform schools and align their curricula, policies, and culture with the cultures of minority students (Madsen & Mabokela, 2000).

There is little in the literature to explain why these conditions result in greater stress for African American males than females, apart from the argument in the Bauman (2002) review, which supports the contention that those African American males explain their motivation to become teachers as driven by their need to serve as role models. More study is needed to define more precisely and specifically what serving as a role model actually means in behavioral terms. For example, there might well be differential effects among teachers who define role models differently. Is a role model one who has succeeded in the dominant European American culture? Is he a model of someone who can succeed in two cultures? Is he a model of someone who pursues learning to develop a particular talent? Is he a model of someone who is willing to sacrifice status and money to serve others? Is he a model of someone who seeks to function as a community leader? This "role model" motivation is directed at teaching in urban schools. A study of 140 African American teachers in suburban schools showed that their primary motivation for teaching was similar to Whites; that is, "imparting knowledge" (Wilson & Butty, 1999).

Several studies have found the reasons African Americans enter teaching are essentially the same as those of Whites. They argue that altruism may not necessarily lead to competence, so the fact that most African American males choose fields outside of education because they are motivated by salary and advancement should not preclude them from being recruited. They may still become good teachers (Shipp, 1999). Others argue that since approximately 25% of teachers are now recruited at the postbaccalaureate level, that this is the greatest pool from which to recruit African American teachers (Clewell & Vallegas, 1999). One 10-year follow-up study of college graduates from fields outside of education who were working as paraprofessionals demonstrated that this could be a viable population for preparing outstanding teachers. After ten years, 94% of this pool, composed of 74% African Americans, was still working as classroom teachers in a highly bureaucratic urban district with debilitating conditions of work (Haberman, 1999b).

There is a growing literature of stories depicting the struggle of individual African Americans as they have pursued teaching careers. These include first-person reports as well as biographies. The stories have a literary and an inspirational quality and are focused on how barriers of discrimination and poverty were overcome. The generalization one might infer from these stories is that great people who want to teach will encounter horrendous obstacles but will overcome them by commitment, perseverance, and ability (Foster, 1997). Stories of personal heroism and sacrifice however are different from analyses of specifically how dysfunctional urban school bureaucracies cause stress, burnout, and attrition, and whether their debilitating impact is different for African Americans or Whites. Stories of great teachers also underscore the fact that these are also great people, and lead to the question of whether a new critical mass of teachers of color can be identified and hired in the twenty-first century.

SUMMARY

A review of the studies focusing on teacher stress indicates beyond any reasonable doubt that classroom management and discipline are cited most frequently and ranked highest as the most pervasive cause of teacher burnout. It is also the most continuously cited teacher concern and dominates teachers' perceptions from student teaching (Cherniss, 2016; Roy, 1974) through retirement (Flook, Goldberg, Pinger, Bonus, & Davidson, 2013; Morton, Vesco, Williams, & Awender, 1997). The second-most powerful cause of stress has to do with teachers' perceptions of administrative support. This is a category of reasons that represents disparities between what teachers believe principals should be doing and what teachers perceive administrators actually doing to facilitate teachers' work. This category is also affected by the climate a principal has established in a school regarding the role of teachers and the specific behaviors they are expected and not expected to perform. Stress is greater in urban schools than rural ones. At the same time, teachers' different personal characteristics lead them to leave, burnout, or cope with the very same objective conditions of work. The attributes which predict burnout, coping, or quitting include age, sex, educational level, grade-level taught, years of experience, religiousness, race/ethnicity, class, and commitment to serving children.

The fact that most teachers are White and that most stress and burnout occurs in schools serving predominantly diverse children in poverty is highly significant. So too is the fact that the highest attrition rates for new teachers is in schools serving minority populations. This relationship between teacher stress and burnout, that tightens with greater student diversity and lower socioeconomic level, was documented decades ago (Goodman, 1980). This trend of traditional teacher education graduates not being able to serve diverse children in poverty in large urban school bureaucracies has not only been thoroughly documented but has continued to worsen during this period. This is in spite of the fact that it is widely known that effective recruitment and selection can reduce job stress. Using screening devices with predictive validity can create a better fit between teachers' abilities and the demands placed on them in bureaucratic school systems. A mismatch between system demands and teacher abilities due to poorly conceived and executed recruitment and selection procedures results in heightened stress levels with negative effects on teachers, students, and school systems (Wiley, 2000).

A set of studies supporting the contention that matching teacher and student ethnicity correlates with greater student learning is accumulating. The evidence indicates that higher teacher retention and greater student achievement is based on positive teacher-student relationships. Since minority teachers relate more effectively with minority students the potential exists for less burnout and attrition to occur if the teaching force were more representative of the students. It would be incorrect, however, on the basis of existing evidence to conclude that simple racial or ethnic matching will decrease teacher attrition and close the achievement gap for diverse children in poverty. If "the" solution were one of simple background matching then school districts such as Washington, DC, or Newark, New Jersey, where teachers and students are from the same ethnic backgrounds, would be among the highest-achieving districts rather than among the lowest. The issue of socioeconomic class differences which separate teachers and students of the same cultural background and which intrude upon the ability of teachers to connect with their students also prevents teachers from establishing the basic relationship required for teaching and learning. There is a paucity of studies dealing with the effects of differences between teachers and students in terms of socioeconomic class.

The literature does not identify differences in the motivation to teach which are related to race or ethnicity, however the historical difference between males and females of all backgrounds remains significant. Teaching is still perceived as a female occupation, and this perception is supported by the content and organization of teacher training and by the ways in which the work of school teachers is organized and administered. In areas where some maleness creeps in (math and science secondary teaching), the shortages of female teachers continues (Ingersol et al., 2014).

The forces that push and pull African Americans into or away from teaching do not seem to differ substantially from those experienced by Whites. Neither do the forces that have thus far been identified as causing stress and burnout. The explanation of the shortage of African American teachers is attributed to the fact that there is a much smaller and shrinking pool of African American males to begin with; that the pipeline from K–12 through university graduation is not increasing; and that African American males who are college graduates have greater access to higher-paying higher-status careers.

At this point the literature can inform us of the causes of stress and burnout, provide some descriptions of the especially debilitating conditions of teaching in urban schools, and summarize the reasons teachers give for entering and leaving teaching. There is no current database to support any expectation that the ethnic/racial gap between White teachers and students of color will be overcome given the demographics of teacher preparation and the conditions of work in bureaucratic, failing school districts. This raises at least three issues worthy of further study. Can the attributes which enable effective teachers to relate to diverse children in poverty and remain working in failing school systems be taught, or should the selection of future teachers focus on individuals who already have these attributes? Given the conditions under which teachers must work in highly bureaucratic school systems and which make burnout and attrition a highly predictable process, what are the most powerful mitigating factors which might counteract or slow down these processes? Do the conditions of work in bureaucratic school systems have differential effects on African American and White teachers? Building a database which answers these questions will enable schools to stop the churn of teachers coming and going at the expense of the children.

CHAPTER QUESTIONS

1. Compare and contrast the terms *stress* and *burnout*. Explain how these terms are similar yet different.
2. In what ways can teachers find job satisfaction, and how important is it for teachers' longevity in the profession?
3. What are reasons that teachers of color enter the profession and how are these reasons different from or similar to their White peers?
4. The 21st century offers new triggers of stress and burnout for urban teachers. Share a list of possible stressors that your 20th century counterparts did not have to deal with in schools. In addition, share some solutions that could support teachers in overcoming these unique new-age stressors.
5. Explore the Internet and search the phrase *teacher stress test*. Take the test and reflect on your score and its meaning. What can you proactively do to continue good stress fitness, and what can you do to reduce stress levels in your life?

ACKNOWLEDGMENT

This chapter originally appeared in *The New Educator* in 2005; volume 1, number 3, pages 153–175; some updates for the in-text citations and references have been included. It is reprinted with the permission of Taylor & Francis.

REFERENCES

Abel, M. H., & Sewell, J. (1999). Stress and burnout in rural and urban secondary school teacher. *Journal of Educational Research, 92*(5), 23–35.

Alliance for Excellent Education (AEE). (2004). *Tapping the potential: Retaining and developing high quality new teachers.* Washington, DC: Alliance for Excellent Education.

Bauman, G. (2002). Motivation for teaching. *The Negro Educational Review, 53*(1), 43–48.

Benner, A. D. (2000). The cost of teacher turnover. *Texas Center for Educational Research.* Retrieved from https://www.tasb.org/About-TASB/Related-Sites-and-Affiliated-Entities/TCER-Reports/documents/17_teacher_turnover_full.aspx

Benya, J. R. (2001, December). Lighting for schools. *National Clearinghouse for Educational Facilities.* Retrieved from http://www.edfacilities.org/pubs/lighting.html

Black, S. (2001). Morale matters: When teachers feel good about their work, student achievement rises. *American School Board Journal, 188*(1), 40–43.

Blasé, J. J. (1982). A socio-psychological grounded theory of teacher stress and burnout. *Educational Research Journal, 18*(4), 93–113.

Blasé, J. J. (1986). A qualitative analysis of sources of teacher stress: Consequences for performance. *American Educational Research Journal, 23*(1), 13–40.

Boe, E. E., Bobbit, S. A., Cook, L. H., Whitener, S. D., & Leeber, A. L. (1997). Why didst thou go? Predictors of special and general education teachers from a national perspective. *The Journal of Special Education, 30*, 390–411.

Brissie, J. S., Hoover-Dempsey, K. V., & Bassler, O. C. (1988). Individual, situational contributors to teacher burnout. *The Journal of Educational Research, 82*, 106–112.

Brownell, M., Smith., S., McNellis, J., & Lenk, L. (1995). Career decisions in special education: Current and former teachers' personal views. *Exceptionality, 5*, 83–102.

Bruno, C. (1983). Equal educational opportunity and declining teacher morale at Black, White and Hispanic high schools in a large urban school district. *The Urban Review, 15*(1), 193.

Buckley, J., Schneider, M., & Yi, M. (2004, February). The effects of school facility quality on teacher retention in urban settings. *National Clearinghouse for Educational Facilities.* Retrieved from http://www.ncef.org/pubs/teacherretention.pdf

Chang, M. (2009). An appraisal perspective of teacher burnout: Examining the emotional work of teachers. *Educational Psychology Review, 21*, 193–218.

Cherniss, C. (2016). *Beyond burnout: Helping teachers, nurses, therapists and lawyers recover from stress and disillusionment.* New York, NY: Routledge.

Cizek, G. J. (1995). On the limited presence of African American teachers: An assessment of research, synthesis and policy implications. *Review of Educational Research, 65*(1), 78–92.

Clewell, B. C., & Villegas, A. M. (1999). Creating a non-traditional pipeline for urban teachers: The pathways to teaching careers model. *Journal of Negro Education, 68*(3), 306–317.

Coates, T. J., & Thoresen, C. E. (1976). Teacher anxiety: A review with recommendations. *Review of Educational Research, 46*(2), 159–184.

Collie, R. J., Shapka, J. D., & Perry, N. E. (2012). School climate and social-emotional learning: Predicting teacher stress, job satisfaction, and teaching efficacy. *Journal of Educational Psychology, 104*(4), 1189.

Corcoran, T. B., Walker, L. J., & White, J. L. (1988). *Working in urban schools.* Retrieved from http://files.eric.ed.gov/fulltext/ED299356.pdf

Corwin, R. G. (1973). *Organizational reform and organizational survival: The teacher corps as an instrument of educational change.* New York, NY: Wiley.

Cox, T., & Brockley, T. (1984). The experience and effects of stress in teachers. *British Educational Research Journal, 10*(1), 83–87.

Cunningham, W. G. (1983). Teacher burnout: A review of the literature. *The Urban Review, 15*, 37–51.

Darling-Hammond, L. (1999). Recruiting teachers for the 21st century: The foundation of educational equity. *The Journal of Negro Education, 68*(3), 254–279.

Darling-Hammond, L., & Sclan, E. M. (1996). Who teaches and why: Dilemma of building a profession for twenty-first century schools. In J. Sikula (Ed.), *Handbook of research on teacher education* (pp. 67–101). New York, NY: Macmillan.

Darling-Hammond, L., & Sykes, G. (2003). Wanted, a national teacher supply policy for education: The right way to meet the "highly qualified teacher" challenge. *Education Policy Analysis Archives.* Retrieved from http://epaa.asu.edu/ojs/article/view/261

Day, C., & Hong, J. (2016). Influences on the capacities for emotional resilience of teachers in schools serving disadvantaged urban communities: Challenges of living on the edge. *Teaching and Teacher Education, 59*, 115–125.

Doyle, D. P., Diepold, B., & DeSchryver, D. A. (2004, September 7). Where do public school teachers send *their* kids to school? *Arresting Insights in Education.* Retrieved from http://files.eric.ed.gov/fulltext/ED485524.pdf

Dunham, J. (1977). The effects of disruptive behavior on teachers. *Educational Review, 19*(3), 181–187.

Ehrenberg, E. L., Ehrenberg, R. G., Ehrenberg, R. A., & Rees, D. L. (1989). School district leave policies, absenteeism and student achievement. *Journal of Human Resources, 26*(1), 72– 105.

Evans, V., Ramsey, J. P., Johnson, D., & Evans, A. L. (1985). The effect of job stress related variables on teacher stress. *Journal of the Southeastern Association of Educational Opportunity Program Personnel, 4*(1), 22–35.

Farkas, S., Johnson, J., & Foleno, T. (2004). A sense of calling: Who teaches and why. *Public Agenda.* Retrieved from http://www.publicagenda.org/files/sense_of_calling.pdf

Fernet, C., Guay, F., Senécal, C., & Austin, S. (2012). Predicting intra-individual changes in teacher burnout: The role of perceived school environment and motivational factors. *Teaching and Teacher Education, 28*(4), 514–525.

Figlio, D. (2001, Fall).What might school accountability do? *National Bureau of Economic Research.* Retrieved from http://www.nber.org/reporter/fall01/figlio.html

Flook, L., Goldberg, S. B., Pinger, L., Bonus, K., & Davidson, R. J. (2013). Mindfulness for teachers: A pilot study to assess effects on stress, burnout, and teaching efficacy. *Mind, Brain, and Education, 7*(3), 182–195.

Florida State Department of Education. (1985). Teaching as a career: High school students' perceptions' of teachers and teaching. Tallahassee, FL. Retrieved from https://ia902707.us.archive.org/15/items/ERIC_ED266088/ERIC_ED266088.pdf

Foster, M. (1997). *Black teachers in teaching.* New York, NY: New Press.

Friedman, I. (1995). Student behavior patterns contributing to teacher burnout. *The Journal of Educational Research, 84*, 325–333.

Gold, Y., & Roth, R. A. (2013). *Teachers managing stress and preventing burnout.* New York, NY: Routledge.

Goldring, R., Taie, S., & Riddles, M. (2014). Teacher attrition and mobility: Results from the 2012–13 Teacher Follow-Up survey first look. *NCES.* Retrieved from http://nces.ed.gov/pubs2014/2014077.pdf

Gonzalez, M. A. (1997). *Study of the relationship of stress, burnout, hardiness and social support in urban secondary school teachers* (Unpublished doctoral dissertation). Temple University, Philadelphia, PA.

Goodman, V. B. (1980). Urban teacher stress: A critical literature review. *ERIC Clearinghouse on Urban Education*. Retrieved from http://eric.ed.gov/?id=ED221611

Green-Reese, S., Johnson, D. J., & Campbell, W. A. (1991).Teacher job satisfaction and teacher job stress: School size, age and teaching experience. *Education, 112*(2), 247–252.

Gritz, R. M., & Theobold, N. D. (1996). The effects of school district spending priorities on length of stay in teaching. *Journal of Human Resources, 31*(3), 477–512.

Haberman, M. (1995). *Star teachers of children in poverty*. Indianapolis, IN: Kappa Delta Pi.

Haberman, M. (1999a). Victory at Buffalo Creek: What makes a school serving Hispanic children in poverty successful? *Instructional Leader, 12*(2), 1–5.

Haberman, M. (1999b). Increasing the number of high quality African American teachers in urban schools. *Instructional Psychology, 26*(4), 208.

Haberman, M., & Post, L. (1998). Teachers for multicultural schools: The power of selection. *Theory Into Practice, 37*(2), 96–104.

Hakanen, J. J., Bakker, A. B., & Schaufeli, W. B. (2006). Burnout and work engagement among teachers. *Journal of school psychology, 43*(6), 495–513.

Hanushek, E. A., Kain, J. F., & Rifkin, S. G. (2002).Why public schools lose teachers? *The Journal of Human Resources, 39*(2), 326–354.

Hanushek, E. A., & Lugue, J. A. (2000). Smaller classes, lower salaries? In S. W. Laine & J. G. Ward (Eds.), *Using what we know: A review of research on class size reduction* (pp. 35–51). Oak Brook, IL: North Central Regional Educational Laboratory.

Henderson, D., & Henderson, T. (1997). *Texas teachers: Moonlighting and morale*. Retrieved from http://files.eric.ed.gov/fulltext/ED398179.pdf

Hicks, F. P. (1933). *The mental health of teachers*. New York, NY: Cullman and Ghertner.

Hultell, D., Melin, B., & Gustavsson, J. P. (2013). Getting personal with teacher burnout: A longitudinal study on the development of burnout using a person-based approach. *Teaching and Teacher Education, 32*, 75–86.

Ingersoll, R., Merrill, L., & Stuckey, D. (2014). Seven trends: The transformation of the teaching force. *CPRE*. Retrieved from http://repository.upenn.edu/cgi/viewcontent.cgi?article=1003&context=cpre_researchreports

Jarvis, M. (2002). Teacher stress: A critical review of recent findings and suggestions for future research directions. *Stress News: International Stress Management Association, 16*(4). Retrieved from http://www.isma.org./uk/stressnw/teachstress1.htm

Jones, N. D., Youngs, P., & Frank, K. A. (2013). The role of school-based colleagues in shaping the commitment of novice special and general education teachers. *Exceptional Children, 79*(3), 365.

Keleher, T., Piana, L. D., & Fata, M. G. (1999). Creating crisis: How California's teaching policies aggravate racial inequality in public schools. *ERIC Clearinghouse on Urban Education*. Retrieved from http://eric.ed.gov/?id=ED458205

King, S. H. (1993a).The limited presence of African American teachers. *Review of Educational Research, 63*(2), 115–149.

King, S. H. (1993b).Why did we chose teaching careers and what will enable us to stay?: Insights from one cohort of the African American Teaching Pool. *Journal of Negro Education, 62*(4), 475–493.

Klassen, R. M., & Chui, M. (2010). Effects on teachers' self-efficacy and job satisfaction: Teacher gender, years of experience, and job stress. *Journal of Educational Psychology, 102*(3), 741–756.

Konert, E. (1997). *Relationship among middle-school teacher burnout, stress, job satisfaction and coping styles* (Unpublished doctoral dissertation). Wayne State University, Detroit, MI.

Koon, J. R. (1971). *Effects of expectancy, anxiety and task difficulty on teacher behavior* (Unpublished doctoral dissertation). Syracuse University, Syracuse, NY.

Kyriacou, C., & Sutcliff, J. (1977). Teacher stress: A review. *Educational Review, 29*(4), 299–306.

Kyriacou, C., & Sutcliff, J. (1978). A model teacher stress. *Educational Studies, 4*,1–6.

Lackney, J. A. (1999). *Assessing school facilities for learning/assessing the impact of the physical environment on the educational process: Integrating theoretical issues with practical concerns.* Retrieved from http://files.eric.ed.gov/fulltext/ED441330 .pdf

Lanier, J., & Little, J. (1986). Research on teacher education. In W. C. Whitrock (Ed.), *Handbook of research on teaching* (pp. 527–569). New York, NY: Macmillan.

Leitman, R., Binns, K., & Duffett, A. (1995). *The American teacher, 1984–1995, Metropolitan Life survey, old problems new challenges.* Retrieved from http://files.eric.ed.gov/fulltext/ED392783.pdf

Lemasters, L. K. (1999). *A synthesis of studies pertaining to facilities, student achievement and student behavior* (Unpublished doctoral dissertation). Virginia Polytechnic and State University, Blacksburg, VA.

Lopez, O. S. (1995). The effect of the relationship between classroom student diversity and teacher capacity on student performance. *ERIC Clearinghouse on Urban Education.* Retrieved from http://eric.ed.gov/?id=ED386423

Lortie, D. (1975). *Schoolteacher: A sociological study.* Chicago, IL: University of Chicago Press.

Love, S. M. (2015). Teaching as urban ministry: Teaching-specific chronic stressors and burnout in urban ministry (Doctoral dissertation). Fuller Theological Seminary, Pasadena, CA. *Proquest.* Retrieved from http://search.proquest.com/docview/1685390202

Lowe, J. M. (1990). *The interface between educational facilities and learning climate in three elementary schools* (Unpublished doctoral dissertation). Texas A&M University, College Station, TX.

Lucas, J. (1981). *Effects of noise on academic achievement and classroom behavior.* Sacramento: California Department of Health Services.

Lumsden, L. (1988). Teacher morale. *ERIC Digest Number 120.* Retrieved from http://files.eric.ed.gov/fulltext/ED422601.pdf

Macdonald, D. (1999). Teacher attrition: A review of the literature. *Teaching and Teacher Education, 15*, 839–848.

Macmillan, R. (1999). Influence of workplace conditions on teachers' job satisfaction. *The Journal of Educational Research, 93*(1), 39–47.

Madsen, J. A., & Mabokela, R. O. (2000). Organizational culture and its impact on African American teachers. *American Educational Research Journal, 37*(4), 849–876.

Miech, R., & Elder, G. H. (1996). The service ethic and teaching. *Sociology of Education, 69*, 237–253.

Morton, L. L., Vesco, R., Williams, N. H., & Awender, M. A. (1997). Student teacher anxieties related to class management, pedagogy, evaluation and staff relations. *British Journal of Educational Psychology, 67*, 69–89.

Murnane, R. J., & Olsen, R. (1989). The effects of salaries and opportunity costs on length of stay in teaching: Evidence from Michigan. *Review of Economics and Statistics, 71*(2), 347–352.

National Center for Educational Statistics. (1996). *The status of teaching as a profession*. Washington, DC: U.S. Government Printing Office.

National Center for Education Statistics. (1997). *The condition of education: Minorities in higher education* (NCES 97-372). Washington, DC: U.S. Department of Education, Office of Educational Research and Improvement.

National Center for Education Statistics. (2014). Highest degree earned, years of full-time teaching experiences, and average class size for teachers in public elementary and secondary schools, by state: 2011–12. *Digest of Education Statistics*. Retrieved from http://nces.ed.gov/programs/digest/d14/tables/dt14_209.30.asp

National Education Association. (1938). *Fit to teach: A study of the health problems of teachers*. Washington, DC: Department of Classroom Teachers.

National Education Association. (1951). Teaching load in 1950. *NEA Research Bulletin, 29*(1), 3–50.

National Education Association. (1967). Teachers' problems. *NEA Research Bulletin, 45*(1), 116–117.

Oliveira, J., & Farrell, J. (1993). Teacher costs and teacher effectiveness in developing countries. In J. Oliveira & J. Farrell (Eds.), *Teachers in developing countries: Improving effectiveness and managing costs* (pp. 7–24). Washington, DC: World Bank.

Pitter, G. W., Whitfield, D., Gjazwan, L., & Posey, J. (2003). Minority participation in majors: A decade of changes in discipline choice and earnings. *The Negro Educational Review, 54*(3/4), 79–90.

Quartz, K. H., Thomas, A., Hasan, L., Kim, P., & Barraza-Lawrence, K. (2001). *Urban teacher retention: Exploratory research methods and findings* (Technical report of the Center X/TEP Research Group, #1001-UTEC-6-01). Los Angeles, LA: UCLA, Institute for Democracy, Education, and Access.

Rollefson, M. (1990). *Teacher turnover: Patterns of entry to and exit from teaching*. Washington, DC: NCES Schools and Staffing Survey.

Ronfeldt, M., Loeb, S., & Wyckoff, J. (2013). How teacher turnover harms student achievement. *American Educational Research Journal, 50*(1), 4–36.

Rowan, B., Correnti, R., & Miller, R. (2002). What large-scale, survey research tells us about teacher effects on student achievement: Insights from the prospectus study of elementary schools. CPRE Research Reports. Retrieved from http://repository.upenn.edu/cpre_researchreports/31

Roy, W. (1974). *The effect of a group dynamic approach to student teaching on cohesiveness, dogmatism, pupil control ideology and perceived problems* (Unpublished doctoral dissertation). University of Wisconsin-Milwaukee.

Rudd, G. A., & Wiseman, S. (1962). Sources of dissatisfaction among a group of teachers. *British Journal of Educational Psychology, 32*(3), 275–291.

Schwab, R. L., Jackson, S. E., & Schuler, R. S. (1986). Educator burnout: Sources and consequences. *Educational Research Quarterly, 10*(3), 40–30.

Shipp, V. H. (1999). Factors influencing the career choices of African American collegians: Implications for minority teacher recruitment. *Journal of Negro Education, 63*(3), 343–351.

Southeast Center for Teaching Quality. (2003). Creating working conditions so teachers can help all students achieve. *Teaching Quality in the Southeast Best Practices & Policies, 3*(2), 1–3.

Spilt, J. M., Koomen, H. M. Y., & Thijs, J. T. (2011). Teacher wellbeing: The importance of teacher-student relationships. *Educational Psychology Review, 23*, 457–477. Retrieved from https://lirias.kuleuven.be/bitstream/123456789/429951/2/Spilt+et+al+2011_Teacher+Wellbeing.pdf

Stephens, C. E. (2001). *Report to the governor on teacher retention and turnover.* Athens: Standards Commission, State of Georgia.

Tapper, D. (1995, May). *Swimming upstream: The first-year experiences of teachers working in New York City public schools.* Retrieved from http://files.eric.ed.gov/fulltext/ED460085.pdf

Tye, B. B., & O'Brien, L. (2002).Why are experienced teachers leaving the profession? *Phi Delta Kappan, 84*(1), 24–32

Walker, E. (1998). *Study of the relationship between burnout and teachers' school schedule: Year-round and traditional* (Unpublished masters thesis). California State University, Long Beach.

West, J. P., & West, C. M. (1989). Job stress and public sector occupations. *ROPPA, 9*(3), 46–65.

Wiley, C. (2000). A synthesis of research on the causes, effects and reduction strategies of teachers stress. *Journal of Instructional Psychology, 27*(2), 80–87.

Wilson, J. W., & Butty, J. M. (1999). Factors that influence African American male teachers' education and career aspirations: Implications for school district recruitment and retention efforts. *Journal of Negro Education, 68*(3), 280–292.

Yasin, S. (1999). The supply and demand of elementary and secondary school teachers in the United States. *ERIC Digests. org.* Retrieved from http://www.ericdigests.org/2000-3/demand.htm

Young, B. B. (1978). Anxiety and stress—How they affect teachers' teaching. *NASSP Bulletin, 62,* 78–84.

CHAPTER 4

THE MYTH OF THE "FULLY QUALIFIED" BRIGHT YOUNG TEACHER

Martin Haberman

Chapter Objectives

The learner will

1. review a brief history of the concentration of young females in teacher education;
2. analyze the ways in which teacher recruitment practices, in teacher preparation programs and candidate selection, maintain young females as America's teaching force;
3. disrupt the falsehood that young beginning teachers are prepared to teach; and
4. consider some suggestions for interrupting the quitter/failure rate of young beginning teachers.

We are not damaged nearly as much by the things we don't know as we are by the things we do know that just aren't so. A myth is defined as "a popular belief or tradition that has grown up around something or some-

Better Teachers, Better Schools: What Star Teachers Know, Believe, and Do
pp. 57–75
Copyright © 2017 by Information Age Publishing

one; especially one embodying the ideals and institutions of a society or segment of society" (Merriam-Webster, n.d.). So how did the myth develop in educational institutions, and accepted by all Americans, that beginning teachers should be young men and women between the ages of 20 and 25?

I recently rented a car at the airport and noticed a large sign on the counter that read: "We do not rent vehicles to individuals under 25." The attendant at a second counter informed me that they had a similar policy of not renting to those under 25. At the remaining three counters I was informed that they would rent cars to those under 25 but that they then required insurance at substantially higher rate. The school bus company in my city has had a "Drivers Wanted" sign out front for as long as I can remember. I stopped in and asked if he would hire anyone below the age of 25 and he said, "No way. The insurance, if you can get it, is triple." In a recent conversation I asked a doctoral student who was an insurance actuary, before developing an interest in educational research, if he knew the reason insurance rates for school bus drivers under 25 would be triple. He explained that young drivers have substantially more accidents and that the official explanation his company used for charging more for those under 25 was, "lacks wisdom and judgment."

I then contemplated my own experiences and those of my friends and colleagues in raising children and grandchildren. We constantly comfort each other when our adolescent and young adult offspring experiment with drugs, tobacco and alcohol, engage in high-risk activities, abuse their health, and waste money on things they can't afford. We worry about where they go, with whom they associate, how late they stay out, and most of all, what they might be doing. My own research, conducted over a period of 55 years, indicates that of those over 30 who claim they want to teach diverse children and youth in poverty, approximately one in three pass my Star Teacher Selection Interview. Of those under 25 who say they would like to teach diverse, children and youth in poverty, the pass rate is 1 in 10.

In reflecting on the implications of the events at the car rental company, the bus company, in my personal life, and in my research, I asked myself what sorts of jobs should be available to young people. After all, we can't discriminate in hiring on the basis of age. The answer was obvious and came to me in a flash. Let's make those lacking the "wisdom and judgment" to drive the school bus the teachers responsible for shaping the mind and character of children and adolescents!

YOUNG TEACHERS: A BRIEF HISTORY OF TEACHER EDUCATION

At the turn of the 19th century, most of the first public school teachers were itinerant males hired into small rural communities. They kept school for a month or two and then moved on. It wasn't long before the local tax-payers realized they could get farm girls to keep school for as long as 8 months a year at much cheaper cost. The typical school marm was a teen-age farm girl, idled by winter, who had the equivalent of a 6th-grade edu-cation. She could read the Bible and do some basic arithmetic. She lived or boarded in the community, meted out the strong discipline expected by parents, and kept order in a multi-age cabin school room. By the Civil War, the teenage school marm was the picture Americans had imprinted in their minds of the "school teacher," and they began reproducing her counterparts en masse. The first public normal schools providing teacher training opened in the 1830s to teenage girls who had completed sixth grade. After the Civil War, there were over 16 publicly supported teacher training schools. By WWI every state had half a dozen or more normal schools training teenage girls to keep school all over America's farm country. These normal schools started as one-year institutions, became two-year institutions in the 19th century and four-year teacher-training colleges in the 20th century (Meyer, 1957).

The normal school movement largely bypassed the urban areas, filled as they were with large numbers of Catholics, newer immigrants and oth-ers regarded as being something less than real Americans. With the exception of Boston, Baltimore, St. Louis, and a very few other cities, there were no publicly supported normal schools in urban areas. The growth and transition from normal schools to teachers colleges to 4-year baccalaureate institutions was essentially a rural phenomenon devoted to the training of teenage farm girls. This history explains the curious fact that the overwhelming majority of America's teachers are still prepared in state colleges located in rural areas surrounded by rural schools; for example, Oswego, New York; St. Cloud, Minnesota; Northern Illinois; Troy, Alabama; and so on. Towns that are inaccessible by bus or rail (e.g., River Falls, Wisconsin) have thriving schools of education. Even today, when most new teacher positions are in cities and suburbs, the "urban emphasis" in teacher training programs is something that had to be grafted on to the "regular" programs as a result of the Civil Rights Move-ment of the 1960s after normal schools had been in operation for 130 years.

After President Lincoln established the land grant universities, they also took on the mission of teacher training. They began by focusing on the training of secondary teachers in need of more subject-matter knowl-edge. After WWI, the land grant universities expanded their programs downward to include the preparation of elementary school teachers. At the same time the teachers colleges, ever on the alert for higher enroll-ments and more male students, expanded their programs upward to include secondary education. The current situation is one in which the preponderance of new teachers are still females under 25, trained in land-grant universities and in former teacher colleges located outside of urban areas.

After WWII, millions of veterans supported by financial aid under the GI Bill began attending colleges and universities. This also increased the number of males entering teacher training programs. The influx of males was accelerated again in the early 1950s when the selective service system (the draft) deferred males from military service if they were enrolled in a college or university. During the Korean War, designated as a "Police Action" but in which over 55,000 soldiers were killed, many young men stayed in college and entered teacher training programs. But these were temporary blips in the history of teacher education. After those eligible for GI benefits graduated, the age of students dropped back down to those under 25, and after the Korean War deferments ended, the number of males entering teacher training dropped significantly. Teaching quickly returned to its normal state of being a predominantly female career and teacher training to regarding "traditional students" as those between 20 and 25.

Why Are Teachers So Young?

It is important to recognize that no group ever consciously decided, on the basis of any theory or research, how old the school marm should be as a requirement for admission into teacher training. The focus was and remains on what level of schooling she has completed and not on her own developmental level and maturity. In the beginning she was only required to have a 6th-grade education and was therefore frequently less than 16 years of age. After the first normal schools developed one-year training programs several mandated that candidates must be 17 but not necessarily high school graduates. It was the lengthening of the teacher training from 1 to 2 years and then from 2 to 4 years that accounted for the increase in the age of beginning teachers and not any concern with the question of the appropriate age at which individuals should be prepared for teaching. Today, since new teachers must have a four-year degree, 90% of graduating teachers are between 20 and 25. The term *nontraditional student* has been coined to designate older adults. The age of the "fully qualified beginning teacher" has advanced simply as a function of the age at which most students typically graduate from college. In recent years, universities and alternative certification programs have recruited college graduates so there are now a substantial number of adults over 30 entering teaching (approximately 10%). Nevertheless, the situation that has remained constant from the 1830s until the present is that a "fully qualified beginning teacher" is typically perceived to be a female under 25. The deep historical and cultural roots of this myth are impossible to shake off.

Added to the power of tradition are the benefits which universities and colleges of education enjoy by training 90% of new teachers while they are late adolescents and young adults. This is the age when students are most likely to be able to devote themselves to full-time study and pay full-time tuition. Schools of education not only support themselves, they are the cash cows that keep the colleges of arts and science stocked with students taking general education courses. The requirement in many institutions that education majors now complete academic majors hasn't hurt the financial state of the university either. Many colleges and universities are able to keep their arts and science colleges as well as their schools of education thriving by admitting and matriculating large numbers of late adolescents as full-time students. As an aside, there is a certain irony in the constant charge that schools of education don't teach future teachers enough subject matter when most of the future teacher's coursework is taken outside of schools of education. In truth, the total university benefits even more than the schools of education by maintaining the myth of the school marm.

The assumption made by all 50 state departments of teacher certification is that the people they certify as teachers are adults who will be teaching children. Without thinking too much about it, the public assumes that teachers represent a mature, adult generation, teaching and socializing a younger generation. The fact of the matter is that late adolescents are declared "adults" at age 18 as a legal matter and not because they have reached an adult stage of development. In the 19th century a teenage girl might have been married, borne and buried children, engaged in the Indian wars, and managed a farm. As a result of her powerful life experiences, a late adolescent growing up in the 19th century was likely to be much more mature than a female college graduate of 20–25 in the 21st century.

When we consider the age and maturation level of youth in high school, it is clear that college graduates between 20 and 25 do not represent an older, mature generation teaching and socializing a younger generation. Today's school marm is in the very same stage of human development as the late adolescents she is supposed to instruct and socialize. She sees the world the same way, listens to the same music, dresses in similar styles, shares the same heroes, and wants the same things. Today's late adolescents and young adults are typically in a state of development that rejects and resists adult authority. They are consumed with concerns such as Will I find someone to love me? Will I be able to earn a living and support myself? How do I become independent of my mother without hurting her feelings? Sociologists and anthropologists who study American society accurately describe the period between ages 15 and 25 as one of self-absorption and a yearning for independence (Bellah, Madsen, Sullivan, Swidler, & Tipton, 1985). I call it the "Age of Me-ness," in which almost every thought and every waking hour is devoted to What do I want? What do I need? What will make me happy? How can I get what I want? In this stage of development, behavior is never independent of, What will my friends think of me if I do this or that? Considering the stages of human development in terms of the needs and drives of people during a particular stage of life, it is clear that there is no more self-centered, anti-establishment period of life than late adolescence and young adulthood. If one considers teaching as an occupation which requires making the needs of others paramount in one's life and in one's work, there can be no worse stage of life to prepare people as teachers than that between 20 and 25.

As a college teacher in the University of Wisconsin-Milwaukee, I received a notice from the university administration specifying what acts constituted student misconduct in campus classrooms and laboratories. The directive specified the student behaviors I should not allow in my classes and provided the telephone numbers of the campus police, health services, and fire department should I need assistance. The student behaviors cited included coming late, leaving early, eating, drinking, reading newspapers, disturbing others, plagiarism, using cells, texting, listening to music, wearing clothing that contained discriminatory slogans, and using laptops for purposes other than those related to the work of the class. This directive was also sent to faculty teaching education courses since, like other college youth, students in teacher preparation programs engage in these same behaviors.

Apparently, a remarkable degree of maturation occurs in education students between the time they graduate from the university in June and the time they assume the roles of fully responsible teachers in September. In 3 or 4 months they are transformed from perpetrators to enforcers. Is it reasonable to assume that over a summer, newly minted teachers transform themselves from impolite, disinterested, disruptive students into the official representatives of adult authority committed to enforcing the rules and regulations of the school systems where they have been hired as teachers? My explanation of why young, beginning teachers find discipline and classroom management so difficult (their number one problem) is that they find it too great a leap to assume the role of rule enforcer and representative of "the system" when they themselves are still mired in the stage of questioning and resisting, even fighting adult authority. If the late adolescent/young adult teacher still perceives herself in the role of a "cool student," she empathizes with students resisting school rules and adult authority. She cannot enforce school rules with the confidence and commitment required to make those rules effective. If the teacher doesn't really believe school rules make sense and are fair, how likely are her students to believe it?

Many high school principals say that they like to hire young teachers because the values and outlook they share with their students enables them to establish rapport and make the curriculum relevant. This naïveté is made evident when the very same principals then complain because so many of their new teachers are not able to establish discipline and elicit respect for school rules. The principals attribute this failure to their teacher training. It is not the case that young teachers do not receive training in discipline and classroom management but rather they are in a stage of development which prevents them from wanting or being able to represent authority. If the teacher is herself still a late adolescent or young adult predisposed to fight "the system" (i.e., adult authority), she cannot serve as a model encouraging high school students to obey and see the value in school rules. The nature of adolescence is to resist all rules per se. Because of the nature of the stage of development she is in, the young teacher is caught in a serious internal conflict. Her emotional attachment will be with students resisting school rules. This empathy will exert a far greater influence on her behavior than any cognitive notion that "schools cannot function without order." This problem of not wanting to be perceived as an authority figure will be exacerbated further by the young teacher's need to be liked and admired by her students; after all, she, like her students in this stage, is desperate for the admiration of friends. The dilemma for many young beginning teachers is that they need the approval of friends more than they want students.

In five years or less 46% of all teachers quit. In some of the major urban districts more than 50% of beginners quit in less than three years. Beginning teacher attrition continues to increase (National Commission on Teaching and America's Future, 2003). Recruiting "the best and the brightest" is an ancillary myth that makes the situation even worse. A Department of Education study found that new teachers who scored the highest on college entrance exams are twice as likely to quit as those with lower scores (Hanushek, 2009). Much of this churn (i.e., the coming and going of beginning teachers) is due to the terrible conditions of work in the schools and to the fact that young women tend to be more mobile as they marry. However, my studies indicate that the primary reason beginning teachers leave is because they cannot handle discipline and because they don't get the administrative support they need to control the students. The studies of why teachers quit give many reasons, however it is clear that their coming and going, especially in schools serving diverse students in poverty, is not a function of racial differences between teachers and students but is clearly connected to the teacher's age and level of maturity (Sabir, 2007).

According to the Alliance for Excellent Education (2005), the school marm myth costs school districts over $5 billion per year in hiring costs. The problems are that these districts keep replacing quitters and failures with new teachers from the same immature population. In some major school districts it is possible to be hired as a teacher without ever having to speak to another human being. Candidates are hired by completing paperwork; supplying transcripts, licenses, references; and sending in the results of medical exams and criminal checks. Interviews are with principals for placement into a particular school only after the candidate has been hired as a teacher in the district. The directors of many of the human service departments who hire the teachers in urban school districts across America believe they are too busy to have all the candidates personally interviewed. In place of a personal interview it is common for these districts to use online screeners. Candidates take a multiple choice test online. (There is no way to prevent a teacher applicant from having a savvier friend take her telephone or computer interview. I have turned down many such requests.) I have never been able to identify another job, even the most menial, which can be obtained without having to speak to another human being in some sort of interview. Even a part-time job as an assistant chambermaid or washing cars requires applicants to speak to someone in a face-to-face situation. The notion that individuals can be hired into sensitive positions such as teachers without being personally interviewed leads one to suspect the intelligence of those in the school districts' human resource departments. If they stopped for a moment to consider why they are too busy hiring people to spend the time needed to interview them, they might come up with the possibility that not using in-depth valid in-person interviews of applicants results in them continually hiring the wrong people, namely, the "fully qualified bright young teacher."

Over 1,200 schools, colleges, and departments of education turn out an estimated 500,000 youngsters each year as "fully qualified." To address critics such as myself, many of these institutions also offer boutique programs for 20 or 30 nontraditional, older students. Colleges and universities ought to reverse their emphasis and should focus on adults over 30 as the primary population to prepare for teaching and maintain their boutique programs for the one in ten students under 25 who are sufficiently mature to actually become "fully qualified." Clearly this will never happen. There is too much at stake financially and structurally for universities to make changes which will threaten their financial stability. Change is something we in the university pronounce as the responsibility of others. Because we will continue to spew out young teachers and therefore continue the churn of quitter/failures passing through the K–12 schools, we can safely predict that public schools will continue to deteriorate. Every 2 years American schools provide enough dropouts to create a city the size of Chicago (Befanz & Rutgers, 2004).

It is interesting that while it is clearly the role of higher education and not the lower schools to provide the schools with effective teachers, this glaring failure is rarely if ever mentioned; it is the K–12 schools that are attacked for having poor teachers, as if their poor teachers sprung from the head of Zeus. After hiring the 21st century school marms, today's school systems then spend billions trying to upgrade teachers they never should have hired initially. Unfortunately, no teacher development programs or merit pay schemes will transform quitter/failure teachers into effective ones. No school can be better than its teachers. The single most important factor affecting student achievement is teacher effectiveness, and teacher effects are cumulative and additive. One bad teacher needs three good teachers in a row to compensate (Sanders & Horn, 1998). The system of schools of education ensconced in universities selling courses to late adolescent and young adult females will never provide a sufficient number of the effective teachers America needs.

The rationale for the certification laws in all 50 states is based on the belief that in order for children to learn they must have teachers who understand the nature of their development. Early childhood teachers are supposed to be expert on the nature of children between 5 and 8, elementary teachers on the nature of children up through age 12, middle and secondary school teachers on the nature of pre-adolescents and adolescents. This great commitment to knowing the developmental stage of the learner as a prerequisite for being able to teach them is completely ignored once students enter the university. College faculty, including those in schools of education, know little if anything about the developmental stages of their students or how instruction should be differentiated to best meet the needs of students in various stages of development. In the university, adults aged 18 to retirement age are instructed in the exact same ways and are expected to learn in the exact same ways. The assumption that school districts make when they assume the teachers they hire between the ages of 20 and 25 are in an adult stage of development is merely an echo of the mistake the universities have made in training individuals in this age group.

It is important to recognize that 25% of the newly minted teachers are male and this translates into foisting as many as 150,000 "fully qualified" young males on children and youth every year. I have not discussed this population since late adolescent, and young adult males in this age group are even less mature than females. I assume the reader will readily extrapolate the argument presented here regarding the school marm to males in the 20–25 age group. The legalized insanity of certifying a 22-year-old male to shape the character and inspire learning among middle and high school youth boggles the mind; it requires us to simply ignore the nature of the thoughtless, self-centered behavior of males socialized into American society at this stage in their development. These irresponsible, self-centered young men, "lacking wisdom and judgment," are somehow transformed into responsible adults capable of serving as role models by virtue of receiving a teaching certificate. The straw man wanted brains and the Wizard of Oz gave him a diploma.

THE NATURE OF ADULTHOOD AND ITS RELEVANCE TO YOUNG TEACHERS

Teachers' knowledge of subject matter is a necessary but not sufficient condition for becoming effective. Adolescents do not care how much their teachers know until after they have accepted them as their teachers. Students accept and respond positively to teachers if they perceive them as being fair, helpful, and concerned with them as individuals. The willingness and ability to encourage students, many of whom are not particularly lovable, is the essence, the very soul of teaching. Secondary students are pushed by hormones and pulled by their friends into attitudes and activities that are not necessarily conducive to learning. Effective teachers, because they are in an adult stage of development, do not allow students' poor or disappointing behavior to shake their positive views of students as individuals worthy of respect. Ineffective teachers cannot separate students' misbehavior from their perceptions of students' worth as persons. Secondary students are not looking for another friend; they already have enough peers. Juxtaposing the demands placed on young teachers who are themselves in need of reassurance and the support of friends, with the needs of students for encouragement from a confident, respected teacher, highlights the irrationality of teachers and students being in the same stage of development.

Lest the reader be misled into believing that this argument is germane to only teaching in urban schools, consider the following interaction I transcribed between a class of all White high school seniors in a high-achieving suburban high school and a young White teacher in her first year of teaching. The class is conducting an end-of-the-year review in preparation for taking the final exam.

> Teacher: You guys need to listen. I already know the answers to the final, so I am not doing this for me.

Student 1:	Can't you just tell us the answers. That way we can just go through them.
Teacher:	No. That's not how it works, but what I can do is give you the information that you need to know to figure out the answers for yourself.
Student 2:	Ms. Parker, I'm not going to lie. I really don't care about this final because this is my least favorite class.
Teacher:	Well, you are my least favorite student so that does not surprise me.
Class:	Whoa!
Teacher:	Okay, calm down. We need to get through this because if we don't you will not be ready for the final.
Student 3:	Isn't, like, your job to teach us? If we are not ready it's not our fault, it's yours.
Student 4:	Yeah. You should let us use our notes for the final.
Teacher:	Okay, enough. If you guys don't want to do anything, then I can't make you! Those of you who want to study please move to this side of the room. Those of you who don't care, just leave. Go home. Sit on your couch where it is a lot more comfortable. We don't want you here anyway.
Student 1:	So we can just leave?
Teacher:	I'm sorry. I am no longer engaging in your idiotic conversation. I will be working with the students who want to learn.
Student 1:	Okay. See you guys later [student leaves room].

This is a teacher with 30 credits of A in education courses including an A in student teaching. I have over 400 of such dialogues which demonstrate how immature teachers cause and escalate their own problems. Lacking "wisdom and judgment" and being in the same stage of development as their students, they quibble with them as peers rather than dialogue with them as a mature adult who is leading and encouraging an adolescent.

In the more than 5,000 observations I have made of teachers, the result of placing young teachers with secondary students is that it is not the teachers who socialize the students but the students who socialize the teachers. The ways in which the classes are conducted, the effort that students put forth, and the amount of learning that occurs is controlled by the students, not the teachers. The dynamic by which this occurs is straightforward. Students reward teachers by complying with their directions and punish them by resisting teachers' instructions. Students' compliance leads teachers to regard a lesson or activity as successful. On the other hand, students' resistance leads teachers to discontinue activities that are hard to manage even if they may be more educative. Through this process, young teachers, dependent as they are on students' compliance, approval, and affection, have their instructional behavior shaped by their students' preferences. In effect, the ways in which young beginning teachers teach are the ways their students want to be taught; teachers who resist having their behavior shaped by students become mired in classroom management issues and are driven out.

Adult Developmental Models

Kohlberg's Theory of Moral Development

The theoretic basis for recognizing the inappropriateness of making late adolescents and young adults teachers has been known for some time from a variety of sources. Adults who attain a more mature level of development will have a stronger and more reasonable sense of who they are and are more self-accepting. Greater maturity increases the likelihood that individuals can become more confident, more inner-directed and more motivated by intrinsic rewards. This does not mean that all adults are capable of becoming teachers. Only one in three of those of aged 30 and above who say they would like to teach can pass my Star Teacher Selection Interview. Teaching is a moral craft. Only adults who have reached the most mature levels of their own development have the potential for focusing on their students rather than on themselves, encouraging learning and providing the skills for succeeding in the world of work. Kohlberg's theoretic formulation of moral development is framed in terms of what concerns people have as they pass through six stages of development:

1. Level I. Concern about obedience
2. Level II. Concern with satisfying needs and wants
3. Level III. Concern with conformity
4. Level IV. Concern with preserving society
5. Level V. Concern with the social contract, that is, "What is right beyond legal absolutes?"
6. Level VI. Concern with universal, ethical principles (Kohlberg, 1976).

According to Kohlberg (1976), many attain Level IV by age 25 and begin to focus on reasoning in accordance with basic democratic principles, but only 10% of those in their twenties ever reach Levels V and VI. Based on their experiences as a college teacher and a psychologist,

Springthall and Springthall (1981) believe that while students are capable of thinking on Levels V and VI, they rarely do.

Erikson's 8 Stages of Human Development

Erikson contends that only mature adults overcome the stage of "self-absorption." His eight stages of human development are trust vs. mistrust (first year); autonomy vs. doubt (2nd and 3rd years); initiative vs. guilt (4th and 5th years); industry vs. inferiority (ages 6–11); identity vs. role confusion (ages 12–18); intimacy vs. isolation (ages 18–25); generativity vs. self-absorption (middle age); and integrity vs. despair (old age). "Generativity" refers to concerns about the next generation either through parenting or in general. In Erikson's formulation, this means an individual must resolve the issue of intimacy vs. isolation before reaching the level of concern for children (Erikson, 1963). A fundamental assumption of all developmental theories is that an individual must pass through all the preceding stages in sequence and that each stage is prerequisite for the next. Using Erikson's model, Marcia studied college youth and found that only 22% developed identity, which Erikson contends should occur between ages 12 and 18. Marcia described the other 78% in states of "identity moratorium, foreclosure or diffusion." She defined and sequenced these states in the following manner: "moratorium" is a search for oneself prior to making a life commitment (28%); "foreclosure refers to accepting whatever authority figures prescribe (26%); and "diffusion" refers to a stage in which there is no commitment to any person, philosophy, or set of beliefs, that is, living for the moment and not delaying gratification (Marcia, 1976). A subsequent study placed 24% in this stage (Waterman, 1985). If those doing follow-up studies on Erikson's model are right, then the number of college youth thinking about people other than themselves is about 22%.

Piaget's Theory of Cognitive Development

The classical developmental model of cognition is Piaget's theory of cognitive development (Inhelder & Piaget, 1958). In this model, it is clear that an individual should reach at least the fourth stage of development before teaching others. This stage describes formal operations and refers to the following abilities: (a) abstract thinking: the ability to think about possibilities and not be constrained by concrete reality; (b) propositional thinking: the ability to think about the relationship among ideas, concepts, and propositions; (c) combinatorial thinking: the ability to generate all combinations of ideas as well as cognitive operations; (d) hypothetical-deductive thinking: the ability to think scientifically about the definition and control of variables, and about the generation, testing, and revision of hypotheses; (e) the ability to think ahead to the solution to problems by defining problems, planning, selecting strategies, and revising; (f) the ability of metacognition, including thinking about cognitive processes, memory, learning, and language; and (g) the ability to be self-reflective about cognitive processes, identity existence, morality, and personal relationships. It should be obvious that those who would teach others would be at this level of cognitive development, however, in my search of the research and theoretical literature of college teaching, I have found no evidence anywhere that these are typical behaviors of undergraduates. When I ask college teachers about the prevalence of these attributes among the undergraduates they teach, their typical response is laughter. If college youth have not attained higher levels of thinking in 4 or more years at the university, how likely is it that they will then develop them in the summer before taking their first teaching position?

In studying the content of college students' reasoning, some researchers have followed them through 4 years of college (Perry, 1981). In the early stages, students are moral and intellectual absolutists: there are correct solutions for every problem and authorities are assumed to know what these are. In the next stage, students are relativistic: one opinion is as good or as useless as another. This seems to be the stage of teacher-education students at the time of graduation. In the final stage of this model, not typical of undergraduates, individuals become committed to a search for and an expression of their own identity.

Ancillary Models

Other models of adolescent and adult development focus on the development of the individual's beliefs and assumptions regarding the nature of knowledge itself (Kitchener, 1986). Beginning with direct experience as the support for an absolutist view, Kitchener moves through stages of weighing conflicting perceptions (relativism) and concludes with a stage in which a mature view of reality combines personal experience with expert opinion, research, and multiple ways of knowing. It is indeed ironic that young beginning teachers are still in a late adolescent stage of focusing on their own personal experiences as the most valuable mode of learning but rarely extend this ideological commitment to the way they try to teach children and youth. It is the hallmark of immaturity that young adults worship their own personal experiences as the ultimate way of knowing but are driven by their need for control to focus on only vicarious learning (i.e., texts and seat work) as the way they teach others. Allowing experiments and hands-on learning all make discipline and class control more difficult.

I believe that most teacher educators would agree with my contentions regarding their preservice students' immaturities and find teaching them a constant battle to get them to think, reflect, and base their actions on a knowledge base rather than on personal preferences and untested beliefs. While they are savvy enough to not admit this publicly, most teacher educators are well aware of the adolescent, even childlike stage in which many of those they certify still find themselves. We have known for a long time that as graduation and certification approaches, preservice students' concerns narrow significantly until they can think of nothing but discipline and classroom management (Roy, 1974). "Will I be able to control the class?" becomes such an all-consuming, overwhelming fear that there is little thinking at any level. In Kohlberg's (1976) formulation, this is a moral stage that precedes even late adolescence and characterizes the need for power and control that is characteristic of early adolescence. Finally, the most complete summary of the research and developmental theory dealing with young adults 18–25 leads to the inescapable conclusion that this is clearly the wrong stage of development in which to locate teacher training (Pintrich, 1990). I find it sad but revealing that I have never encountered a teacher educator who has ever referred to, cited, or even read this definitive summary of young adult development.

SOME FINAL NOTES

What I have argued may very well support the contention that all university-level education is wasted on most people before the age of 25 but such an analysis is beyond the scope of this paper. The decade after WWII is often referred to as the "Golden Age of Higher Education," because the millions of war veterans who entered universities under the GI Bill were older and more mature as a result of their life experiences. University faculty found them much more amenable to higher levels of thinking. Similarly, the period from 1963–1973, when the National Teacher Corps attracted 100,000 more mature college graduates into teaching, was considered by many to have been a golden age for teacher education.

This analysis has focused on the preparation of young adults who become secondary teachers because it is undeniable that this is peer teaching rather than an older generation teaching and socializing a younger one. I believe, however, that the case for not using young adults as beginning teachers of elementary age children is equally strong but would require a more elaborate analysis than space here permits. Essentially, the same degree of cognition and emotional development is necessary for teaching at every level, and I am just as concerned with immature young adults teaching 4-year-olds as I am with them trying to teach geometry to adolescents.

Nowhere have I taken the position that all experienced teachers are good simply because they have aged and not quit. Many should be removed. It is important to recognize that many people simply grow older and never attain the levels of maturity and development described by any of the theorists. Many experienced teachers are not learners and therefore do not grow. As a result, they do not have 30 years of experience; they have one year of experience 30 times. My contention is that selecting, preparing, and hiring individuals over 30 will be three times more effective than maintaining the myth of the "fully qualified young teacher," who will never take a teaching job or who is likely to be a failure/quitter teacher if she does. This analysis is not an advocacy for preventing all individuals younger than 25 from becoming teachers but for being more selective. If hiring officials used validated forms of interviewing, I would estimate that as many as 50,000 young teachers under 25 could be identified each year who have reached the level of maturity needed for teaching and who could meet the demands of functioning as teachers of record in even the most challenging situations. While this is only 1 in 10 of the teacher education graduates, it represents a sizable population who are needed and who should not be overlooked. It should.also be noted that many of the very same individuals who are not sufficiently mature to be teaching before age 25 may be highly effective teachers if they enter the profession in their 30s or later.

In the final analysis, whether or not an individual comes down on the side of wanting teachers to be more mature or younger depends on how complex he perceives the teacher's job to be. According to Thies-Sprinthall and Sprinthall (1987),

> We need to specify which kinds of behaviors can be predicted by developmental stage and which are irrelevant. If, for example, we wanted persons to perform some kinds of mindless, jejune task, their level of cognitive stage would probably demonstrate little correlation to successful performance. On the other hand, if the task required higher-order abilities such as understanding and applying abstract concepts in a humane mode, then indeed the level of psychological maturity and the level of cognitive development may be important predictors. And it probably comes as no great surprise to say that such outcomes are supported by multiple research studies. The most general study was done by Douglas Heath (1977) in his studies of adult success in four countries. He used a multiple index of success and quality of life, and he used over 200 predictors. He found that there were four general developmental characteristics which were highly relevant to success: a) symbolization of experience, b) allocentrism i.e. empathy, c) autonomy, and d) a commitment to democratic values. The common or standardized predictors such as academic grade point average and scores on the Scholastic Aptitude Test were meaningless with one exception: in his American sample there was an inverse correlation between success in adulthood and SAT score. (pp. 68-69)

RECOMMENDATIONS

I have four specific recommendations. University based teacher education needs to continue to expand the trend of making its programs more available to older adults. In addition to the traditional criteria, entry into university based programs of teacher preparation need to include validated interviews of candidates' values and predispositions to ascertain their level of development. School districts need to use validated interviewing instruments to determine the likelihood that the young adults they hire will be effective and remain in teaching for 5 or more years. A career ladder needs to be developed for young newly certified teachers who have not yet reached the level of mature adulthood so that they may be hired as paraprofessionals and work toward becoming regular teachers after they have attained an appropriate level of development.

Given the unlikelihood that these changes will be made, it is not difficult to predict that the quality of schools will continue to deteriorate. As large numbers of immature quitter/failure teachers continue to pass through the profession, they will waste their own time and money, the precious school years of their students, and broaden the educational wasteland. The myth of the young school marm is alive and well. Our society's traditions and convictions can be greater enemies of the truth than outright lies.

CHAPTER QUESTIONS

1. At what age and why did you decide to become a teacher? What function did gender roles, by you and your family, have on your decision to pursue teaching as a career?

2. Reflect on your teacher preparation program. What were the qualifications for becoming a teacher in your program? Are these qualifications rigorous enough for today's K–12 schools? Why or why not?

3. What was the average age of the graduates in your teacher preparation program? What percentage of the teachers in your teacher preparation program is female and male? What were the overt and covert recruitment practices that may have contributed to the numbers reflected in your teacher preparation program?

4. What is the nature of adulthood and its relevance to beginning teachers? In your response, cite a minimum of two human development theories.

5. There are four recommendations offered in this chapter to identify
    mature beginning teachers. Please speculate if any of these recom-
    mendations could be successfully implemented and share the sup-
    portive structures and/or roadblocks for each.

ACKNOWLEDGMENT

This was the last piece written by Martin Haberman and it was
bequeathed to the Haberman Educational Foundation, Inc.; all rights
reserved.

REFERENCES

Alliance for Excellent Education. (2005). *Teacher attrition: A costly loss to the nation
and to the states.* Washington, DC: Author.

Befanz, K., & Rutgers, C. (2004). *Locating the school dropout crisis.* Baltimore, MD:
Johns Hopkins University Press.

Bellah, R. N., Madsen, R., Sullivan, W. M., Swidler, A., & Tipton, S. M. (1985).
Habits of the heart. Berkeley: University of California Press.

Erikson, E. (1963). *Childhood and society: The landmark work on the social significance
of childhood.* New York, NY: Norton.

Hanushek, E. A. (2009). Teacher deselection. In D. Goldhaber & J. Hannaway
(Eds.), *Creating a new teaching profession* (pp. 163–180). Washington, DC:
Urban Institute Press.

Heath, D. H. (1977). Academic predictors of adult maturity and competence. The
Journal of Higher Education, 613–632.

Inhelder, B., & Piaget, J. (1958). *The growth of logical thinking from childhood to adolescence.* New York, NY: Basic Books.

Keating, D. P. (1980). Thinking processes in adolescence. In J. Adelman (Ed.),
Handbook of adolescent psychology (pp. 211–246). New York, NY: Wiley.

Kitchener, K. S. (1986) The reflective judgment model: Characteristics, evidence
and measurement. In R. A. Mines & K. S. Kitchener (Eds.), *Adult cognitive
development: Methods and models* (pp. 76–91). New York, NY: Praeger.

Kohlberg, L. (1976). Moral stages and moralization. In T. E. Likona (Ed.), *Moral
development and behavior: Theory, research and social issues* (pp. 2–15). New York,
NY: Holt, Rinehart and Winston.

Marcia, J. (1976). Identity six years later: A follow-up study. *Journal of Youth and
Adolescence, 5,* 145–160.

Merriam-Webster. (n.d.). *Myth.* Retrieved from http://www.merriam-webster.com/
dictionary/myth

Meyer, A. E. (1957). *An educational history of the American people.* New York, NY:
McGraw-Hill.

National Commission on Teaching and America's Future. (2003). No dream
denied: A pledge to America's children. *National Commission on Teaching and*

America's Future. Retrieved from http://nctaf.org/wp-content/uploads/no-dream-denied_summary_report.pdf

Perry, W. G. (1981). Cognitive and ethical growth: The making of meaning. In A. W. Chickering (Ed.), *The modern American college* (pp. 76–116). San Francisco, CA: Jossey-Bass.

Pintrich, P. R. (1990). Implications of psychological research on student learning and college teaching in teacher education. In W. R. Houston (Ed.), *Handbook of research on teacher education* (pp. 826–857). New York, NY: Macmillan.

Roy, W. E. (1974). *The effect of a group dynamics approach to student teaching on group cohesiveness, dogmatism, pupil control ideology and perceived problems* (Unpublished doctoral dissertation). University of Wisconsin-Milwaukee.

Sabir, M. (2007). *The impact of the conditions of work in urban schools on outstanding African American and European American teachers* (Unpublished doctoral dissertation). University of Wisconsin-Milwaukee.

Sanders, W. L., & Horn, S. P. (1998). Research findings from the Tennessee Value-Added Assessment System. *Journal of Personnel Evaluation in Education, 12*(3), 247–256.

Sprinthall, R. C., & Sprinthall, N. A. (1981). *Educational psychology: A developmental approach*. Reading, MA: Addison-Wesley.

Thies-Sprinthall, L., & Sprinthall, N. A. (1987). Experienced teachers: Agents for revitalization and renewal as mentors and teacher educators. *Journal of Education, 169*(1), 65–77.

Waterman, A. (1985). Identity in the context of adolescent psychology. *New Directions for Child and Adolescent Development, 30*, 5–24.

CHAPTER 5

CHARACTER IS DESTINY

My Journey to Becoming a Star Teacher

Sherese Mitchell

Chapter Objectives

The learner will

1. identify characteristics of a star teacher's beliefs;
2. consider how reflection and self-awareness of one's life history can provide insight into one's character; and
3. evaluate how closely aligned one's core beliefs are to Haberman's seven midrange functions.

While attending a national conference in the spring of 2013, I had the pleasure of meeting Mrs. Delia Stafford-Johnson. We discussed Dr. Martin Haberman (1932–2012) as well as my experience as an educator. I learned that much of Haberman's life was dedicated to researching teachers' success in urban schools and teaching children in poverty. The longer we spoke, the more I came to realize that perhaps I too was a star teacher. Like stars, I truly value student learning and realize that I have a place in education to assist in shaping young minds. Star teachers are defined as

Better Teachers, Better Schools: What Star Teachers Know, Believe, and Do
pp. 77–99
Copyright © 2017 by Information Age Publishing

teachers who are "so effective that the adverse conditions of working in failing schools or school districts do not prevent them from being successful teachers" (Haberman, 2004a, p. 53).   I am a good teacher, but am I a "star" teacher? The evidence for such a query would inevitably be found in my students' academic success, which was nurtured by our positive relationships in the classroom.

Teachers are tested in America's classrooms and schools daily. Those who can draw from a lifetime of strengths and understanding of who they are at their core will not only just survive, but also thrive. The experiences that teachers encounter in their personal lives and teaching careers will shape their character and, in turn, determine their academic success with learners. Haberman elaborates in *Star Teachers: The Ideology and Best Practice of Effective Teachers of Diverse Children and Youth in Poverty* (2004b) that there are background aspects that foretell who will remain in schools serving diverse students in poverty and who will be effective doing so. Haberman (2010) deduces "[Star] teachers are not born. They develop the appropriate ideology and relationship skills by reflecting upon, learning from and benefiting from their life experiences" (p. 216). Taking his lead, I chart the development of my character, critically examine my own life history alongside Haberman's seven midrange functions or dispositions as my guide, and offer a rationale for why critical star assessments by new and seasoned teachers are important.

MAPPING THE DEVELOPMENT OF MY CHARACTER

As I reflect on my childhood, academic training and volunteerism, and teaching career, I now realize that these were the experiences that formed the core of my core and set the stage for the type of classroom leader I would become. My experience in the trenches of a variety of schools including parochial, charter, and public institutions—ranging from elementary school through the community college systems—has been the overarching influence that shaped me as an educator. Until recently, I had no idea that I had special assets that positioned me in a small category (approximately 8%) of educators in the 120 major urban school districts (Haberman, 2004b). Take a journey back in time with me as I recall events that support qualities that Haberman outlined as the midrange functions of a star teacher.

Father Knows Best

When I was a young girl, my father, in my mind, was very strict and unreasonable. However, at that time I did not stop to think that other students did not have a father at home or in their lives at all. I remember being reprimanded for not doing my best and being pushed hard to do well in school. It was not a good feeling to know that my best (or so I thought) was not good enough. He was not a tyrant who was fueled by a desire for discipline and control during my childhood. My father's tough love was there, but so were his tenderness, and above all, his time. He took time to talk to me and to listen. He is someone who took the time to foster self-directed learning and independence. He has shown me that nothing is impossible when I put forth effort and that the rewards of hard work are priceless. He is an inspiration to me and has helped me get where I am today. My life could have taken different turns based on his methods of encouragement. Perhaps I could have grown to resent him, men, or even authority figures. Another option could have ended with me feeling helpless, hopeless, or inadequate, and eventually giving up on life on life's terms. His persistent methods worked for me, and I realize now that he was doing the best he could. This was the only way he knew how to raise me to survive in society.

I concur with Haberman's assessment that "Miseducation is, in effect, a sentence of death carried out daily over a lifetime" (Haberman, 2007, p. 180). My father's strong influence in my life was something I resented when I was younger. He was encouraging me because he wanted me to achieve more than he had. He knew the importance of an education based on his failure to attend college and his lack of opportunity and options in life. Honestly, I do not know where I would be without an education today—perhaps dead, incarcerated, addicted to drugs, or on the streets. My father never went to college, but he knew that school was important in shaping an individual's future. This was a lesson he learned the hard way when he decided to work and raise a family at a young age. I know he has always done his best, and that is all I could ever ask of him or anyone. My father's presence and consistent motivation were constant drives in my desire to be successful, not only in academia but in life. I always sought his approval and looked for his congratulatory remarks when I succeeded. I remember scoring eighties on tests, and being questioned about why those marks were not 100s. This went on throughout my years in high school. But my father's encouragement helped me to graduate not only from high school but college with an educational doctorate. I will always be grateful for the lessons my father taught me.

Teaching as a Professional Calling

In college I started to ask myself, how could I perform better? I was an undecided major and pursued a degree in liberal arts while in the process of making a career decision. My circumstances made that choice for me. I have always loved to help and volunteer. I learned this from those around me. There were always individuals willing to give their last dollar; sacrifice eating so someone else wouldn't go hungry, or provide their time when it was limited. Of course, it was not easy and was stressful for them, but somehow they always managed to give to others. Through observation, I learned it was not hard or challenging to give of myself in any way I could so someone else could benefit, especially children (who I have always believed are instrumental in shaping the future). After all, I had been very fortunate in my life, so there was no other option but to pay it forward. Once I began to be kind to people and volunteer, it became second nature. There were times when I was tired, but learned how to multitask and use my gratitude for the opportunity to help drive me to continue helping others. Most of my volunteer and early work involved young children. Previously, I was a Sunday school teacher, hospital playroom volunteer, camp counselor, assistant director of the camp, assistant teacher, and substitute teacher. I felt comfortable working with children. This is where I began to develop a sense of where I belonged in my career at the age of 19.

One day, while I working with kindergarten students as an assistant teacher, everything fell right into place. I was grading some papers when two girls came over to me with Lego building blocks on a plate. At first, I wondered why I should take time to listen to them. They said, "Ms. Sherese, this is for you. It's your birthday, so we made you a cake." My heart melted at that moment, and I realized I wanted to be a part of their world even though it was not my birthday. I had finally seen the light—the light into my future as an educator. I understood the cake—I could see it even though it was not tangible. The sweet smell of the vanilla frosting permeated my senses, and I saw the light on the candles atop the cake. That was the same imaginary play that my father and mother encouraged when I was young. I remember including them in my imaginary play just as those young girls did with me using the Lego birthday cake. I noticed that more Lego birthday cakes, breakfasts, dinners, and lunches followed—and were accompanied by great conversation. I truly enjoyed listening to young children when I was interacting with them in the classrooms, at the camp, or Sunday school. I later came to realize that many of them were not listened to at home or by other teachers who did not have time to listen. Whether I wanted it or not, my students were available to me and actively listened to my concerns. As a teacher, there is so much preparation and time that is dedicated to instruction. Naturally—I wanted to listen because I discovered so much about them. They were not only students, they were small people with feelings, dreams, and opinions that mattered. It was not always easy to be there for my students, but I was committed to being there for them.

I had the steady hand of support and honest parents in my life—good or bad, they told me what I needed to hear, not what I always wanted to hear. Children sense honesty; they speak and detect the truth. This is why I never lie to students; lying was never encouraged in my family. In fact it was strongly discouraged, and telling the truth was always commended. The value of honesty was instilled in me, and I instill it in my students. When I taught elementary school, students expected to see me daily and, when they did not, they would worry (because it was their routine). When I was going to be absent, they always knew. Similarly, older students enrolled in my community college classes expected to see me as well. However, the situation was more involved. Some students traveled long distances to get to the lecture (sometimes 90–120 minutes). Additionally, I hear murmurs of disgust from students when colleagues cancel their classes. I empathize with the students because I remember traveling 1 hour and 45 minutes to my college classes and seeing a note on the door that they were canceled. The negative reaction of students takes me back to those times. Trust and empathy are two things that I foster in my students. This is accomplished by being direct, informing and including students in the learning process. It is only fair, and something I expect in return. When I could not follow through on a promise, they knew why. There were no surprises and they knew what to expect. I ensured the classroom environment was routine and predictable since many of my students lacked stability at home. Many students have come to believe in my word throughout my 15 years as an educator.

It was through volunteer work with children of many ages that I realized teaching is my calling. Teaching was almost a pleasurable pastime as opposed to a job. It was something I enjoyed and never questioned if I was being effective, especially in the earlier years of my career. Haberman (1995) explains that there are seven midrange functions or dispositions of effective educators of underserved urban learners that are based on neither specific behaviors nor personality attributes. Unwittingly, I had no idea that I possessed these attributes.

SEVEN MIDRANGE FUNCTIONS OF STAR TEACHERS

Haberman's research helped him identify characteristics and beliefs of individuals who were considered "quitters" and "failures" in today's public schools. His research has also assisted him in developing a two-part protocol that involves a prescreener questionnaire and interview, which hones in on what teaching should be for children, especially those living in poverty. The results of the protocol form what the best educators believe their job should and will be and detailed in Haberman's seven mid-range functions that star teachers possess (Haberman, 2004b). When I reflect on my personal history and instructional career, I can connect with these functions. But am I a star teacher? In Table 5.1, I conduct a self-analysis on whether or not I embody Haberman's seven midrange functions of star teachers and critically excavate my instructional practice for substantiation.

Approach to At-Risk Students

Regardless of adversity, star teachers believe it is their responsibility to ignite the desire to learn in their students (Haberman, 1995). My approach to at-risk students is something that I have demonstrated throughout my career. There were so many times that I could have played the victim but my students who came from backgrounds that placed them at risk were more victimized. I had to make it about supporting them and teaching them to save themselves.

> Miseducation is, in effect, a sentence of death carried out daily over a lifetime. It is the most powerful example I know of cruel and unusual punishment, and it is exacted on children innocent of any crime. Most Americans avoid the personal tragedy aspect of this massive miseducation by not sending their own children to school in these failing urban districts. This includes the majority of the teachers who work in them! (Haberman, 2004b, p. 1)

My ideology about serving diverse children in poverty aligns closely with that of Haberman. I too realize that I "do not control all the out-of-school and life experiences that impinge on student achievement," but I still "accept accountability for students' learning" (Haberman, 2004b, p. 98). It has always been challenging to watch students struggle and encourage them to give me their best despite their situations. In most cases, I have felt helpless to know that their life beyond the classroom was out of my hands. Yet I have learned to do the best I can during the time I share with my students.

Many K–12 students who I have educated through the years were at risk due to their tenuous home life, financial status, and general attitudes about learning. My college students were in the same boat; several of them were single parents and first-generation college attendees. A great deal of our K–12 students leave the K–12 system un/underprepared for college and the real world; the at-risk learners in K–12 schools become at-risk learners in community college (Martin, Galentino, & Townsend, 2014; McCabe, 2003; Perin, 2013). Even though these learners had the deck stacked against them, we would not use these roadblocks as

Table 5.1.   Seven Midrange Functions of Star Teachers and the Author's Personal Assessment of These Dispositions

Seven Core Functions	Brief Description of Functions	Personal Evidence of Functions
Approach to at-risk students	• Regardless of adversity, it is their responsibility to ignite the desire to learn in their students.	• Held college students accountable for tracking their grades. • Trip to Chinatown to continue learning about Chinese culture and etiquette.
Persistence	• Acceptance of responsibility to make classroom interesting and engaging for all children to learn in a variety of formats based on their individual needs. • Constant searching for best practices for every student. • Engagement in reflective practice to find better ways of doing things in the classroom.	• Accommodated learning styles in the classroom. • Studied hermit crab as an interdisciplinary approach to learning and maintained it as a class pet.
Protection of students' learning	• Bring their outside interests and activities in the classroom to involve students in learning. • Find ways to expand the traditional curriculum and sometimes are seen as being noncompliant with the academic agenda (redefine the boundaries within they work.) • Courteous, patient, and professional when redefining boundaries and negotiating with authority figures. • View protecting and increasing students' involvement in academic activities as their highest priority.	• Wiggle walks with young students and adults. • Variety show on challenging topics. • Plate spinning.
Fallibility	• Admit and accept their own mistakes, which enables them to accept the mistakes of their students without attacking them.	• Misspelled words on board. • "I need a break from you."
Professional versus personal orientation	• Do not take children's misbehavior as a personal attack. • Expect that all students will be able to learn regardless of how they feel about the student and vice versa. • Sense of authentic respect.	• Philosophy of *How important is it?* • Promoted positive and ignored negative behaviors.

(Table continues on next page)

Table 5.1. (Continued)

Seven Core Functions	Brief Description of Functions	Personal Evidence of Functions
Burn out: The care and feeding of bureaucracy	Protect selves from burnout by not subjecting self to constant stress from interfering bureaucracy. • Seek others who are positive-minded, team teach, and realize they are not alone … have a support system.	• Collaborated with colleagues in instruction.
Putting theory into practice	• Engage in reflective practice. • Cite clear, observable examples that all children can learn. • Translates theory into practice.	• Solicited feedback from college students about my teaching style.

excuses—failure was not an option! So we jointly became accountable for their learning. For example, I implemented a strategy of insisting that my college students write down their grades and maintain them. We had many conversations throughout the semester about what grade they feel they have "earned" in the course. Another thing that we discussed was their attendance. Some students were not aware that they'd accrued so many late warnings or absences. When I spoke to them, I found that these problems decreased or stopped. Our discussions made them accountable. Most professors do not take the time to ask students' thoughts or take the time to provide feedback as to how students are performing in class. When I took the time to speak to students or solicit their opinions, I showed them that I care—and I really do. It is my duty to care; it is my calling.

Motivating these underserved college students would take the work of the community to support me in my efforts. I always explain to my students how I was raised and what was instilled in me, so I introduced my father to them. I enlisted my father and he has made appearances in my elementary and postsecondary classrooms, and he spoke to them the same way he spoke to me. He begins his speech by telling them how proud he is of them for being in college and encourages them to continue working hard. Some students do not have any support, so that one visit from him can go a long way in their lives. I encourage my students to work hard, and I tell them I believe in them because I know they need to hear it.

Initially I was so stressed about the difficulties that my students faced that I took all their issues home. At times, I let their situations get the best of me and lay awake at night wondering how I could help them. Whether it was a child being ignored by parents or a college student with several children and no support at home, I felt helpless. Everyone has temporary issues, including me. Yet how we face the issues is key. Having teachers in my life who helped me feel safe in school and encouraged me as my father did was very motivating for me as a young student. I wanted that for my students. However, in time I realized we all needed to leave those painful situations outside the door of the classroom. "Stars respond as professionals and are not easily shocked" (Haberman, 2004a, p. 53). Making the educational environment a safe place where we were a team—and in some cases family—went a long way.

Children are children. They all want similar things, no matter what environment. However, I learned that the more at-risk they were, the more I had to give them in order for them to be successful. I became a surrogate mother to many students because of their distressing situations. This was not only true when I was working at the public school, but also all the environments where I have interacted with students, whether children or adults. My approach to at-risk students was employed throughout my career. Regardless of my students' situations, I always felt it was my responsibility to ignite that academic spark in them. I provided meaningful learning by taking the students to Chinatown in Manhattan to dine at an authentic Chinese restaurant. Everyone can eat Chinese food. However, not everyone knows how to eat with chopsticks, place a napkin, or has other dining skills. These are skills I learned when I got older. No one showed me these things when I was 7 years of age. I wanted that for them. I wanted them to be aware of things that helped them to function in society and be good citizens. Haberman (1995) supports this as a positive approach to at-risk children because it was my responsibility to spark the desire to learn in my students despite their background and life challenges.

Persistence

Constantly searching the best practices that meet every student's needs and the responsibility to make the classroom engaging is another function of a star teacher (Haberman, 1995). Once I accepted these uncontrollable factors, I was able to teach students using a variety of methodologies. Everyone is a distinct learner who learns in a very unique way. A variety of learners can benefit from the use of hands-on instruction (Lauria, 2010). Dr. Rita Dunn, an authority on learning styles, my mentor, and college professor, said on many occasions, "When students cannot learn the way we teach them, we must teach them the way they learn." Initially I resisted this theory and all resources associated with it. To my mind, Dr.

Dunn never forced learning styles into my mind. I saw them for myself in her methods and by taking a step back and realizing she could be right.

Something else that I believed in when I was teaching young children was instructional methods that were not from the textbook. There were many theories that I learned in college and in my field work. However, that information took on a different reality once I began to actually see and expand on that information in my own classroom. There was an entirely new perspective that came with the new experience of having a classroom where I was the lead teacher. I saw the theory put into practice, but studying learning styles took my learning to another level. According to Dr. Haberman, theory is important, but putting it into practice for the sake of students is paramount to their success. Additionally, I have never been one to stick with routine or what everyone else is doing. "Variety is the spice of life" is a true statement that my father once told me. I did teach lessons from the textbook. However, I expanded upon them by taking the lessons even further. I assisted the students in making a connection to the real world. This connection helped the students to grasp the material even quicker. Money was a topic my class struggled with year after year. This topic puzzled me. How could I teach it effectively? I tried all kinds of things: play money, repetition, worksheets, and more! On one occasion, I provided each of my 2nd-grade students with a quarter and went to the corner store. I allowed them to get whatever they wanted with the quarter. It was so nice to see how they managed their money based on what they knew from our classroom activities. There was a big difference in seeing them use what they learned as opposed to completing examples in a workbook. I realized that I was helping them to function in society. It was meaningful learning. It worked better than all the other methods I had tried in the past. I knew that I should continue with this activity because the students retained the best. However, I still sought additional activities for the students to acquire money skills. This was an example of persistence. I accepted that it was my responsibility to make the classroom engaging for all children in a variety of formats. "Teachers engage in systematic self-reflection" (Haberman & Post, 1998, p. 99) and constant deliberation on my teaching methodologies helped me to sharpen my teaching skills to best engage my students in academics.

One afternoon, my 2nd-grade students were rather noisy and full of energy. There was one period left before dismissal, but I was overwhelmed and did not feel as though I could make it to the end of the day. At that point, I said to my students "Here, take these materials." I put my head down on the desk. These were the materials that I had prepared for my evening graduate class with Dr. Dunn, and were scheduled to be submitted. However, I wanted to do something different because the routine that the students had become familiar with was no longer working. The materials consisted of hands-on learning materials about an Uromastyx, a strange lizard. Part of my reason for offering the materials to my students was my frustration with a familiar routine, and the other part was to see if these materials really worked. Reluctantly, I distributed the materials to the children, and my previously loud and energized class became quiet. They were so silent that I walked around and really studied their behavior. The students were learning new and difficult material. Some students were even trying to pronounce the name of the lizard. I never believed that the hands-on materials I was encouraged to create in Dr. Dunn's graduate class would actually work. However, that day, I came to believe it was not only effective but also a strategy that I could employ for many years to follow.

I employed direct instruction as a teaching strategy. I used this method to remediate students in the area of reading. There was a presentation book that I placed on my lap. Through my modeling and student repetition, students who were behind in reading levels managed to improve over time. My remedial students responded well to this strategy. Direct instruction goes beyond giving orders daily. The components contribute to a well-rounded approach to ensure that all students' needs are addressed. A true format of direct instruction was required by many of my students. Haberman (2004b) states, "There is substantial evidence that the achievement of children in poverty improves markedly when they are taught with direct instruction. Many children growing up in poverty are left to their own devices with few controls and little structure." I was providing students the structure and routine that so many of them needed.

I also learned to expand my horizons and taught a gifted first grade and even prekindergarten as time progressed. I adapted to teaching both of those new grades and found great lessons through the experience. I saw so much growth in the first grade. Their reading levels soared as I incorporated topics that were of interest to them. I bought a hermit crab for our classroom. We read fiction and nonfiction literature about this pet. Additionally, the students had done research on the animal before I even brought it to the classroom. They learned how to take care of it, what it ate, and how to handle it. Science, math, writing, and literature were all included in their study of the hermit crab. Integration of a host of subjects was also a successful strategy because students became used to the incorporation of all subjects. Moreover, they were provided with the opportunity to gain practice in subjects in which they were weak. The topic based on their shared experience made the different curricula areas easier to digest academically. "Star teachers push students to even more advanced levels of important forms of knowledge" (Haberman, 2004b, p. 102). I had no problem encouraging students to perform beyond the boundaries the academic society placed on them.

Another example of my persistence with learners was when I was teaching 1st-grade students how to add two-digit numbers using manipulatives. However, there were two children who continued to struggle. One drew sticks to add, and the other counted on her fingers. This was the way that they were taught. It seemed almost impossible to reteach a skill that was ingrained. I continued showing them different ways to add using not only manipulatives but a number grid and number line. After about 6 weeks of using repetition and allowing them to use the tool that helped them best, they finally developed the skill to add more efficiently. It required a great deal of patience to continuously providing tools, asking them to try again and being encouraging without becoming frustrated. I knew they were doing their best, so I owed them my best as an educator.

There are countless other illustrations from my instruction that demonstrate persistence. I also encouraged the students to learn in other ways besides learning directly from me. Students engaged in small group learning, partner learning, independent learning, and informal learning. They were always encouraged to learn in a way that was comfortable for them. If they felt like standing, walking around or lying on the carpet, it was fine as long as they accomplished the task and did not disturb others.

Protection of Students' Learning

In my classrooms, nothing was going to get in the way of my students' education; "For star teachers the ultimate value to be preserved is learning" (Haberman, 2010, p. 139). I wholeheartedly believed that teaching and learning were my highest priority and was vigilant in the protection of students' leaning at every cost. We worked in my elementary schools from 7:30 a.m. until about 4 p.m. I realized that they needed a break at times. Sometimes these young learners needed to just break free from their seats and stretch their little bodies. It helped them to refocus their brains when learning challenging material or as we came closer to holiday breaks. It was a long day. It was even longer for the children. Sitting still for long periods of time did not work for young children. Most needed to move. I noticed this as I recall children falling out of chairs "by accident," tapping their pencils or feet as they struggled to retain the information I was providing. There was a strategy I used called "wiggle walk" in the protection of students' learning. Students were encouraged to raise their hands and wiggle their fingers. When I saw this sign, I knew they needed a few minutes to stretch their legs. At that point, I acknowledged them with a nod, and they paced back and forth. This was done in the back of the room so they did not disturb their classmates. After students began to practice this, no one "fell out" of a chair and the tapping of pencils and feet decreased. While pursuing my doctoral degree in learning styles, I found that some learners are kinesthetic and need to move. Equipped with this new information, I added the option of allowing students to stand while working. It was interesting that it became a way of life within our classroom community. Students learned as I became knowledgeable that people learn in a variety of ways. The objective is that students acquire academic information. When students were comfortable in the classroom environment, I noticed that their academic achievement increased. When I worked at the college level, wiggle walks worked well in a modified way. The wiggle walk and accountability measures were methods that I employed for protecting the learner at the college level. Students were encouraged to leave the room whenever they wanted or to sit in the back of the room on a couch. Remember, the objective was to ensure that they were comfortable learning. If they needed to eat while they learned, that was okay as well. Providing students with an opportunity to leave the room prevented them from devaluing the lecture. My students were learning in a way that worked best for them because the wiggle walks served as a safeguard for learning.

My tenure at a charter school allowed me to tap into my creativity and allowed me to include my outside interests. "Star teachers incorporate their outside interests, search for ways to expand the traditional curriculum, and are courteous and patient while redefining boundaries in an effort to protect students' learning," (Haberman, 1995, p. 779). Again, experience with father guided my classroom interactions as he had taken the time to teach how to juggle and plate spin. Years later, I passed that skill on to my 2nd-grade students. I recall a variety show in which our 2nd-grade students took part in a production that incorporated the history of China, the Water Cycle, Western Expansion, and the War of 1812. This was accomplished through songs, dances, poems, and plate spinning! I noticed student reflexes sharpen as we practiced plate spinning for brief times during our long days. I worked collaboratively with another 2nd-grade teacher in arranging the performance. The principal did not question why they were juggling or plate spinning. In fact, she provided even more reasons for why they should be doing a variety of things besides academics. Having the principal on my side further motivated and encouraged me to continue what I was doing. One reason for her support of these activities was that they can help students' hand-eye coordination—and that is what happened. The exercises helped them to be well rounded. The bonus was being able to show their parents and school community what they learned as a culminating event. I saw pride in their eyes as they performed and a sense of accomplishment once the event concluded. Everyone had a role, and these at-risk students felt empowered because it was not really academics to them. I used this engagement to scaffold academic exercises in the classroom. They were "secretly" learning the curriculum and having fun.

Following the charter school experience, I wanted to try teaching at a public school. At the charter school, I developed a reputation for being different and getting results. However, I needed to prove myself as a teacher in the public school because I was new. I remember organizing at least one arts-based performance per academic year based on the content, and I even let my students practice plate spinning for a short time every Friday. One afternoon, the assistant principal visited our class and looked very surprised when he found the students spinning plates. I was very courteous and professional; I negotiated with him in protecting the students' learning. Many of the things that I had learned to do earlier transferred to this environment. I knew it had worked before, and I realized these strategies worked here as well. The only difference was that I had to be a little imaginative and detail oriented when teaching these strategies to the students. Here I learned to be more diligent in finding research to support what I was doing in the classroom—in case someone wanted to know. There was never a time when I behaved like I had something to hide. My classroom door remained open at all times, and I always encouraged visits from the administration, colleagues, and parents. In this way, my actions were transparent. Through transparency, I gained respect and support from others.

Fallibility

Star teachers acknowledge their own errors and in turn can accept those of their students and not attack them (Haberman, 1995). I remained professional at all times. However, there was one student who constantly sought my attention while I was teaching a 2nd-grade class. Once I told him, "I can't wait for the winter break!" I was frustrated with him, but I had to develop patience. He told his mom. At first I was a bit nervous, but realized I had nothing to be nervous about. I could have used kinder words when speaking to the young boy. However, as I explained to his mom, "We both need a break from each other." She was very accepting of the comment and understood why I said it. Together we had a conversation with her son, so he did not feel that I was attacking him. I was able to admit my mistake and carry out the *fallibility* midrange function.

I can also remember misspelling words on the board through the years. I invited the students to point out those errors to me and did not get upset. By correcting each other over the years, my students and I were only making each other better. Haberman explains that teachers should admit their mistakes in order to reach higher levels of understanding and greater self-awareness (Haberman, 2012). "Children cannot learn in classroom where mistakes are not allowed" (Haberman, 1995, p. 780). Teachers can accept the mistakes of their students when they can accept their own mistakes. Accepting correction did not make me resentful, but grateful for an opportunity for improvement. There were numerous mistakes I made through the years, but I was able to face them. In facing them, I was more accepting of the children when they made mistakes and did not attack them when they messed up. Everyone makes mistakes. I knew that and wanted them to know it as well.

Professional Versus Personal Orientation

Star teachers expect all children to have the capacity to learn and do not take children's misbehavior as a personal attack (Haberman, 1995). I found preventative solutions to dealing with students with behavior problems because "star teachers expect problems" (Haberman, 2004b, p. 103). I took the time to listen to them, show them I care, and not give up on them. In my experience, students craved structure and guidance—but most of all they craved ATTENTION. Sometimes situations in life cause students to misbehave—the desperate cry for attention. The fact that students act out is not necessarily stimulated by not knowing what was right or wrong, but because they want to be noticed. In my experience, this method works in most households and in classrooms. When my elementary school children performed undesirable actions, they would get punished. Being reprimanded was attention and they took what they could get, whether it was transmitted positively or negatively. Many parents are overworked and tired. This contributes to their lack of patience with their children in most cases when they arrived home late after a long day of work. When their child decided to misbehave, these parents need to address that behavior. When a child wants to discuss his day of plate spinning or setting butterflies free, many adults in their lives are often distracted or too tired to listen attentively and practiced pseudo-listening and respond in an insensitive manner.

Haberman (1994) explains,

> Teachers in schools serving children in poverty have no choice other than gentle teaching. Children growing up in neighborhoods where they are socialized to violence, physical abuse, and even death will not be brought readily into submission by such punishments as a time-out room, suspension, or even expulsion. (pp. 240–241)

After second grade, teachers have difficulty disciplining children with the endorsement of minor punishments or fear. Students growing up in areas where they are witnesses to violence, abuse, and death "will not be readily brought into submission by certain punishments. Escaping from the power mission, and adopting the theory that each child controls themselves and their learning is key" (Haberman, 1994, p. 240).

I was never a teacher who wanted to be in control. I often heard K–12 teachers saying, "Don't rock your chair," or "Stop tapping your pencil," or "Sit still." My philosophy was, "How important is it?" I had learned to choose my battles and that some behaviors could definitely be ignored. Furthermore, students would eventually stop the behavior (i.e., tapping a pencil) because I did not provide negative attention. Instead, I gave positive attention in other ways: listening, showing them alternative skills (how to plate spin, dance, poetry, etc.), or by allowing them to see that I was a real person too. Therefore, I was proactive as opposed to reactive. When a student feels beaten down, he will no longer seek to win the power struggle but will shift the goal of revenge, distrust, inadequacy, or discouraged (Haberman, 2012). I did not want to attack students or make them feel uncomfortable. I wanted them to feel safe. This approach eliminated so many of the behavioral issues that my colleagues found challenging. There were not many behavioral problems in my classrooms. Moreover, I did not take those minor incidents that did occur personally and did my best to respond in a professional way. There was a genuine sense of respect and I expected all students to learn.

A community college in the South Bronx hired me and again I felt like a small fish in a big pond. In this new environment, I was challenged by my adult students and did not know how to deal with it because now I was dealing with adults, not young students. I sought advice from a counselor who was very clear when she said, "You need to maintain a positive classroom environment." Even though some students challenged me, I put my principles above our personalities. I recalled that being true of the elementary teaching years as well. The objective was for students to learn; and if they were not, I had to find a solution. I developed strategies to ensure that the classroom environment was positive and to relate to my students in a "supportive professional manner, even when they did despicable things" (Haberman, 2004, p.170).

Burnout

Star teachers seek other positive-minded people for support to protect themselves from burnout and do not subject themselves to stress from interfering bureaucracy (Haberman, 2004a). The more meaningful activities that I shared with my elementary students, the more support I received from the principal, colleagues, parents, and my students. My methodologies were different, but they were accepted and encouraged.

Eventually, other teachers came to me to help them express their creative side. I was more than willing to help. There was never a time when I felt uncomfortable that someone was copying my style or trying to be different too. I was happy that my colleagues were trying different things in the classroom because the end result was that the students would be comfortable and thirst for more knowledge. We fed off of each other's ideas. We were positive about what we were doing for and with the children. This is what kept my spirits up and motivated me to teach. We were a community of learners and forming a cohort with my colleagues is an example Haberman's midrange function of *burnout.*

But the year that I taught prekindergarten was completely different from my first and grade assignments. I was reluctant to teach prekindergarten at first, but it was one of the many turning points in my teaching career. Parents were very hands-on and inquisitive because I was new to the grade and did not have any children of my own. It was hard for them to trust a new, young teacher with their beloved children. At first, this made teaching a little challenging and uncomfortable for me. I felt like all eyes were on me—and they were. Quite a number of parents hovered over me for about 3 weeks into the school year. After the first week of considering a solution, I realized I needed to make them feel safe and trust me. There was no time to stop and take any of this personally. I stopped and imagined myself in their position instead of getting defensive. Being a part of a solution is much more than playing the victim. That experience taught me that everything that I want to do can be accomplished when I pause, change my perspective, and think about a solution. During this challenging time I began to reflect on my career as an elementary school teacher. There were so many lives that I touched and inspired. There were so many parents, teachers, students, and administrators who came to believe in another way of learning. I had made an impact, but I developed a strong desire to make an even bigger impact. It was at that time that I decided to pursue educating future teachers. The impact I had on a class of 25–40 students was big, but the impact I could have on 25–40 future teachers who could make an impact on hundreds of students would be tremendous. It was a turning point where I yearned for something more. There was so much more that I could be doing for many more students, but where? I wanted to retreat, I was becoming burned out.

Yet I had learned that the best way to face anything was to ask questions, do the best I could, and stay focused. When I was experiencing tinges of burnout in my final year as an elementary instructor, a colleague asked me, "Sherese, what is going on with you?" I told her there was something bigger that I needed to do, make a bigger impact, but I wasn't sure how to go about it. She told me to "dress for success and fake it until I made it." She was right! That was the best advice that I received and best lesson from the public school experience. Even when I was dealing with the toughest behavioral problems of one of my young students, I never let the student or anyone else see me sweat. I took it in stride and regrouped. This was only another speed bump to roll over. The same philosophy that I preached to my students about seeing their progress, and not perfection, was something that I needed to remember and apply to myself. Getting my second wind through self-reflection helped me to avoid burnout at this critical turning point in my career and propelled me into the college classroom.

Putting Theory Into Practice

Star teachers know how to articulate teaching theories and rearticulate these ideas into real classroom practice. They can also explain a specific teaching strategy that they use in their classroom and direct you to the general teaching theory or philosophy that informs their practice. For instance, the concept of student feedback is highly valued in K–12 as well as postsecondary classrooms (Spooren, Brockx, & Mortelmans, 2013) because it serves as a type of evaluation of student achievement (Kane & Staiger, 2012). Therefore, I solicited students' feedback on surveys that I developed or by asking students to go online to the college survey or rate-myprofessor.com; these tactics helped me to understand their personal feelings and gain instructional insight. My reputation was such that I could not yet ask them directly for feedback and expect an honest answer. Students felt more comfortable being anonymous. In this way, they did not feel judged or that their views would affect their final grades. It was difficult to hear feedback at first, but now as I reflect on that experience, I realize it was the students' feedback that shaped me into the educator that I am today. Taking the time to listen to college students really helped the class move along well and reveals my ability to perform the *theory into practice* midrange function. There was so much that I had learned in my own academic career that I was able to translate into practice. Some things did not flow right away. However, I reflected on how certain things would work for the students that I was teaching and everything seemed to fall into place.

When I taught elementary school, the young students did not provide feedback. Administrators, colleagues, and parents provided peer evaluations to help me grow. After a peer review, I remember wanting to exit the classroom immediately; it was uncomfortable to speak in front of adults who could judge me. One of the concerns was that students were receiving too much information in a class session. Decreasing the amount of information that I presented and allowing a brief time after class for questions proved useful. Providing students the time that they needed was something that my younger students had needed and I needed as well. According to Arslan (2014), the peer observation is one of the most "eye opening experiments as it allows the teacher to view himself/herself from the perspective of an equivalent sharing his/her neutral comments for the sake of providing better teaching and learning in the end." Peer observers who serve as mentors can help other practitioners, especially inexperienced teachers. As a new teacher, advice from experienced educators helped me to grow into a confident, competent teacher who values feedback. Education in the 21st century does not support teaching in isolation (Rodgers & Skelton, 2013). Experienced teachers can learn from new teachers, become empowered by their mentor relationship, and develop their own body of knowledge as a result of their interactions with colleagues. Reviewing years of working with children and adults, I was able to connect the dots and see my journey into my career evolve as a star teacher. Regardless of the classroom level, Haberman (2012) explains that star teachers listen to students and peers to improve their practice.

IMPLICATIONS: WHY TEACHERS MUST ASSESS THEIR STAR POTENTIAL

A teacher's journey is very personal, but there are two larger implications of this chapter for the field of education: teacher turnover and teacher self-reflection as a form of professional development.

Teacher Turnover

One third of all beginning teachers are gone by their third year of teaching and half are gone by year 5 (Ingersoll, Merrill, & Stuckey, 2014). There is a correlation between high teacher turnover and stagnant student achievement (Rodgers & Skelton, 2013). Moreover, teacher turnover is highest year after year in schools located in disadvantaged areas (Haberman & Rickards, 1990). It is a challenge to retain educators in institutions with inadequate funding. Limited resources and low salaries cause an increasing number of teachers to quit or transfer to higher-paying districts (Rodgers & Skelton, 2013). In addition, these schools are often staffed by great numbers of inexperienced teachers. The increased demand for educators is evidenced in the growing demand to replace educators who leave. The public school system loses money after investing in teachers who leave after just a few years on the job. It is imperative to reach them before they go.

The devastating attrition rates of K–12 can be thwarted by effectively identifying teachers who are committed and invested in being there for the students (Chingos & Peterson, 2011). The character or core of people cannot be assessed through an essay or GPA for teacher candidates, but the Star Teacher Prescreener Questionnaire and Star Teacher Interview, a two-step protocol, can help principals and administrators identify and select the best possible candidates for children and youth in poverty.

Self-Reflection

Any educator must extend their knowledge base and be a lifelong learner in order to be effective in the classroom. Practice should include ongoing professional development and self-reflection (Tavil, 2014). It is an empowering practice to consider what transpired in the classroom because it allows you to reevaluate what works and what doesn't, what demonstrates growth in teaching skills and what is not quite working. Reflective practice can begin by asking yourself certain questions, such as "What worked in that lesson?" "Did the students grasp the information?" and "What did I do differently today that made this class a success?" I personally continually educate myself on best practices and current class-room-based research in order to be as effective as possible, particularly with at-risk students. I have found that I have been able to support and facilitate the success of my students in the classroom through self-reflection and professional development.

Ward and McCotter (2004) propose that reflection among preservice teachers must be a detectable feature of their teacher preparation; to truly view their beginning instruction experiences can provide valuable insight (Farrell, 2012). However, teachers who have been in the field can also benefit from self-reflection. There is always an area that could benefit from development. Arslan (2014) explains that self-reflection, done correctly, drives a never ending feedback loop of professional development competence.

> Self-reflection or self-criticism is one of the most effective ways to help teachers on the way to professional development. There are a variety of methods such as keeping diaries, journals, notes, video records (Brock, Juand Wong, 1991) that can be employed in self-reflection and they all provide significant means to alter oneself accordingly. (p. 14)

Self-reflection practices are generally noted by listing positive and negative aspects of an individual's teaching style followed by an action plan for change. Self-reflection is a careful introspection that is highly purposeful and contemplative in nature.

Self-reflection is definitely a valuable tool that I used in my career. It helped me to improve, not only for myself but for the students. Putting in time, effort, and acknowledging progress are not easy tasks, nor is it for everyone. Personally, I did not think about the work involved. My ultimate goal was helping students learn. I knew the best way to do this (without analyzing theories) was to look at my actions. This is what worked for me based on my experience. When I began teaching and I noticed many students failing, I asked the question, "Why did the majority fail?" I took time to investigate my teaching practices, test content, learning environments, seating arrangements and more! Because of my self-reflection, I realized that I played a part in many students not doing well. It was early in my career and I could not say I was a star teacher or even an above-average educator. This is what forced me to look at my actions. Although I made many mistakes in the classroom, what separates me from the average teacher is that I reflected on those mistakes and moved forward. It was my on-the-job experiences that were opportunities for application of theory into practice and contributed to my growth. The examination of our strengths and weakness, and taking action in areas that improvement, is the cornerstone of a star teacher's development.

SUMMARY: CHARACTER IS DESTINY

The midrange functions assessed in the Star Teacher Interview appear evident in my personal and educational history. I had many transformative moments in my life that have shaped the core of who I am as a person and educator. My cumulative life and professional experiences have informed my character and predicted my instructional destiny. I found a way to survive in an educational bureaucracy by understanding why at-risk students can succeed with a different type of teaching. Yet the culmination of my education as a child and as an educator truly came full circle when I came to learn about the great work of Haberman.

I look back with humility and realize that everything that I did or said in the classroom was not a coincidence. Haberman's research about teachers' success in urban schools has not only benefited me in making sense of my educational career, but many others who have a strong passion for teaching. By paying attention to my childhood, academic training, and teaching career, I was able to determine my star potential. Teaching is not for everyone, and I know I was preordained to be an effective teacher for several reasons. I am doggedly persistent about finding "what works" to help children learn; I am committed to the protection of students' learning from the noise of the world; I readily admit my mistakes; I don't blame students when they have a bad day and keep my professional composure; I have survival skills that help me avoid burnout; and I use reflection to help me make sense of my instructional practices. Am I a star teacher, one of the 8% that Haberman describes? I'll defer to you, the reader, for your judgment.

CHAPTER QUESTIONS

1. Is the author a star teacher? Explain your response.
2. How can a review of your life history help you understand your teaching philosophy and improve performance?
3. Has reflection or self-awareness influenced your instruction methods? Explain.
4. What are your core beliefs about education? Using Table 5.1 as your guide, reflect on whether or not you are a star teacher. Can you connect any of your beliefs to Haberman's midrange functions and explain if there are any alignments to the evidence you provide?

REFERENCES

Arslan, E. (2014). To assess the students or ourselves? *Journal of Educational and Instructional Studies in the World, 4*(3), 11–15.

Chingos, M. M., & Peterson, P. E. (2011). It's easier to pick a good teacher than to train one: Familiar and new results on the correlates of teacher effectiveness. *Economics of Education Review, 30,* 449–465.

Farrell, T. S. C. (2012). Novice-service, language teacher development: Bridging the gap between pre-service and in-service education and development. *TESOL Quarterly, 46*(3), 435–449.

Haberman, M. (1994). Gentle teaching in a violent society. *Educational Horizons, 72*(3), 238–248.

Haberman, M. (1995, June). Selecting star teachers for children and youth in urban poverty. *Phi Delta Kappan, 76*(10), 777–781.

Haberman, M. (2004a). Can star teachers create learning communities? *Educational Leadership, 61*(8), 52–56.

Haberman, M. (2004b). *Star teachers: The ideology and best practice of effective teachers of diverse children and youth in poverty.* Houston, TX: Haberman Educational Foundation.

Haberman, M. (2007). Who benefits from failing urban schools? An essay. *Theory Into Practice, 46,* 179–186.

Haberman, M. (2010). *Star teachers: The ideology and best practice of effective teachers of diverse children and youth in poverty* (1st ed., 3rd printing). Houston, TX: Haberman Educational Foundation.

Haberman, M. (2012). Teacher talk: When teachers face themselves. *Haberman Educational Foundation*. Retrieved from http://www.org/Articles/Default.aspx?id=89

Haberman, M., & Post, L. (1998). Teachers for multicultural schools: the power of selection. *Theory Into Practice, 37*(2), 96–104.

Haberman, M., & Richards, W. (1990). Urban teachers who quit: Why they leave and what they do. *Urban Education, 25*(3), 297–303.

Ingersoll, R., Merrill, L., & Stuckey, D. (2014). *Seven trends: The transformation of the teaching force*. Philadelphia, PA: Consortium for Policy Research in Education.

Kane, T. J., & Staiger, D. O. (2012). Gathering feedback for teaching: Combining high-quality observations with student surveys and achievement gains. *Bill & Melinda Gates Foundation*. Retrieved from http://files.eric.ed.gov/fulltext/ED540960.pdf

Lauria, J. (2010). Differentiation through learning-style responsive strategies. *Kappa Delta Pi Record, 47*(1), 24–29.

Martin, K., Galentino, R., & Townsend, L. (2014). Community college student success: The role of motivation and self-empowerment. *Community College Review, 42* (3), 221–241.

McCabe, R. H. (2003). *Yes we can! A community college guide for developing America's underprepared*. Washington, DC: Community College Press.

Perin, D. (2013). Literacy skills among academically underprepared students. *Community College Review, 41*(2), 118–136.

Rodgers, C., & Skelton, J. (2013). Professional development and mentoring support of teacher retention. *Journal on School Educational Technology, 9*(3), 1–11.

Spooren, P., Brockx, B., & Mortelmans, D. (2013). On the validity of student evaluation of teaching the state of the art. *Review of Educational Research, 83*(4), 598–642.

Tavil, Z. M. (2014). The effect of self-reflections through electronic journals (e-journals) on the self efficacy of pre-service teachers. *South African Journal of Education, 34*(1), 1–20.

Ward, J. R., & McCotter, S. S. (2004). Reflection as a visible outcome for preservice teachers. *Teaching and Teacher Education, 20*(3), 243–257.

CHAPTER 6

THE LIFEGUARD

Confessions From a Novice
Star Teacher of Children in Poverty

Lauren Ashley Williams

Chapter Objectives

The learner will

1. explore a case study which demonstrates the ideology or core beliefs of a beginning star teacher; and
2. understand the importance of building relationships among children in poverty.

The summer after my first year of teaching, I studied abroad through Texas A&M University in Costa Rica. All of the students on the trip were teachers in the university's Master of Education Post-Baccalaureate program. During the short week I was there, I had the great pleasure of being introduced to a professor of history who had a passion for teaching and devotion for those who were in the process of becoming teachers. While he and I discussed my first year of experience as a teacher, I explained to him how tough it was that year. I had felt very alone in trying to discover

Better Teachers, Better Schools: What Star Teachers Know, Believe, and Do
pp. 101–117
Copyright © 2017 by Information Age Publishing
All rights of reproduction in any form reserved.

ways in which I could reach students in poverty. Most of the texts I had read only explained what it meant to be in poverty but had little explanation for how to specifically reach those students through my teaching. Thank goodness the professor knew exactly what book would be helpful for my concerns. When we got back to the United States, I received a copy of *Star Teachers of Children in Poverty* (1995b) by Dr. Martin Haberman in the mail from that supportive professor. After reading the book, before the start of my second year of teaching, my professional life (and possibly my personal and spiritual life) was changed forever. In the passages that follow I share how I wrestled in college to find a career in teaching, then chronicle my first three years as a novice teacher.

LIFEGUARD AT THE "GHETTO POOL"

I never wanted to be a teacher. My dream career was something that would allow me to be financially cushioned in life because, in my mind, that was the definition of success. After graduating high school, I began college as a biomedical science major to begin my path to becoming an anesthesiologist (which is what every other freshman at Texas A&M University seemed to have decided as well). My first year in college went about as well as a fish climbing a tree and I headed back home for the summer to rethink my career choice. After 2 months of researching high-paying jobs, I changed my major to communications, hoping to become the next great marketing agent at a major public relations company in New York, California, Paris, or any stunning and well-known city in the world. By my junior year I was on the path I wanted to be, so I thought. I loved the creativity that my degree plan gave me, and I was so excited about the lavish life that I had dreamed of for so long.

During the summer before my senior year, I visited my hometown and decided to go hang out with some friends of mine who were still lifeguards at one of the community pools. It was fondly called "the ghetto pool" by the citizens of our small town; I suspected because it was patronized by so many poor kids of color from the poorer part of town. Friends of mine and I, from the more affluent part of the community, had all worked at this pool since we were 16. While catching up on the latest town gossip, two boys that had come to the pool every summer since they were in elementary came up to me to say hello. When I first started working at the pool, these boys were in middle school. They, like many of the other young visitors to this pool, grew up in poverty with very little adult supervision. Additionally, these boys had a very dark view of education and anyone with any sort of successful life due to an education.

"Say, Lauren! Where you been?! We ain't been kicked out at all this summer so far! You'd be so proud of us," shouted one of the boys as he stood no more than six feet away from me. "That's awesome!" I laughed. "What are y'all up to lately? You graduated last month didn't you?"

"Sure did! And let me tell ya, those college essays were tough, but we got in!" replied the same boy. The other boy tried to hold back his smile, but it didn't last long when he began laughing at the expression on my face. I was in shock. These two, like many of the poverty-stricken children that came to this pool, never seemed like "the college type" to me. "That's so great! I'm so proud of you two! So, what college are you going to and what made the essays so hard? Tough topics?" I was really interested to find out what their plans were for their future. I had never felt so invested in someone else's future plans other than my own before this discussion.

"It's just a community college, but the essay we wrote was supposed to be about the most inspirational person in our life, so it made it hard because I don't get inspired much," the second boy responded. These boys were cousins, and I knew they were somewhat close to their grandmother, who lived with them, and they had several other cousins. One of the cousins became a running back at the University of Texas, and then was kicked off the football team for drug abuse. Therefore, I understood why trying to find a role model to inspire them was a little difficult. As they described the excruciating pain of having to write and edit, and write some more, and edit again, and use correct grammar, the curiosity stirred in my mind of who they each had picked to be the topic of their essay.

"Writing's not that bad," I said. "So, who did you end up writing your essays about?" I expected to hear about some basketball or football player that they looked up to in their athletic lives, but what came out of the second boy's mouth next caught me completely off guard. "You. We both wrote about you," he stated so matter-of-factly, as if I should have already known that. I was, for the second time within the past 10 or 15 minutes, in a state of shock. "Me?" I questioned. "Why me?" They looked at me with the same shocked and confused look that I'm sure was written on my own face.

"You were always so pushy towards us to do better in school," the first boy stated. "We only ever saw you in the summer and it was always like we were still being lectured at by a teacher from school or something." Then the second boy continued, "Yeah, but you was the only person who ever really made me realize that I needed to go to college if I ever wanted to fill my bank account with some big money! No one ever made me realize how important getting a degree from school was except you." The words of the second boy brought on some crazy feelings. I felt proud of myself for helping these boys (even if it was unknowing). Additionally, I was proud of them for putting in such hard work and effort. My excitement seemed similar to what a mother would feel about her own children in this situation, and I had never intended to be an inspiration to anyone but my own children someday.

This was when I realized my purpose and calling in life. I had, for the past 20 years, believed that the most important reason to choose a career was for the comforts and luxuries that the salary could provide. But at this moment during the summer of 2010, income was not the most important qualification of my future anymore. The possibility that my career choice could impact lives was worth so much more to me. So, the educational world began screaming out my name and I ran to it as fast as I could during the last year of being an undergraduate.

MY FIRST YEAR TEACHING: LEARNING FROM STUDENTS IN POVERTY

Being fresh out of college with no teaching experience, I decided to take the first offer I received from the first high school I interviewed with, just to make sure I had some sort of financial security in my first year out of college as a "grown adult." Really, I was hoping to go back to my hometown and work in the same hallways that I had grown up in, but this city was not far from home. It was only about 20 minutes, and in all reality was very similar in the diversity and types of students who attended my former high school: a high percentage of students of color as well as a high percentage of learners from families with a low socioeconomic status.

This was a military-oriented city because one of the largest Army bases was located just down the road from the high school where I began my teaching career. The average age of the city's citizens was only around 35 or 40 years old, with an average income of less than $40,000 a year. Over half of the citizens were African American, Hispanic, or a mix of the two, and the crime rate of the town was nearly double of what the average crime rate was for the entire nation. From homeless children to fostered children and students with soldier parents to students with unemployed parents, I knew that I was going to be up against some very challenging student lives.

Throughout my entire first year, I did not have a lot of help. The school's mentor program was a joke. Most veteran teachers in the school viewed mentorship as an obligation they had to complete in order to meet a requirement on their end-of-year assessment. I worked harder than I ever thought I would, getting to school at 7:00 A.M. and not leaving until 7:00 P.M. or later. My first year of teaching was a major struggle, and I wasn't sure if I would be able to get through it.

The first semester, similar to my first year in college, was extremely difficult for me. I felt like I had made the wrong decision to go into this career field. I knew my content, I knew how to explain the English language to these sophomores and juniors, but there were very few students that seemed willing to work for themselves, let alone for me. There were students who I got along with really well, but they had similar lifestyles as I did when I was growing up; middle to upper-middle class with strong support systems outside of school. The problem was the majority of my students were not from a similar background; around 70%–75% of my students lived in the poorest part of the community. In my mind, I had no idea how to connect with them. Additionally, co-workers did not offer any legitimate help. They would simply tell me I just needed to try to understand where the students were coming from and try to work and deal with what I had.

In search for help, I read Ruby Payne's *A Framework for Understanding Poverty* nearly four times over that Christmas break. I was searching for answers in her book that were not there. While Ruby Payne gave me information for grasping the meaning of poverty and the issues that students may be facing outside of school, there was nothing to tell me how to reach them in order to gain their trust and their hard work. I realized that I needed to focus on taking "principles and concepts from a variety of sources (i.e., courses, workshops, books, and research) and translate them into practice" (Haberman, 1995b, pp. 779–780).

How do you get a student to do homework and to study if they are dealing with taking care of their four or five younger siblings as soon as they get home? What makes school work something that is important to a student who leaves school wondering if they will get dinner that night or if they will have to wait until they can get a free lunch the next day at school? Who am I to tell a student who lives in fear of being shot in a drive-by shooting that they need to find the time to come to tutoring or to study their notes? My mind was filled with these questions, and I felt extremely hopeless and lost. I felt like I had failed my duty as a teacher. My passion was helping kids, but I did not seem to have the ability to do so. I did not know how to "fix" the issues that many of my kids were dealing with outside of their 51 minutes a day in my classroom.

One of Haberman's (1995a) midrange functions for effective teaching includes *fallibility*. I expressed this dimension because I was a teacher "who [could] accept their own mistakes" (p. 780) and not just the mistakes of my students. I had to realize that I had made mistakes within this first semester of school in order to become a better teacher for the benefit of my students. I continued to carry this characteristic with me throughout my teaching career. For example, there was a student who never turned in any homework. After asking him why he wasn't getting his assignments completed he explained that his single mother worked nights and he had to take care of his three younger siblings once he got home from his own afterschool job. Instead of finding a way to help him with his missing assignments, I simply told him he would have to manage his time better if he wanted to pass the class. Later, I continued to ponder how I had handled the situation and I felt terrible for not helping him find a solution. Therefore, the next day I apologized to him for not offering helpful and realistic suggestions to his problem and asked what time he had to be at his afterschool job each day. His job started at 5:00 P.M. each afternoon, but he did not have a seventh or eighth period class. I offered him my teacher desk for those class periods where he could work on his homework while I taught. He accepted my invitation and thanked me for my sincere apology.

After Christmas break, I went back to school with a more accepting and open attitude toward my underserved students. Haberman (1995a) explains that when star teachers exemplify *persistence*, the third of his seven midrange functions, they "accept responsibility for making the classroom an interesting, engaging place and for involving the children in all forms of learning" (p. 779). Thus, I did everything I could to find ways to make getting their education in my classroom easier and more available outside of class on their own time. While researching ways to communicate with students, I found a technology application called Remind101. This application allowed me to send mass text messages to students when I needed to give them a message before or after school. It proved to be a great tool for helping my students (all of my students, not just the ones in poverty) to keep up with things they may have forgotten about or pushed to the side because of other life demands.

My lesson plans changed dramatically. Instead of giving out homework (since in reality it was never completed), I began giving in-class assignments. This led to less of me at the front of the classroom lecturing and more of my kids working with some basic notes/information to discover and learn the greater depths of those minilessons that I gave each day. I noticed a complete turnaround in my students' attitude toward learning. My classroom atmosphere was more positive and encouraging. Students were learning together, and I was getting to know my students on more personal levels because I could spend nearly 40 minutes a day talking with them instead of talking to them.

While my relationship with my students was much stronger, I still had one major issue; the State of Texas Assessments of Academic Readiness (STAAR) test. This annual end-of-the-year standardized test was tough, and the majority of my sophomores did not know how to study for a test. For that reason, in an effort to encourage my students to engage in class (and hopefully outside of class, too), I utilized kinesthetic games that incorporated course content and skills. The games were sports-based, but in order to score points, students had to know their English/language arts content in order to answer the questions correctly. It was amazing to watch the growth of my students as they began to really take their education into their own hands in order to be successful at the game. I still wasn't quite where I wanted to be with regard to encouraging education with my students, but I was at least getting them to have fun in class and actually learn something.

By the end of the year, I had created a very strong relationship with the majority of my students. Those who didn't take the state test seriously for themselves certainly showed that they were going to take it seriously for me, their teacher. I ended up with 79% of students passing their test. At first, it seemed like a low percentage rate, until I looked at the same students' scores from the test the year before when only 52% of them passed. From the one year spent in my class, 27% more of these kids were able to be successful on a test that would determine their graduation out of high school. I wasn't sure, though, if it was the strength I had in teaching the content or if it was the relationships that I had built, until I gave my last assignment of the year.

Students were asked to write a letter (see Figure 6.1) to the most inspirational person in their lives within their past 2 years of high school. Many wrote to their parents, their coaches, their siblings, and their boyfriends or girlfriends. When the assignment was due, students were able to mail out their letters to those people. I received several, but two of them stuck out to me.

Student A had a very difficult time in school in general. He had a tendency to follow the wrong crowd—a crowd that did not benefit him in his academics and kept him from really succeeding in school. This was the first moment I realized that even if I reached only one student, the difficulties of being a teacher were completely worth it. His gram-

> Dear, Ms. Spurlock,
>
> You have been a great influence on me because you helped me go down the right path, and made me focus on my work. Also you help me get a better grade in our fifth period class. So I thank you and everything you have done to prepare me become a successful writer.

Figure 6.1.   Letter from Student A to Lauren Williams (formerly Lauren Spurlock).

Dear Ms. Spurlock,

As the year has progressed, I feel as though you have become one of the biggest inspirations in my life this year. When I first met you in the summer I thought, "Wow. She's super pretty and really nice. I hope this class is worth staying in IB." Believe it or not, I was going to quit IB after the first month of this year. However coming to your class everyday seemed to cheer me up and made me stay. Not only have you been an inspiration to me, but to most of the other students in IB. You say what's on your mind and take nothing from no one.

When I was severely depressed and had thought the only way of getting rid of it was through suicide, your little note hit home. I still have it and read it every day. After the incident of me going to the hospital for mental treatment happened, I did not blame you at all for worrying. In fact I was happier that someone cared enough to help me even when I couldn't help myself. I've grown a lot over the last few years as a brother, a son, and a student. You helped me grow as a person. You've helped me

You may not know it, but I want to go to Texas A&M, College Station because of you. I already thought of applying but now it's one of my top choices for college. You have inspired and influenced me in so many ways I don't think just this one letter can cover everything I must express. You are my favorite teacher and want you to know that you have changed my life. For that, I want to thank you so much.

Figure 6.2.   Letter from Student B to Lauren Williams (formerly Lauren Spurlock).

mar wasn't perfect and his overall writing was still far below grade-level standards. However, between his first piece of writing at the beginning of the school year and this letter, there was a major gain in sentence structure. The fact that he recognized the improvements made in his writing during my class touched my heart like nothing had ever touched it before.

The second of these two letters (see Figure 6.2) was from a boy who had seriously contemplated suicide. In his letter, he told me that a simple note that I wrote him made a huge impact on his entire life.

On the last day of school, I received an email from a parent of one of my female students (see Figure 6.3). It was after these letters and this email that my final question of the school year was answered. Did my relationship-building with my kids in the second half of the school year help them to become better students? Yes. Yes, it did. And my goal for my second year of teaching would be to discover how exactly I had built those relationships and why they seemed to be the most important aspect of my teaching style.

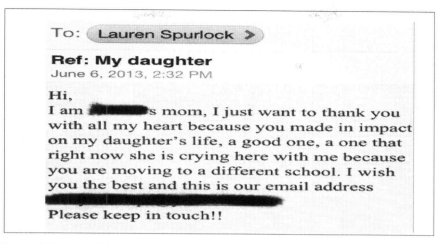

To: Lauren Spurlock >

Ref: My daughter
June 6, 2013, 2:32 PM

Hi,
I am ▮▮▮▮▮'s mom, I just want to thank you
with all my heart because you made in impact
on my daughter's life, a good one, a one that
right now she is crying here with me because
you are moving to a different school. I wish
you the best and this is our email address
▮▮▮▮▮▮▮▮▮▮▮▮▮▮▮▮▮▮▮▮▮▮▮
Please keep in touch!!

Figure 6.3.   Email from parent to Lauren Williams (formerly Lauren Spurlock).

THE SECOND YEAR:
BUILDING RELATIONSHIPS FROM THE BEGINNING

Because of the lack of support and mentoring at the high school I worked at during my first year of teaching, I chose to apply and interview with schools in the district that I grew up in. After landing a job teaching 8th-grade English/language arts and reading, I was a little nervous. This was the youngest grade level that my certification would allow me to teach, and in all reality, I had never thought I would teach any grade level lower than freshman in high school. While this was not the same middle school in which I had experienced my awkward preteen years, it still produced kids who would end up in the only high school in our district. In fact, the students who spent their 6th-, 7th-, and 8th-grade years there were the same students who lived near and went to the "ghetto pool" that I worked at during high school and college. This was a little ironic considering that it was teenagers from that pool whose conversation put me on the path to this career that I was beginning to truly love.

I was not the only 8th-grade English/language arts and reading teacher—there were two of us. It was a nice surprise to discover that I had attended high school and been on the dance team with my new partner teacher's daughter. We immediately bonded and were able to work together from the first day of school. This was the first major difference I saw between my first year of teaching and this year. I actually had someone with whom I could plan lessons; with whom I could discuss my struggles with students, and on whom I could lean when I needed help or advice. Little did I know that these small collegial acts helped me to avoid burnout and help to "set up a network of a few like-minded teachers ... and use these support systems as sources of emotional sustenance" (Haberman, 1995b, p. 780). Our only problem at the beginning of this year, though, was that our content leader requested that we begin using the curriculum and teaching our content on the second day of school. Luckily, my partner teacher had already built relationships with these eighth graders the year before when she was their 7th-grade English/language arts and reading teacher. It took me about two days of abiding by my content leader's request to push curriculum and content on my students before I decided that in order to make sure that these lessons really stuck in the minds of my students, I needed to create a foundation of relationships with all of my students.

Haberman's (1995a) fifth midrange function of effective teaching is *protecting learners and learning*. I was able to "persist in searching for ways to engage [my] students actively in learning ... and resolve [my] struggles with bureaucracy patiently, courteously, and professionally ... and seek to negotiate with authority" (p. 779). I effectively performed this function because I sought to create relationships with my students before forcing content onto them; this approach provided the best foundation for success in my classroom. In his book, Haberman (1995b) explains, "Stars learn about their children's lives ... to become sensitive to the children's backgrounds because they genuinely care about them" (p. 53). So, that's what I did. I put the strong focus of content on the back burner for the last couple of days of the first week of school, opened up about my own hardships, triumphs, and tribulations in my life while modeling how to write an autobiography and then assigned my students to write their own autobiography. The effect was amazing. Because I had become transparent to my kids, they were completely willing to become transparent to me in return. I was able to learn about my students on a personal level over a weekend of reading their autobiographies, and from the second week of school until the end of the school year, I could speak to my students on much more intimate levels. Knowing them in this way allowed me to adjust my teaching style to be very personalized to each and every one of my students. This was the moment that I knew that building relationships with my students was the first and most important part of becoming an effective teacher to my children in poverty, something that I learned through my interpretation and inspiration of Haberman's book.

Unlike my first year of teaching, the first semester of my second year went very smoothly and exceptionally well. My relationships with my students gave them a trust in me as their teacher. The majority of them sincerely knew that I had their best interest in mind. Instead of taking half of the year to get my students to work and to learn for me, I was able to "convince [my] students that learning is itself the reward" (Haberman, 1995a, p. 18). While many of my co-workers used extrinsic rewards on a regular basis, those types of rewards were a rarity in my classroom. Instead, I pushed my students to become excited about learning. Student tardiness and skipping class were also rare. The students relished coming to class because they enjoyed the sense of empowerment gained from self-directed learning. In fact, they enjoyed being in my classroom so much so that I had to push students out of the door nearly every period of every day to get them to go to their other classes throughout the day.

Our district required all grade levels to give common-based assessments (CBAs) in which every student of each grade level took the same test across the district. After the first 8th-grade English/language arts and reading CBA, my partner teacher and I received an email (see Figure 6.4) from one of the assistant superintendents with a congratulations on how well our students had done on the test as opposed to the other 8th-grade classes in the other middle schools within the district. We had over 80% of our students pass a test that is very similar to the state's STAAR test. While

---

High Five
October 14, 2013 at 11:04 AM
High Five

I wanted to give both of you a TISD high-five. Your CBA scores are outstanding. 8th grade ELA at LMS is the best in the entire district. You guys make a wonderful team and your scores show. Both of you are WELL above the district CBA passing average. I want to thank you for your hard work and commitment. What an outstanding job. Keep up the good work!

Figure 6.4.   Email from district administrator to Lauren Williams (formerly Lauren Spurlock) and peer teacher.

this was great news as a teacher, it was even greater news for our students. In their 7th-grade year, these same students had a passing rate of less than 65%. Within less than 2 months of being in our classes, we had brought our students' passing rate up by nearly 20%. Instead of taking all of the credit for this, however, we went back to class and showed our students the email and the passing rate for our school and the other middle schools. We were so excited for them and showed them that excitement. We spent the last 15 minutes of class really celebrating their growth. Our students' confidence level was boosted so much that our students' scores on the remaining CBAs that the district gave throughout the year were just as high, sometimes higher.

Because I taught underserved learners, I was painfully aware of my *approach to at-risk students*, yet another one of Haberman's midrange functions. Because my students were plagued by poverty and other ills, it was a function I had to exercise every day in my class. It became so important to me to continue to build students' self-esteem in their learning because I knew that, "For children in poverty, succeeding in school is a matter of life and death ... they must succeed in school to have any hope of occupational mobility" (Haberman, 1995a, p. 40). When school was out at 3:45 in the afternoon, I had between 10 and 15 students in my room each day. All of them who came to visit were living in poverty. It was during these afternoons that I expressed the importance of education for them. "Regardless of the life conditions [my] students faced, [I as their teacher] had a primary responsibility for sparking [my] students' desire to learn" (Haberman, 1995b, p. 780). While I had a strong relationship with nearly all of my students, my strongest was with these types of students because I felt responsible for them and wanted to encourage that desire for an education that I knew was within them.

Similar to my first year of teaching, I decided to have a lesson over letter writing after state testing was finished and the year was coming to an end. Again, many students wrote to their parents, siblings, grandparents, and coaches, but I ended up with several myself. One letter was from a young lady who had struggled with school her whole life but passed the state test for the first time since she was in third grade. We had created such a strong bond that she had even begun referring to me as "Mom." She credited me with that outcome, though I credit her with becoming the person I knew she truly was.

This young lady and I originally had a very hard time getting along. She would fight me tooth and nail about learning and participating in class. Her attitude was so bad that she would curse at me, tell me she hated me, and even attempted to get other students to act the same way nearly every day. But I did not crumble, I could see right through her. "Star teachers have extremely strong, positive feelings toward their students, which in many cases might be deemed a form of love," (Haberman, 1995b, p. 780). My personal feelings kept at bay and my professionalism did not waiver, and I drew upon every ounce of strength I had to exhibit Haberman's seventh midrange function of *professional versus personal orientation to students*. While this student showed hate toward teachers, school, and educational success, I knew that she was a smart girl, someone who could do great things if she put her mind to it, so I never gave up on her. She would get angry at me for pushing her to do her best and expressed her anger through hate and rage. Then one day she and I spent her entire lunch detention talking about our brothers. She had lost her older brother a couple years before and I had also lost my older brother a bit earlier. We created a bond through our conversation on that topic and it was the first time that I had seen her without that thick wall erected around her.

That was the moment that I finally broke through to the most difficult student I had taught so far in my teaching career. In her letter to me, in which she affectionately called me Mom, I knew things were turning around for this young lady. Not because her circumstances had changed,

Dear Mom,

I really appreciate all the work you do for me, thank you for all the things you have done for me. You are a great teacher. I have learned so much from you. Now I was sure I passed the STAAR thanks to you. I am really glad that you are my teacher because you really know how to make things fun. I know sometimes that I make mistakes but I don't mean to. I also wanted to thank you for being so supportive. You taught me that I should never say never. That when things get hard, I really shouldn't give up. I really think you are a great teacher. I appreciate the personal time and extra time you spent helping me. Thank you for teaching me what no other teacher has.

I am really appreciative to have you as a teacher. I remember when school started I hated your class, I honestly hated ELA and I didn't want to repeat it again. I judged you before I even knew you. Over the year you've shown me what it's like to have a teacher that truly cares for me. I walk in everyday willing to learn and do my work, because I enjoy coming to your class. Every day I sit back I learn something new. I do it because you deserve it and because you taught me that I deserve it, too.

Remember when we didn't like each other because you said I was disrespectful and rude? I really respect all my teachers now and I try to stay out of trouble. Remember the day we started to talk about our brothers and you told me that my brother would love to see me graduate and how happy he was going to be? Thank you for telling me that because I really never thought about it. I always told myself I was going drop out of school and work at McDonalds. I remember how we had talks about it every day and every single day I wanted to come to school because of you. Well now I want to finish school and be a probation officer thanks to you. You really helped me through a lot.

Remember when you told me to do something that would make me happy? Well I want to help others and I believe I can change into a way better person. You have always been there for me through thick and thin and I really appreciate that. I love you. You better be there when I graduate. Where ever I go in life I will always remember that I had an excellent guide. I will always be thankful to you for all the hard work and effort you have put in. I'll miss you next year! I will always keep my promise.

Figure 6.5.   Email from Student C to Lauren Williams (affectionately called "Mom").

but her outlook had done a 180 degree turnaround. In student C's letter to me (see Figure 6.5), she discovered that she "deserved" to be acknowledged, loved, and affirmed. I would like to think that because I affirmed this student, I was able to help her, in whatever small way, to own her self-worth. Children in poverty battle self-image and self-concept that robs them of their sense of value. Once their value and dignity are validated, then they can be encouraged to chart their own paths in life.

At the end of the school year, my partner and I each ended up with an 81% passing rate on the state STAAR test. Our school and our district were so happy and proud of us, but in reality we could not take the credit. We gave all of the credit to our students. Our students knew how proud we were of the amount of hard work that they had put into this school year. Nearly every single student, whether they had passed the STAAR test or not, had grown in their scores, and while the standardized test is the state's way of labeling and grading a student, I knew that all of my students had grown in their own personal achievements. I could not have felt more pride for them.

It was this second year of teaching that my questions from the end of my first year of teaching were answered. How had I built the relationships I had with my students? I became completely transparent. I showed my students that I loved them as people and as learners. I gave them every encouragement I could think of throughout the year in order to build them up and get them to believe in themselves as well.

Why did my relationships with students seem to be the most important part of my teaching style? Without my relationships with my students, there was no reason to teach. I had to believe in my underserved students in order for them to ever believe in themselves. The majority of my students who lived in poverty had no role models at home to encourage education; there are so many other issues that they had to deal with in their lives outside of school. Many would leave school knowing that they wouldn't get their next meal until they got their free breakfast the next day in the school's cafeteria. Some walked out of the school building wondering where they were going to sleep that night. I learned from Haberman that I had to build trusting, warm, loving, respectful relationships with children in order to become a role model that could push them to want to learn and want to become educated. When this second year of teaching ended, I had never felt more thankful and blessed to be in the career of teaching children of poverty.

THE THIRD YEAR: "WITHOUT YOU, I WOULD PROBABLY BE DEAD ..."

The following year, 2014, I met up with the young lady who had written me the letter above during my second year of teaching. We met at Chick-Fil-A right after school, before the high school football game began, to catch up on how school was going so far this year for her. School had only been in session for a week so far, and I was really hoping that she would still be on that same path that she seemed to be on when she left my classroom at the end of her 8th-grade year.

After grabbing our food, we sat down and began to talk about her first week of high school and her plans and goals for these next 4 years. The things she told me gave me goosebumps and made me feel like a proud mother. She explained that she had lost many of her friends because she did not want to skip classes with them. Her goal was to finish high school with all A's and to go on to a 4-year university where she could become some sort of probation officer or social worker. As a way to make sure that she kept herself out of trouble, she joined the Junior Air Force Reserve Officers' Training Corps (ROTC) at the high school and she was learning about respect for authority and for herself.

I was in complete shock. I could not believe that this same young lady was the girl who was cursing at me every day at the beginning of school just a year ago. I told her this and that I was so proud of her. She chuckled and said, "You made me, Mom. Without you, I would probably be dead, in jail, or on the way to one of those things. You showed me what success is and what success feels like. I don't ever want to go back to my old ways. This is who I am, and this is what I am going to continue to be." My watery eyes smiled at her, I gave her a big hug, and we continued talking about her future for another 2 hours. This was the reason that I had become a teacher, and I could not have done this without the help of Haberman; his words directed me, and now I was helping learners to help themselves. I will continue to use his book as a guide to help me through the remainder of my career.

My relationships with my students are never ending. I am still very connected with many of my students, even those from my first year of teaching. As star teachers, it is important to know that your job is never done. Every year you get a new set of students in your classroom, but those former students will always be there. If you create the strong relationships with your students each year, those bonds will last for many years to come. Teachers don't work for just 9 to 10 months a year; your work continues throughout your entire life and the lives of your students. Keeping that philosophy playing on a constant loop in your mind and heart, throughout your career, will give you the motivation to be a star teacher for your students every day, every week, every year. A student in your classroom is not a student of yours for just a school year. A student in your classroom is a student of yours for the rest of your life and their lives.

SUMMARY

In an odd way, I am still that same lifeguard at the community pool where I found my career path. "[Star teachers] see the need for diverse children in poverty to succeed in school as a matter of life and death for the students and the survival of society" (Haberman, 2010, p. 216). I grew to realize the incredible impact that I can have on the children who need me the most. Since becoming a teacher, many people dare to utter that they think I am crazy for choosing this career. Many times I hear, "I could never be a teacher because they don't make enough money for what they have to deal with," or "You must hate your life for those 9 months." I now understand the sphere of my influence and know that, while teaching is definitely not an easy job, and there are days when I am surprised I don't get home and see a bald version of myself in the mirror, I can't imagine doing anything else. The pay is not great, but I believe that what I do every year, every month, every week, and every day is worth more than gold or silver itself. While I only have a few years of teaching children from impoverished backgrounds under my belt, I have already discovered that the relationships with these incredible underserved learners are the greatest "pay" I could ever receive.

CHAPTER QUESTIONS

1. The author explored several majors before teaching. Describe your path to teaching. Are teachers who were always decided on teaching as a career less or more committed that those who go into teaching after they have failed other majors? Explain your response. Are teachers whose original decision had always been on teaching as a career less or more committed that those who go into teaching after a second or third career? Explain your response.

2. The author used the trope "ghetto" in the description of the community pool where she worked as a lifeguard. Is her use of the word acceptable? Why or why not?

3. It is a widely held belief that poor kids of color do not want or value an education. Where did this belief originate and does it have any validity? Explain. What are the repercussions if teachers believed this idea?

4. Teacher and student relationships are a central theme in this chapter. At what point should a teacher work on his or her relationships with students? Defend your answer. Next, make a list of relationship-building strategies that you can exercise in your classroom that are specific to your grade level, subject matter, and the background of your learners.

5. In 30 to 50 words, describe your teaching philosophy. Were you prepared to teach diverse learners or kids in poverty, and is this commitment a part of your teaching philosophy?

6. Teachers must be careful and act as supportive figures in their students' lives and not saviors; what does this statement mean to you?

7. The author's journey with Haberman's work began when a professor gave her one of Dr. Haberman's books. Many teachers are often motivated by other teachers. Reflect on the supervisors and peers in your life and share how one of them positively influenced your teaching career.

REFERENCES

Haberman, M. (1995a, June). Selecting 'star' teachers of children and youth in urban poverty. *The Phi Delta Kappan, 76*(10), 777–781. Retrieved from http://faculty.washington.edu/cwj/edci469a/6/starhaberman.pdf

Haberman, M. (1995b). *Star teachers of children in poverty.* West Lafayette, IN: Kappa Delta Pi.

Haberman, H. (2010). *Star teachers: The ideology and best practice of effective teachers of diverse children and youth in poverty* (1st ed., 3rd printing). Houston, TX: Haberman Educational Foundation.

Payne, R. K. (2005). *A framework for understanding poverty* (4th ed). Highlands, TX: aha! Process.

CHAPTER 7

DOES "HIGHLY QUALIFIED" MAKE YOU A "STAR"?

**Sueanne E. McKinney, Sherell Fuller, Stephen Hancock,
Robert H. Audette, and Jack Robinson**

Chapter Objectives

The learner will

1. disentangle the terms *highly qualified* or *effective* teachers and *star* teachers;
2. formulate a rationale for the impact of national reform like No Child Left Behind on schools and teacher quality; and
3. assess the characteristics of effective teachers versus star teachers.

A well-prepared teacher is vitally important to a child's education, and he or she plays a significant role in children's intellectual, social, and emotional development. There is an expanding body of evidence in the research that validates an unmistakable correlation between student achievement and teacher quality (Carter, 2001; Good & Brophy, 1997; Haberman, 1995, 2005; Haycock, 2001; Ladson-Billings, 2000; Mehan, Hubbard, & Villanueva, 1994; Pollard-Durodola, 2003; Rice, 2003; Sanders & Rivers, 1996; Wenglinsky, 2002). Despite the support, there is much debate regarding what actually characterizes a quality teacher.

Better Teachers, Better Schools: What Star Teachers Know, Believe, and Do
pp. 119–135
Copyright © 2017 by Information Age Publishing

The Interstate New Teacher Assessment and Support Consortium, the National Board for Professional Teaching Standards, and the National Council for the Accreditation of Teacher Education define quality teachers according to a set of structured standards, such as "the ability to understand the process through which children learn and develop, and be committed to furthering students' learning," and "deep knowledge of the subject they teach and [the ability] to convey this knowledge to students in ways that engage student inquiry" (NRC, 2001). Exactly how these standards will be demonstrated and measured remains elusive. Other proxies used to define quality teachers include degree level and certification type, experience level, graduating institution, and standardized test scores, such as the SAT and Praxis (Goldhaber, 2003). Still others treat teacher quality "as a teacher's quantifiable ability to produce growth in student achievement" (p. 6). The professional literature clearly shows that there is no consistency in defining teacher quality.

Having an effective teacher is especially crucial for urban students. Kincheloe (2004) states, "Nowhere are the obstacles to success and the existential needs of the students as great as in urban areas" (p. 4). Concentrated poverty, family instability, and early exposure to violence are but a few hardships and difficulties that urban students must confront in their attempts to meet personal, academic, and social success. Because challenges are constant and prominent in the lives of these children, teachers who can make a difference are especially needed in inner-city schools—and the condition is critical. According to Haberman (1995), the majority of students placed in high-poverty schools "have no life options for achieving decent lives other than by experiencing success in school" (p. 1). However, many high-poverty schools continue to fall short in their attempts to provide equitable and rigorous educational opportunities for the disadvantaged (Bartoli, 2001; Carter, 2001; Haberman, 1995, 2005; Kozol, 1991). Will the No Child Left Behind (NCLB) mandate of having only highly qualified teachers in public school classrooms be the cure-all for the ills of urban schools (NCLB, 2001)? Because the stakes are so high and so formidable in this era of school accountability, educators must carefully examine the question whether a "highly qualified" teacher, as defined by the NCLB legislation, identifies them as being highly effective in an urban school environment.

THE PROMISE OF NCLB

In his 1964 State of the Union address, President Lyndon Johnson announced, "This administration today, here and now, declares unconditional war on poverty in America." The "War on Poverty" was an ideal that sought to combat many of America's social and economic ills. It was designed to address problems in "chronically distressed areas" of the country and promote ideas such as a youth employment plan; extension of the food stamp and employment assistance systems; and support for schools, hospitals, and libraries.

A Legacy for Concern

A landmark educational product of the war on poverty was the Elementary and Secondary Education Act of 1965, which was the first extensive federal aid ever targeted for K–12 education. Through this act, the federal government allotted more than $1 billion to assist schools in the purchase of materials and to begin programs for students with special needs.

A fundamental goal of the Elementary and Secondary Education Act was the support of compensatory education designed to expand and improve educational programs for children and families living in poverty. President Johnson, a former schoolteacher, believed that "if poor children were provided a higher quality education they could attain the same levels of educational and occupational outcomes as their more advantaged counterparts, and ultimately, could escape the vicious cycle of poverty" (Borman, 2003, p. 453). Through the act, Title I was established as a form of compensatory education. Currently, Title I serves more than 10 million children in nearly 50,000 schools, and it continues to be one of the largest single investments that the federal government has made in U.S. public schools. Drawing from the act itself (Elementary and Secondary Education Act, 1965, 79 Stat. 27, 27), Borman describes the mission of Title I as providing

> financial assistance to ... local educational agencies serving areas with concentrations of children from low-income families to expand and improve their educational programs by various means ... which contribute particularly to meeting the special educational needs of educationally deprived children. (p. 453)

Schools with populations of students that qualify for Title I funds can use them at any grade level, K–12. However, most students are served in elementary school classrooms. Ideally, Title I was established to help close the achievement gap between economically disadvantaged students and their more advantaged peers.

With the passage of NCLB in January 2002, Congress reauthorized the Elementary and Secondary Act and focused the challenge of improving America's schools on the long-standing concern for closing the achievement gap between students from high and low socioeconomic backgrounds. Because Title I schools are home to many students from low socioeconomic backgrounds, they are subject to much of the focus under NCLB. To continue the legacy of the Elementary and Secondary Education Act, the current administration developed seven key components to be implemented through NCLB. *Improving Teacher Quality: All Students Taught by Quality Teachers* mandates the placement of highly qualified teachers in every classroom, especially those with a high proportion of children in poverty.

Offering a Promise for America's Toughest Schools

NCLB has established guidelines and criteria that describe highly qualified teachers and paraprofessionals. According to these standards, highly qualified teachers must (a) hold a minimum of a bachelor's degree, (2) have obtained full state certification or licensure, and (c) have demonstrated subject area competence in each of the academic subjects in which the teacher teaches. Beginning with the 2002–2003 academic year, newly hired elementary teachers must have also passed required state tests (U.S. Department of Education, 2016). New middle school and secondary school teachers must show successful completion of an academic major, a graduate degree, coursework equivalent to an undergraduate academic major, or advanced certification or credentialing in each of the academic subjects in which they teach. All teachers who are teaching core subjects (English, reading/language arts, mathematics, science, foreign languages, civics and government, economics, arts, history, and geography) in Title I schools who were hired after the 2002–2003 school year must be highly qualified. In addition, all teachers currently teaching in core subjects must be highly qualified by the end of the 2005–2006 school year. Although this NCLB legislation promised pedigrees and test scores as a means to quality and effective teaching (Schul, 2011), research regarding pedigrees and test scores as the means to quality and effective teaching, research regarding the traits of successful teachers in the urban context illustrates the importance of specific skills, dispositions, and attitudes as the essential attributes needed to be of high quality.

CHARACTERISTICS OF EFFECTIVE TEACHERS AND "STARS"

Urban environments present unique challenges for high-poverty schools and differentiate them from their suburban and rural counterparts (Delpit, 1995; Foster, 1994; Ladson-Billings, 1994; Olson & Jerald, 1998;

Sachs, 2004). For example, the culture of poverty and its blighting effects affect more African American children than it does any other racial or ethnic group and is considered an "urban phenomenon" (Olson & Jerald, 1998). Dr. Martin Haberman (1995), nationally recognized as a leader in effective urban teacher research, described the experience of urban teaching as "an extraordinary life experience—a volatile, highly charged, emotionally draining, physically exhausting experience for even the most competent, experienced teacher" (p. 1). He further states, "The pressures, intensity, and emotional commitments are beyond belief and almost beyond description" (p. 1).

In *Star Teachers of Children in Poverty* (1995), Haberman identifies 15 characteristics and seven midrange functions of effective urban teachers and refers to those educators who possess them as "star" teachers. These individuals

> are outstandingly successful: their students score higher on standardized tests; parents and children think they are great; principals rate them highly; other teachers regard them as outstanding; central office supervisors consider them successful; cooperating universities regard them as superior; and they evaluate themselves as outstanding teachers. (p. 1)

Through his extensive research on effective urban teachers, extending over a period of 50 years, Haberman identified the ideologies of these teachers that enabled them to be outstandingly successful with children in poverty. Star teachers also share histories of personal success in coping with significant personal trials (e.g., death of loved ones, bankruptcy, experiencing violence), and their dispositions and attitudes about effective urban teaching most likely emanated from those trials (Haberman, 1995, 1996).

Haberman (1995) argues that a teacher's disposition in his or her approach to working with at-risk students is the most powerful indicator of an effective urban educator. Teachers not successful in urban contexts tend to blame societal factors such as violence, gangs, drugs, and the like for the cause of the high percentage of at-risk children. These teachers also tend to blame the children for their lack of success. Haberman contends, however, that effective urban teachers fault the school, curricular, and teaching methodologies for placing the students at risk for academic failure. Furthermore, he states,

> Of all the functions that discriminate between stars and failures, this dimension [approach to at-risk students] is the most powerful predictor. There is no question that those predisposed to blame the victim will fail as teachers, while those whose natural inclination is constantly to seek more effective teaching strategies, regardless of youngsters' backgrounds or the obstacles

youngsters face, have a fighting chance of becoming effective teachers of children in poverty. (p. 53)

Protecting learners and learning is another disposition identified by Haberman (1995). Because star teachers place a high value on learning, they are able to capitalize on any learning opportunity, including "problems, questions, discrepant events, current crises, and emergencies" (p. 29). Haberman further states that star teachers are able to capture their students' spirit of learning by modeling their own passion for learning. Another characteristic intimately related to teacher commitment and effort is persistence. Star teachers believe that it is their responsibility to meet the needs of their students, and they constantly search and create meaningful, authentic activities to do so. These teachers do not give up on the children regardless of the circumstances that they bring to the classroom. An example of this star teacher mindset is provided in Figure 7.1 through a comparative case study of two 3rd-grade teachers who work at a Title I school.

Star teachers have the disposition, knowledge, and skills to transcend theory into practice. They are able to transform ideas, strategies, and generalizations into actual practice, and they can adapt professional development opportunities, teacher education courses, and clinical experiences into meaningful practice. These effective teachers have the necessary dispositions and skills to handle the demands of the bureaucracy without letting any pressures infringe on their teaching or the learning opportunities that they provide for their students. Emotional and physical stamina is also needed to assist and help students endure the depressing and difficult conditions that many of them must face and to sustain the necessary energy needed to create active classrooms that are student centered and engaging. Additional effective urban teacher characteristics as identified by Haberman (1995, 2005) are presented in Table 7.1.

Other scholars have investigated the characteristics of successful urban teachers. For example, an extensive review of the literature conducted by Baron et al. (1992) identified the characteristics and competencies of effective urban teachers that encompassed both internal and external effects. A few of their findings identified as essential characteristics include active teaching, the dispositions and skills to create a positive classroom environment, the dispositions and skills to use a variety of methods, applicability, and knowledge of urban and multiethnic sociology. Foster's (1994) research identified the following skills and attributes needed by teachers to promote excellence and success in teaching urban students: a disposition of cultural congruency, skills of cultural compatibility in communication patterns, a disposition to focus on the whole child (intellectually, socially, and emotionally), and the dispositions and skills to

Meadowview Elementary School has an enrollment of 457 students. It has been identified as a Title I School, with 94% of the students at or below the poverty level. Title I schools receive additional funding from the U.S. Department of Education with the intention of closing the gap between minority and majority student population. Meadowview Elementary did not meet the state guidelines and standards for accreditation, and has been "Accredited with Warning." Mrs. Susie Graham, the newly hired principal, is excited about the upcoming school year. She has been recognized by the district for her effective leadership and managerial skills. Susie has many ideas and interventions to share with her faculty to improve student performance.

Mrs. Graham had to hire two third grade teachers, and she used the *Star Teacher Selection Interview*, developed by Haberman (1995), to assist her through the process. The first prospective candidate, Mr. Glen Barr, is fully licensed, and has 12 years of teaching experience. His references were in order and noted his positive interactions with students. Mrs. Graham is impressed with his credentials, but knows she has to look beyond credentials to hire the best teacher for the position. Mr. Barr passed the *Star Teacher Interview*, and was hired to teach the third grade. Mrs. Graham secretly expected great things from him. The second candidate, Patty Thompson, is also a seasoned teacher with 15 years of experience. Mrs. Thompson is also fully licensed. Mrs. Graham, again, administered the *Star Teacher Interview*, but Patty does not receive a passing score. Never the less, Mrs. Graham hired her since the start of school was just a few days away, and she wasn't sure if more candidates would be available to be interviewed.

Although both teachers are licensed and fully qualified, Mrs. Graham noticed a remarkable difference on many elements between the two teachers. Take for example, *Theory into Practice*, a function of Star Teachers (Haberman, 1995, 2006). Both Mrs. Thompson and Mr. Barr claimed to have high expectations for their students, but their behaviors to support this ideal was very different. Based on Teacher Expectations-Student Achievement (TESA), Mrs. Thompson found it difficult to take the ideals behind the Pygmalion Theory and implement them in her classroom. As a result, she believed that giving students more busy work was the answer and the pedagogy of poverty reigned in her classroom. Such acts as giving information, giving directions, and monitoring seatwork were targeted in her classroom.

Mr. Barr, on the other hand, believed that his expectations in regards to student performance, influenced his teaching methodology which affected student achievement. He demonstrated such behaviors as being in close proximity to the students, taking a personal interest in their out of school lives, praising the performance of students, and using higher level questions. Mr. Barr clearly was able to put *Theory into Practice*.

As Mrs. Graham was making teacher observations, she noticed another distinctive difference between the two teachers. Mrs. Graham observed both teachers teaching a math lesson. Mrs. Thompson continued to utilize the Pedagogy of Poverty in her classroom. She simply gave information to the students in regards to the algorithm being taught, and she blamed them for not understanding. During the observation, it was apparent that her students became frustrated, and Mrs. Thompson easily gave up on her students.

Mr. Barr's lesson was active and student centered, and he included all students in the learning process. He developed an exciting lesson to teach the math algorithm that highlighted *Persistence*. It was obvious that Mr. Barr focused on meeting the needs of each student in the class, and searching for ways to determine "what works."

During Mrs. Graham's observation, she also noticed a difference between the two teachers in regards to *You and Me Against the Material*. Both classes were experiencing difficulty learning the new math algorithm, but how they handled the situation was very different. It was apparent that Mrs. Thompson was annoyed with the students who were having difficulty. This annoyance was easily conveyed to her students, which caused many to give up. She put the material first by letting her students know she will have to move on.

Mr. Barr did the opposite. He offered encouragement to his students that were experiencing difficulty. He served as their coach, noting that if they tackled the material together, success was inevitable. Mr. Barr felt great satisfaction in creating lessons that broke down information so that the child could learn with understanding. He demonstrated to his students that they all have potential in meeting success.

Both teachers are highly qualified and have a state teaching license, yet both teachers have a different teaching philosophy and behave differently in the classroom. Mrs. Graham contributed this difference to a passing score on the *Star Teacher Selection Interview*. She is convinced that if she is able to recruit more Star Teachers for her school, student achievement is foreseeable.

Figure 7.1. Comparative case study offers a glimpse of a star and traditional teacher in action.

connect classroom content with the life experiences of students. Additionally, McDermott and Rothenberg (2000) triangulated data from three focus groups made up of parents, teachers, and students to identify the characteristics of effective teachers in high-poverty schools. Their findings identified necessary characteristics and practices of high-performing

**Table 7.1.   A Comparison of the Identified
Effective Urban Teacher Characteristics**

Haberman (1995)	Baron et al. (1992)	Foster (1994)	McDermott & Rothenberg (2000)
Protecting children's learning: Teachers are able to capitalize on all learning opportunities.	X		
Persistence: Teachers constantly pursue strategies and activities so all children can meet success.	X		
Approach to at-risk students: Teachers take responsibility for children's learning, regardless of the conditions they face.	X		X
Putting ideas into practice: Teachers can relate theory and practice.	X		
Profession/personal orientation to students: Teachers expect and are able to develop rapport with children.	X	X	X
The bureaucracy: Teachers can adjust and cope with the demands of the bureaucracy.			
Fallibility: Teachers take responsibility for their own errors and mistakes.			
Emotional and physical stamina: Teachers are able to endure the challenges and crises of urban settings.			
Organizational ability: Teachers have extraordinary organizational and managerial skills.	X	X	
Explanation of teacher success: Teachers believe that success is met by effort and hard work and not by ability alone.	X		
Explanation of children's success: Teachers are committed to student autonomy and individual differences.	X	X	X
Real teaching: Teachers engage in active teaching instead of direct instruction.	X	X	X
Making students feel needed: Teachers are able to make the students feel needed and wanted in the classroom.	X	X	X
The material versus the student: Teachers find approaches that will assist students in mastering the material.	X	X	X
Gentle teaching in a violent society: Teacher's ideology is promising, even in light of a violent society.	X	X	X

teachers as the dispositions and skills to build trusting relationships with both students and families, communicate frequently with families, demonstrate high expectations, and integrate student's cultural knowledge throughout the curriculum. An analysis of these findings illustrates considerable correspondence across researchers, as shown in Table 7.1.

MAKING A DIFFERENCE IN URBAN SCHOOLS

There is much debate among policymakers and educators alike when conversations focus on the appropriateness of the NCLB Act as the means to improve the prospects of urban schooling and the scholarship of historically underserved children. Advocates embrace the law's admirable goals: accountability in the academic proficiency of all students and high expectations and standards in core content areas. Critics fear that this legislation makes it easy for schools "to exclude students who are low performing on high-stakes tests" (Schul, 2011, p. 2). Using the designation of "highly qualified" teachers without acknowledging, supporting, and promoting the characteristics of star teachers who define effective teaching in urban schools may very well threaten the academic future of most urban students and schools.

According to Haberman (1996), the criteria used to identify "highly qualified" or "the best and the brightest" typically are "white, monolingual, female teacher education students in undergraduate, preservice, teacher education programs" (p. 752); interestingly, these are the very teachers most likely to quit or fail in urban district schools (Haberman, 2003). For example, those teachers who quit and leave urban districts have higher grade point averages and standardized test scores when compared to those of stars. Additionally, teachers with content majors and advanced degrees leave at an extremely high rate. Because most of these teachers come from different socioeconomic environments than those of their students, they find it difficult, if not impossible, to provide culturally responsive methodology to urban students, thus fueling their decision to leave (Kincheloe, 2004).

In her research, Ladson-Billings (2001) found that there are many experienced teachers who have the ability "to teach well in challenging circumstances" (p. 3). Again, the criteria that NCLB proposes for highly qualified teachers do not include the criteria that she refers to as "teaching well," which "means making sure that students achieve, develop a positive sense of themselves, and develop a commitment to larger social and community concerns" (p. 16). This description, along with the characteristics put forth by Haberman and other scholars in the field, acknowledges the importance of qualitative characteristics that are vital in the education of students in urban settings and are not remotely similar to the pedigree and test-based characteristics of highly qualified teachers as defined by NCLB.

According to Haberman (2003),

> While being an effective teacher of diverse children in poverty has some intellectual and academic aspects, it is primarily a human relations activity demanding the ability to make and maintain positive, supportive connections with diverse children, school staff, and caregivers. (p. 23)

Gay (2000) also contends that effective teachers set consistently high expectations and demonstrate those strands of behavior that support a nurturing and caring environment. She further states that star teachers have moral courage and the desire to make the educational enterprise culturally responsive. The enactment of NCLB presented many challenges for urban schools as they move forward to comply with the regulations stipulated by the Department of Education. Clearly, the attraction and retention of effective teachers, as well as the preparation of teacher candidates, are fundamental concerns for all schools, especially those in urban districts.

Attracting and Retaining Effective Urban Educators

The National Commission on Teaching and America's Future (2002) predicts over three million teaching vacancies over the next 10 years, with an overwhelming number in urban schools (U.S. Department of Education, 2002). This is especially critical because urban districts face a greater challenge with hiring and retaining fully credentialed teachers, especially in the areas of mathematics, science, special education, and bilingual education, when compared to their suburban and rural counterparts (Dill & Stafford-Johnson, 2003; Olson & Jerald, 1998; Stafford & Haberman, 2003; U.S. Department of Education, 2002). Of utmost concern is that, even when urban districts are able to hire teachers for their most challenging schools, many of them are inexperienced and leave after a short tenure, some within the first 3–5 years of their professional careers as educators (Dill & Stafford-Johnson, 2003; Haberman, 1995, 2005; Olson & Jerald, 1998; Stafford & Haberman, 2003).

Responding to the NCLB legislation, many urban districts have initiated programs and incentives to attract and retain highly qualified teachers. For example, the Charlotte-Mecklenburg County School System in North Carolina implemented the Equity Plus Program, which includes such incentives as (a) $10,000 a year for 3 years to teach in high-poverty schools, (b) a $500 critical-needs bonus, (c) stipends for teachers who hold master's degrees or are enrolled in graduate-level programs, and (d) financial assistance for teachers to enroll in graduate-level programs. Initiatives of other urban districts include retirement credits, low-interest home mortgages, and forgivable student loans (Claycomb, 2000). Although these initiatives have yet to be fully evaluated, rhetoric and compensatory measures will not attract or retain a high-quality cadre of teachers needed for urban districts.

Teacher preparation programs have played a significant role in urban teacher recruitment. Many colleges of education have responded by providing alternative licensure routes tailored specifically for nontraditional students. Such models include the Retired Military Transition Program and Career Ladders for Teacher Aids. According to Claycomb (2000), headway has also been made in developing and implementing programs for the recruitment of urban teachers. Interventions designed for the retention of urban teachers beyond the first 5 years continue to remain elusive, and the outcomes of these efforts are not well known.

Challenges to Teacher Preparation Programs

Colleges of education traditionally implement a universal approach to teacher education. There continues to be much contradiction and controversy among researchers when the idea of an "urban track" for teacher preparation is proposed (Haberman, 1996). Some scholars assert that effective teachers are able to implement strategies and techniques that are sensitive to all cultural differences, thus supporting programs that focus on the generalization of best practices (Swisher & Deyhle, 1989). Others argue that teacher preparation programs should concentrate on urban pedagogy, and they believe that doing so would contribute to more culturally responsive and competent teachers (Guyton, 1994; Haberman, 1996; Irvine, 1990).

Numerous studies have supported the need for colleges and universities to prepare teacher candidates specifically for the urban context. For example, McKinney, Robinson, and Spooner (2004) report that traditional college experiences do not adequately prepare student interns for the demands of urban school teaching. Audette's (1999) investigation assessed elementary school principals in an urban metropolitan district to determine their levels of satisfaction with the preparation "of newly hired teachers." Over 80% of the 267 respondents indicated overall satisfaction, and 91% ranked dispositions as the most important factor in the eventual success of new teachers. One principal noted, "If a teacher is reasonably intelligent and has an excellent attitude, we can help them to be successful by modeling, mentoring, and filling voids in their preparation. If they have a bad attitude, they taint the entire atmosphere of our school." These studies strongly support the premise that to have highly qualified teachers in urban schools, teacher preparation programs have a serious responsibility to screen for and address the needed characteristics and dispositions of teachers in urban schools where the environmental conditions and learning needs of children are sufficiently distinctive. Until professionals preparing teachers acknowledge the need for an urban-skill and dispositional-knowledge base, it is expected that highly qualified teachers will not be equipped to meet the demands and challenges of urban teaching and that "savage inequalities" will continue to pervade many urban school communities (Kozol, 1991).

Changing Course to Achieve Intended Outcomes

Effective teaching requires documentary knowledge of curricular content, pedagogical skills, and dispositions ranging from a passion for learning to empathy for the challenges that urban students face. It is clear from the review of the NCLB legislation and the evidence of research literature that there is no connection between the set criteria for highly qualified teachers and the characteristics of successful urban teachers. To ensure that no urban child is left behind, attention needs to be given and significant changes need to be made by federal policymakers, teacher preparation programs, state education agencies, and professional development opportunities.

The NCLB legislation does recognize the instrumental role that teachers play in the academic achievement of students; however, bachelor's degrees, state certification, and subject matter competency, although necessary, are not sufficient for teaching success in the urban classroom (Stafford & Haberman, 2003). Federal policymakers must move to expand the qualifications and criteria for highly qualified to include those characteristics that describe urban teaching at its best. Although many urban schools fall short in attracting and retaining high-quality educators, the research contends that those teachers who are identified as highly qualified based on the NCLB standards still experience difficulty and failure in this challenging setting (Haberman, 1996, 2003; Kincheloe, 2004). Clearly, merging these designations will successfully support the imperative that children are provided with a highly qualified teacher.

From the perspective of teacher preparation programs, new models for teacher education must be explored and developed. Colleges of education must transcend the traditional, universal context of teaching and move to place emphasis on understanding, screening for, developing, and evaluating candidates specific for urban school environments (Stafford & Haberman, 2003). Sensitive and validated instruments, such as Haberman's (2004) Urban Teacher Selection Interview, should be developed and utilized to measure potential candidates' dispositions and their likelihood of being successful in the urban school setting. Furthermore, teacher candidates need earlier and additional opportunities to interact with teachers who have proven to be effective in urban schools with students in poverty. The "capstone" experience of student teaching and short-term field experiences have demonstrated their ineffectiveness in developing the ideology to be effective in this type of environment (Haberman, 1995, 2005; McKinney, Haberman, Stafford-Johnson, & Robinson, 2006; McKinney et al., 2004).

State education agencies also need to make adjustments to teacher licensure requirements. Although there is variation in each state's licensure policies, many state departments issue generic elementary school certifications, meaning that those certified can practice their craft in all elementary school settings. Contextual specializations need to be offered, such as certification for teaching in urban school environments or working with at-risk students. The National Council for Accreditation of Teacher Education (2016) now recognizes professional dispositions as an essential element of teacher preparation and expects teacher preparation programs to ensure that candidates "demonstrate dispositions that value fairness and learning by all students" (p. 1). Furthermore, it recommends that higher learning institutions assess teacher candidates' dispositions based on observable classroom behaviors, although it has not communicated the guidelines and criteria for doing so. Because of the new attention given to teacher dispositions, state agencies should also require increased dispositional evidence for certification, given that teacher dispositions have been identified as a vital link to student achievement (Haberman, 1996, 2003; Ladson-Billings, 1994). Finally, urban school districts need to provide extensive professional development opportunities that are rooted in the continual growth of urban teachers (Briars & Resnick, 2000). "A vital step toward school improvement, especially for at-risk children, is making each teacher's learning as important as each child's learning" (Freppon, 2001, p. 159). When districts invest their efforts into improving teaching quality through professional development opportunities, the instructional methodology and practices of the participating teachers are greatly improved (Wenglinsky, 2002). Furthermore, ongoing professional development opportunities can greatly enhance the professional knowledge base of all urban teachers and build a sense of community among them, which in turn can improve the climate of the school building (Berry, Johnson, & Montgomery, 2005). A multiple-dimension effort focusing on teacher inquiry and reflection, cognitive coaching and mentoring, and action research should be made to address how teachers grow, change, and develop throughout their career (Freppon, 2001).

Although NCLB is undoubtedly the most important education legislation enacted since 1974's special education law, its arrival caused great concern for professional educators in urban districts. Although many agree that the intent behind the NCLB legislation was to improve all schools across the nation, the law's narrow focus of defining "highly qualified" excludes the essential skills, knowledge, and attributes that teachers need to be of high quality in urban schools (Berry, Hoke, & Hirsch, 2004). Until policymakers and professional educators acknowledge that a highly qualified urban teacher entails more than subject matter competence, students in poverty may have "highly qualified" teachers but not necessarily "stars."

CHAPTER QUESTIONS

1. Describe the process of state licensure for teachers in the nation and in your state.
2. How do the latest reform efforts in teacher education affect the teacher licensure process? Be specific and name a reform initiative and share a minimum of two potential influences on teacher licensure.
3. Compare and contrast the terms *highly qualified* and *star* teachers.
4. Table 7.1 gives a comparison of several characteristic for effective urban teachers. Identify four from the list and demonstrate the way in which you perform each attribute in your classroom.

ACKNOWLEDGMENT

This chapter was originally published in *The Journal of Teacher Education and Practice* in 2006, volume19, number 1, pages 80–93. Reprinted with permission of Rowman & Littlefield Publishing Group. All rights reserved.

REFERENCES

Audette, R. (1999). *A follow-up survey of graduates' teaching performance in elementary education.* Unpublished manuscript, University of North Carolina, Charlotte.

Baron, E., Rusnak, T., Brookhart, S., Burrett, K., & Whordley, D. (1992, March). *Collaborative urban education: Characteristics of successful urban teachers*. Paper presented at the American Association of School Administrators Convention, San Diego, CA.

Bartoli, J. (2001). *Celebrating city teachers: How to make a difference in urban schools*. Portsmouth, NH: Heinemann.

Berry, B., Hoke, M., & Hirsch, E. (2004). The search for highly qualified teachers. *Phi Delta Kappan, 85*(9), 684–689.

Berry, B., Johnson, D., & Montgomery, D. (2005). The power of teacher leadership. *Educational Leadership, 62*(5), 56–59.

Borman, G. (2003). Compensatory education. In *Encyclopedia of Education* (Vol. 2, pp. 453-458). New York, NY: Macmillan.

Briars, D., & Resnick, L. B. (2000). *Standards, assessments, and what else? The essential elements of standards-based school improvements* (CSE Tech. Report No. 528). Los Angeles: University of California, National Center for Research on Evaluation, Standards, and Student Testing.

Carter, S. (2001). *No excuses: Lessons from 21 high-performing, high-poverty schools*. Washington, DC: Heritage Foundation.

Claycomb, C. (2000). High-quality urban school teachers: What they need to enter and to remain in hard-to-staff schools. *The State Education Standard, 1*(1), 17–20.

Delpit, L. (1995). *Other people's children*. New York: New York Press.

Dill, V., & Stafford-Johnson, D. (2003). *Can teachers be found and certified to teach students at risk?* Houston, TX: Haberman Educational Foundation.

Elementary and Secondary Education Act (ESEA) of 1965, Pub. L. No. 89-10, § 79, Stat 27.

Foster, M. (1994). Effective black teachers: A literature review. In E. Hollins, J. King, & W. Hayman (Eds.), *Teaching diverse populations: Formulating a knowledge base* (pp. 225–241). Albany: State University of New York Press.

Freppon, P. (2001). *What it takes to be a teacher: The role of personal and professional development*. Portsmouth, NH: Heinemann.

Gay, G. (2000). *Culturally responsive teaching: Theory, research, and practice*. New York, NY: Teachers College Press.

Goldhaber, D. (2003). *Teacher quality and student achievement* (Urban Diversity Series No. 115). Retrieved from ERIC data base. (ED477271)

Good, T., & Brophy, J. E. (1997). *Looking in classrooms* (7th ed.). Bloomington, IN: National Educational Service.

Guyton, E. (1994, April). *First year teaching experiences of early childhood urban teacher.* Paper presented at the annual meeting of the American Educational Research Association, New Orleans, LA.

Haberman, M. (1995). *Star teachers of children in poverty*. West Lafayette, IN: Kappa Delta Pi.

Haberman, M. (1996). Selecting and preparing culturally competent teachers for urban schools. In J. Sikula (Ed.), *Handbook of research on teacher education* (pp. 747–760). New York, NY: Macmillan.

Haberman, M. (2003). *Who benefits from failing urban school districts? An essay on equity and justice for diverse children in urban poverty*. Houston, TX: Haberman Educational Foundation.

Haberman, M. (2004). *Star teacher selection interview training manual*. Houston, TX: Haberman Educational Foundation.

Haberman, M. (2005). *Star teachers: The ideology and best practice of effective teachers of diverse children and youth in poverty*. Houston, TX: Haberman Educational Foundation.

Haycock, K. (2001). Closing the achievement gap. *Educational Leadership, 58*(6), 6–11.

Irvine, J. J. (1990). *Black students and school failure: Policies, practices, and prescriptions*. New York, NY: Greenwood.

Kincheloe, J. (2004). Why a book on urban education? In S. Steinberg & J. Kincheloe (Eds.), *19 urban questions: Teaching in the city* (pp. 1–32). New York, NY: Peter Lang.

Kozol, J. (1991). *Savage inequalities*. New York, NY: HarperCollins.

Ladson-Billings, G. (1994). *The dreamkeepers: Successful teachers of African American children*. San Francisco: Jossey-Bass.

Ladson-Billings, G. (2000). Fighting for our lives: Preparing teachers to teach African American students. *Journal of Teacher Education, 51*, 206–214.

Ladson-Billings, G. (2001). *Crossing over to Canaan: The journey of new teachers in diverse classrooms*. San Francisco, CA: Jossey-Bass.

McDermott, P., & Rothenberg, J. (2000, April). *The characteristics of effective teachers in high poverty schools: Triangulating our data*. Paper presented at the annual meeting of the American Educational Research Association, New Orleans, LA.

McKinney, S., Haberman, M., Stafford-Johnson, D., & Robinson, J. (2006). *Developing teachers for high-poverty schools: The role of the internship experience*. Unpublished manuscript, Old Dominion University, Norfolk, VA.

McKinney, S., Robinson, J., & Spooner, M. (2004). A comparison of urban teacher characteristics for student interns placed in different urban school settings. *Professional Educator, 26*(2), 17–30.

Mehan, H., Hubbard, L., & Villanueva, I. (1994). Forming academic identities: Accommodation without assimilation among involuntary minorities. *Anthropology and Education Quarterly, 25*(2), 91–117.

National Commission on Teaching and America's Future. (2002). *Unraveling the "teacher shortage" problem: Teacher retention is the key*. Washington, DC: U.S. Government Printing Office.

National Council of Accreditation of Teacher Education. (2016). *NCATE glossary*. Retrieved October 16, 2016, from http://www.ncate.org/Standards/ UnitStandards/Glossary/tabid/477/Default.aspx#P

National Research Council. (2001). *Testing teacher candidates: The role of licensure tests in improving teacher quality*. Retrieved October 16, 2016, from https:// www.nap.edu/read/10090/chapter/1

No Child Left Behind (NCLB) Act of 2001, Pub. L. No. 107-110, § 6319, Stat 20 (2008).

Olson, L., & Jerald, C. D. (1998, January 8). Barriers to success. *Education Week, 17,* 9–23.

Pollard-Durodola, S. (2003). Wesley Elementary: A beacon of hope for at-risk students. *Education and Urban Society, 36*(1), 94–117.

Rice, J. K. (2003). *Teacher quality: Understanding the effectiveness of teacher attributes.* Washington, DC: Economic Policy Institute.

Sachs, S. (2004) Evaluation of teacher attributes as predictors of success in urban schools. *Journal of Teacher Education, 55*(2), 177–187.

Sanders, W. L., & Rivers, J. (1996). *Cumulative and residual effects of teachers on future student academic achievement.* Knoxville: University of Tennessee, Value-Added Research and Assessment Center.

Schul, J. (2011). *Unintended consequences: Fundamental flaws that plague the no child left behind act.* Retrieved October 16, 2016, from https://nau.edu/uploadedFiles/Academic/COE/About/Projects/Unintended%20Consequences.pdf

Stafford, D., & Haberman, M. (2003). *Can I be a star teacher of diverse children in poverty?* Houston, TX: Haberman Educational Foundation.

Swisher, K., & Deyhle, D. (1989, August). The styles of learning are different but the teaching is just the same: Suggestions for teachers of American Indian youth. *Journal of American Indian Education,* (Special Issue), 1–14.

U.S. Department of Education. (2002, October). *Student achievement and school accountability conference.* Washington, DC: Author.

U.S. Department of Education (2016). *New no child left behind flexibility: Highly qualified teachers.* Retrieved October 16, 2016, from http://www2.ed.gov/nclb/methods/teachers/hqtflexibility.html

Wenglinsky, H. (2002). How schools matter: The link between teacher classroom practices and student academic performance. *Education Policy Analysis Archives, 10*(12). Retrieved October 1, 2016, from https://www.researchgate.net/publication/246392082_How_schools_matter_The_link_between_teacher_classroom_practices_and_student_academic_performance

CHAPTER 8

VICTORY AT BUFFALO CREEK

What Makes a School Serving Low-Income Hispanic Children Successful?

Martin Haberman

Chapter Objectives

The learner will

1. critique a case study of a successful elementary school serving low-income Hispanic learners; and
2. appraise the 33 indicators of a successful school for underserved learners.

What makes a school serving low-income Hispanic children successful? The short answer is the quality of the teachers and the principal. The long answer deals with specifically what they do and the nature of the school climate they create.

The literature explaining school effectiveness for children in poverty is often alluded to in superficial ways. Experts seem to agree that effective schools have regular testing, a strong principal, high teacher expectations, and parental support. Unfortunately, these rubrics also describe

Better Teachers, Better Schools: What Star Teachers Know, Believe, and Do
pp. 137–159

many urban poverty schools which are failing. Each week I visit middle schools which seem to have these four characteristics but from which 60% of the students disappear before they get to or finish high school. What is needed in greater detail is what effectiveness looks like. What are the identifiable behavioral indicators which can be observed and assessed in a successful school? In this chapter, 33 such indicators are identified. Hopefully, this level of detail will begin to explain what actually leads to success in schools serving children in poverty. It should also become easier to improve less effective schools once there are clearer, more specific indicators to emulate.

THE CONTEXT

Buffalo Creek is an elementary school in Houston, Texas, and is part of the Spring Branch Independent School District (SBISD). It opened in 1997 to 586 children and currently serves 630 children in a typical PK–5 organization. The student body is 85% Hispanic, almost entirely of Mexican background. The free lunch program includes 86% of the student body, and 75% of the children are bused. The staff includes a full-time principal, assistant principal, school secretary, 5 custodians, and 29 classroom teachers. The following specialists are also full time: one art teacher, one and a half music teachers, one physical education teacher, four special education teachers, a half-time math specialist, a half-time reading specialist, and two reading recovery teachers. There is also a full-time librarian, one social worker, and one counselor. Part-time staff includes six full-time teaching assistants. There are also six staff in food preparation who work 8 hours per week. The children attending the school were selected by creating boundary changes to relieve overcrowding in four surrounding schools. The teachers were all selected using the Urban Teacher Selection Interview. So too was the assistant principal. The principal is trained to interview using both the Urban Teacher Selection Interview and the Urban Principal Selection Interview.

Why is Buffalo Creek Elementary Successful?

The 33 indicators of this school's success have been gathered from direct observations, school records, speaking with the principal and staff, conducting formal interviews of staff, and reviewing written questionnaires of staff. These indicators are not grouped or summarized because grouping them changes their character. For example, several items relate to having a "strong principal" but what exactly does that mean? The indicators of what the principal actually does and doesn't do involves more than being a "strong" principal. Some indicators are stated in two sentences. Others require a few paragraphs. A discussion of what might be learned from Buffalo Creek concludes the chapter.

After its first year of operation, the school was officially designated as "recognized." Passing rates on the Texas Assessment of Academic Skills (TAAS; the state test at the time) included 97% of the children passed the TAAS, 85% of the students passed the TAAS in reading, and 81% of the students passed the TAAS in math.

Teachers' Children Attend

Other indicators of the school's success are even more compelling. Eight teachers have their own children attending the school. These children were enrolled prior to the achievement test results reported above. In the city where I live there are approximately 6,500 teachers and over 100,000 students. I know of no school where teachers enroll their own children. Indeed, when specifically asked, a majority of our teachers state they would not send their children to the schools where they teach.

Children's Needs Trump Schedule

An obvious indicator of school success relates to scheduling. Most of the extra things plus all the expected things that the staff in Buffalo Creek is willing and eager to do are done by teacher decision. In most urban school districts teachers are required by union contract to leave the building at a common time: as early as 2:30 or 3:00 p.m. in some cities. Such an agreement which controls teacher practice would be inconceivable in Buffalo Creek. Teachers, staff, students, parents, administrators are free to make their own decisions about their presence in the building. Even more, the children's bus schedule is not an iron control over children staying after school for extra activities or additional help. The fact that the staff at Buffalo Creek controls their own time rather than being told when they must leave the building or cut the children's activities off is a source of empowerment for the faculty and staff. It is a truism in the world of work that those with greater control over their own time have higher status and receive greater recognition. This is especially true for teachers who must work within highly organized time schedules. At Buffalo Creek it is a clear and agreed-upon principle of operation that the educational and human needs of children and teachers will take precedence over even the time schedule. This is no mean feat. It is typical in most schools that the rigidities of the time schedule will trump any other consideration. For the Buffalo Creek faculty to be able to give numerous examples of how they make children's needs and their professional preferences a dominant factor over the time schedule is a clear indicator of their empowerment.

Identifiable Priorities

A clear indicator of this school's success deals with the absence of "projectitis." This is a common disease of schools in districts serving children in poverty. Every conceivable program is overlaid on a panoply of existing programs, none of which is ever implemented long enough to matter and none of which can be evaluated because of the contamination from all the other programs. Where everything is special, nothing is. Even worse, the "regular" curriculum disappears. Most school districts serving impoverished students ricochet from one priority to the next as short-term superintendents pass through them. Projects and programs are adopted and dumped into schools because federal or state monies are available. Typically, teachers are barraged with "innovations." Their response cannot be one of hurling themselves wholeheartedly into the next initiative because there are simply too many. Indeed, many districts and individual schools adopt initiatives which require contradictory assumptions about how children learn and what constitutes teachers' best practice. It is understandable that even good teachers as well as burnouts will respond to endless initiatives with, "Don't get excited. This too shall pass." And they are usually right. In a year or two the program, its advocate, and the funds are likely to be gone.

In Buffalo Creek there are only a few new initiatives, everyone buys into them and they are evaluated on an ongoing basis. Buffalo Creek is implementing the Tribes program to combat school violence, a bilingual program, and thematic teaching. Before the faculty would take on any new initiative they would consider its impact on these existing priorities. It is clear that the faculty and staff know what their priorities are and are sticking with them.

Effort as the Explanation for Success

An indicator of school success not typically used is how the faculty and administration account for their own success and that of the children. The Buffalo Creek staff is unanimous in their commitment to effort as the most powerful predictor of success. They do not buy into the ability paradigm. This ideology defines their work as teachers. They believe their job involves engaging learners, getting children to persist, be active, and work hard. They use effort to explain their own successes and those of the principal and school staff.

Such an ideology leads them to believe that if they do not reach a particular objective, they can do something about it. Their belief in the effort paradigm contributes to their feeling of empowerment; that the things they really value for the school are achievable.

Demonstrated Effort as the Basis for High Expectations

High expectations become realizable only as a result of the faculty and staff commitment to the effort paradigm. If the staff of a school were to state high expectations but believe in the ability paradigm, they would be stating a vacuous goal over which they had no control. If children's ability were the cause of their school success then teachers could be essentially unaccountable since acts of teaching, whatever they were, would not be the primary cause of children's learning—innate ability would. Buffalo Creek teachers assume all their children will learn because they feel accountable for generating students' effort and engaging them in learning.

The principal shares the teachers' commitment to student effort. She also explains teacher success and her own success using the effort paradigm. This means there is a logical and consistent basis by which all the Buffalo Creek staff explain their own, each others', and the children's success. To merely announce a belief in high expectations or to place a high expectations flag on the building or to have a logo printed on school stationery is not an implementation strategy. A commonly shared ideology held by 100% of the staff who buy into the effort paradigm is that "everyone who works will achieve and our job is to generate meaningful work," will implement a program of schoolwide high expectations.

Widespread Peer Teaching

An overall but clear indicator of school success is that the students believe their school is a learning community. The children themselves see learning as the school's primary activity and themselves as capable of realizing this goal. The behavioral indicator that most directly substantiates this student perception is their willingness to help each other. Cooperative learning is regularly practiced for some portion of time in all classrooms. A singular indicator of this student commitment is that fourth graders regularly give up their recess period to teach kindergartners comprehension skills. When asked, the faculty can give numerous examples of Buffalo Creek children taking advantage of similar opportunities to teach each other.

Interconnected Teachers

A related indicator of school success is that Buffalo Creek teachers are not limited to dealing with problems by themselves. The isolated teacher who can rely on only her own resources to solve problems is a condition that has been well documented, particularly in large impersonal school systems. Buffalo Creek teachers however expect to and actually do consult with each other, the principal, staff, and community resources as a regular, normal procedure. They are not evaluated as effective if they shut their doors and keep problems away from the principal. The operating value in Buffalo Creek is not that it is a sign of weakness when a teacher seeks help but that it is a natural expectation of a good teacher to seek the advice and cooperation with others. The operating value of the entire staff is "we are in this together. We fail and succeed together."

As a result, teachers regularly seek the advice, ideas, and suggestions of others; develop action plans; and then conduct evaluations of how well particular treatments work. This is no minor characteristic, it's merely item #8 on a list of school attributes. The teachers at Buffalo Creek do not feel isolated. When faced with what seems to be an insolvable problem, they tackle it rather than merely cope with it or sweep it under the rug. As a result, there is a professional willingness by teachers to admit to problems, to seek and accept suggestions, to willingly try implementing treatments, and to engage in evaluations. Teachers are not expected to suffer in silence but to be proactive and team players.

The Faculty as Family

A clearly observable indicator of school success flows from how the teachers work together. The staff has created a community, almost a family, in the Buffalo Creek School. In many large districts the only one who knows a teacher is even absent is the school secretary. And frequently even the school secretary may not know if there is an automated system for teachers to call in sick and for the school to ring up a substitute. The staff in this school derive personal as well as professional support from participating in the life of Buffalo Creek. The various adults who work in Buffalo Creek do not perceive of their school society as an associational one: that is, a work setting where strangers go to practice their profession. The teachers perceive the society they have created in Buffalo Creek as communal: a place of shared values where "everyone knows and cares about me just as I care about them." This communal dynamic creates a bonding similar to that found on a winning team or in an effective military or medical unit as participants realize that their best interests as individuals can only be realized by the success of the group. If a new teacher were to suggest to this faculty that they not work so hard one of two things would happen. The newcomer would have to change and learn to wholeheartedly accept being socialized into the communal ideology that puts kids first, or start thinking about transferring out.

In effective schools, children are seldom late or absent. Less obvious but of equal importance is the behavior of teachers and staff. It is now common in many school districts serving children in poverty for teachers to take "mental health" days off. These are instances in which teachers are not ill but take off the maximum number of days for which they can be paid. In some schools, one third of the faculty may be absent on a given day and if the teachers' contract permits one sick day every two weeks, the entire staff takes that full number. In contrast, Buffalo Creek teachers have a low rate of absenteeism. Indeed, they frequently work when they are ill and are loathe to be away from their children. The operating norm at Buffalo Creek is to routinely place the needs of the children ahead of the teachers' convenience.

Teachers Control Curriculum

Teachers at Buffalo Creek do not report that they feel pressured to cover a certain amount of content each day or even each week. This means that teachers on the same grade level do not feel they are in a race with each other or that they must cover a certain number of chapters in a book in a given time. What they do is set out some global or major points of where they want to be during the year and then discuss with each other where they are and why. An individual teacher can decide how much time to spend on a specific area of content. What this flexibility does is enable teachers with specific groups of students to decide how much time they will devote to studying particular amounts of subject matter. This is a form of curricular empowerment which permits each teacher to focus on her students' needs. If more or less time is needed the teacher can make that determination. Rather than the curriculum serving as a force which controls teacher behavior, the teachers control which content will be emphasized for particular time periods. It is a truism of school success that the more curricular decisions made at the classroom level rather than at the district or state level, the more likely it becomes that the curriculum will actually be learned and not merely covered. What this indicator means in practice is that the Buffalo Creek teachers begin with the annual curriculum goals in each subject area. They then use several long-term goals as markers or guidelines. Within these broad guidelines the teachers are free to decide how quickly to move their classes through each of the content areas. This aspect of teacher empowerment gives every teacher at Buffalo Creek a strong sense of personal input (even control) over what will be studied and for how long. Having this power contributes to the faculty's perception that they are professionals. Teachers without such decision-making authority (i.e., most teachers) report feeling they are written off as mere "how-to-do-it" people who merely follow the texts and implement the curriculum decisions of others.

The Integration of Teacher Specialists

A daily indicator of school success is how the Buffalo Creek teachers work with and utilize specialist teachers in art, music, physical education, and library. In this school, a class period or block of time with a specialist does not mean children stop what they are doing in order to sing or do some artwork while their teacher has a free period. The teachers use and integrate the specialists into their curriculum. Rather than have the children's studies interrupted to do some extraneous activity, the classroom teachers and specialists plan and work together. This means in practice that the content taught by a specialty teacher will fit with, enhance, and extend the science, social studies, math, or language arts being taught in the classroom. If the students are engaged in a particular science or social studies activity for example, there are numerous ways in which special teachers may teach their subject-matter concepts in ways which mesh with and enrich the classroom activities. In this way children gain a sense of how learning seemingly diverse subjects can fit together and interrelate. This planning between teaching specialists and classroom teachers leads students to their curriculum in more integrated, holistic ways rather than as bits and pieces of unconnected knowledge.

Thematic Teaching

Related to and supporting this cooperative planning across disciplines is how most Buffalo Creek teachers deal with subject matter within their individual classrooms. They use thematic teaching; that is, they organize chunks of subject matter drawn from various fields to answer particular problems and questions which hold meaning for their students.

For example, the study of electricity can include science, math, reading, history, music, art, and any number of other subjects. Beginning with particular themes which are relevant to the students, teachers may draw on various subject matters. For children in poverty who often lack the life experiences assumed by those who write textbooks, and who assume there is a common body of knowledge shared by all 6- or 8- or 12-year-olds, thematic teaching seeks to provide the common experiences all children need to learn particular content. This is a major difference between Buffalo Creek and the failing schools in most districts serving children in poverty. Typically, poor children behind in basic skills are subjected to endless hours, days, weeks, months, and years of "drill and kill" activities. Following directions and completing endless worksheets (or computer screens) of drill and kill might be worth the price of student unhappiness if it worked. But it does not. In some cities, endless meaningless skill drills have actually been endorsed by the school board as the official method of instruction to be followed. I refer to this as the pedagogy of poverty. No school board or educational experts would dare inflict such a methodology on advantaged or affluent children.

Thematic teaching requires trusting that teachers have the ability to interest children in almost everything they will need to learn and to keep drill to a minimum. Obviously, everything children need to learn is not necessarily pleasurable and cannot always be made fun. Thematic teaching permits dedicated, hardworking teachers to make a good portion of learning engaging and useful. The bottom line here is that inadequate teachers can be ordered to follow a regimen of drill but they cannot be mandated to use thematic instruction. Such instruction requires great knowledge of content, pedagogy, and the relationship skills needed to connect the children with key concepts in the curriculum. The teachers at Buffalo Creek have all been selected on the basis of having the relationship skills needed to work with children; they are also willing to learn whatever else they need in the areas of subject-matter content and teaching strategies.

Teacher Control of Methods

A pedagogical indicator of success is related to the previous two. While teachers generally use thematic units and integrate their planning with specialists, they still retain some freedom over their teaching methods. Each teacher can determine how much direct instruction, cooperative learning, peer teaching, or individualized or whole-group instruction she will use on a given day or within a week or month. It is within each teacher's power and discretion to teach the whole class or a subgroup, to give a lesson using direct instruction, cooperative learning or some other method. Just as teachers are empowered to control the curriculum, each is empowered to control her pedagogy. As with almost everything else at Buffalo Creek, this is a shared topic of open discussion. Teachers are aware of and supportive of the similarities and differences in their preferred teaching styles. As they share what works for them they are able to put advice and suggestions in context since they know how their colleagues teach.

Risk Takers, Not Change Agents

Another critically important indicator of school success is that the Buffalo Creek faculty are risk takers not change agents. They do not begin by rejecting or seeking to alter state mandates or district policies. At the same time they are willing to try anything reasonable to help their children become engaged in learning and achieve. Effective teachers are focused on their children's learning. They devote whatever physical and psychic energy they have toward this goal. They do not become teachers to function as system changers. Their primary emphasis is on the children in their classes not on school organization or district policies. They see themselves as working directly for the children and their families.

Frequently the Buffalo Creek teachers do things differently, creatively, or spur of the moment. They are risk takers and willing to try anything reasonable that will help their children. This is markedly different from perceiving themselves as change agents. These teachers are trying to make their children successful within the existing system. Again, the faculty and principal support one another in these efforts. At one session in which the faculty was sharing things they had tried, one teacher reported how she took the legs off a table and the children seemed better able to access materials. She then discussed it with the children and they decided to take all the legs off all the tables. Other teachers immediately joined in with similar examples of things they did in their classrooms which helped the children work more effectively. The teachers never asked permission for taking these actions. They felt they had the decision-making authority to do whatever it takes to help their children learn. These examples of teacher actions were not necessarily major but in typical school systems they could not have been made at the teacher's discretion and in many districts not at the discretion of the principal either. In the climate created at Buffalo Creek, however, "destroying school furniture" becomes a reasonable activity and one within the purview of the classroom teacher. For this reason, the term *risk taker* or *creative problem solver* is more appropriate than *change agent*.

Parents as Partners, Not Consumers

Important indicators of this school's success are the ways in which parents and caregivers are communicated with and involved. Parents and caregivers are not dealt with as merely the consumers of the school's services but as genuine partners in the process of education. This approach is demonstrated by a school staff that does not define "parental relations" as informing the parents and caregivers of how their children are doing. Naturally, there are report cards and parent conferences in which teachers explain children's progress in the various subjects. But the Buffalo Creek faculty interpret their primary role as working with and involving parents in ways that emphasize positive partnership. When asked specifically what they want of parents and caregivers, it is not uncommon for Buffalo Creek teachers to respond in terms of how much they can learn from parents. After all, they know their children better than the faculty does and can provide valuable information regarding their children's out-of-school lives, interests, and activities. Teachers frequently seek out and use such information to help them connect the children with the school curriculum. In this approach, teachers' contact with parents and caregivers is a two-way street—teachers explaining children's progress; parents providing important information and insights about their children. Buffalo Creek teachers also involve parents as resources with particular knowledge and skills who can make valuable contributions to their classroom programs. Some parents can explain about their jobs, others their travel, war experiences, or hobbies. The point is that when teachers sincerely believe they can learn important things from parents and caregivers, a new form of home-school relationship is developed in which parents feel respected rather than inferior. It is not possible to overemphasize the importance of this approach when dealing with families in poverty. It is typical of parents and caregivers in poverty to feel they are failing at raising their children. The typical approach in impoverished schools is to emphasize the several things parents should do to help their children do better in school. This merely makes the parents feel more defensive and alienated.

Service to Children and Their Families

A related indicator of school success is that the Buffalo Creek staff seeks to help its families as well as its children. In weekly (sometimes daily) examples, the school principal and staff connect children and families with health and human service opportunities that they need. In a very real sense, Buffalo Creek regards the child's family as well as the child as its client. In cases of neglect or abuse, the school administration and staff will devote the extra hours and effort needed to place a child or secure appropriate services. In a school serving the extreme poverty population that Buffalo Creek serves, this is an ongoing activity. The children and their families need a broad range of health and human services. The school staff interprets its accountability for its children very broadly; that is, achieving the child's total well-being is regarded as prerequisite to the child's doing well in school. Referrals to community agencies and then following-up to check on the resolution of children's problems is a common practice at Buffalo Creek. The children are not viewed as important only between the hours of 8:00 and 3:00 but as valuable all day, every day, including weekends and holidays.

Teachers Visit Homes

A straightforward indicator of this school's success is that the teachers are willing to make home visits. Further, most of the contacts whether in person, by telephone, or in writing are positive. The Buffalo Creek faculty buy into the ideology that parents and caregivers respond to encouragement more than criticism and that such encouragements are most likely to support positive practices and reduce negative ones. It is not typical in poverty schools where teachers perceive neighborhoods as unsafe or uninviting to make home visits a common practice.

Teachers Accept Accountability

A critical indicator of this school's success is how the staff explains the causes of children being at risk and how accountable they as teachers feel for ameliorating these conditions. When asked about the causes of their children's problems in school, the faculty cites their children's limited life experiences and language problems. Such responses are typical of teaching staffs in impoverished schools serving Hispanic children. However, Buffalo Creek teachers do not regard such explanations as excuses for less learning or lowered expectations. Indeed, they talk about "what we can do about counteracting condition X, Y, or Z." They demonstrate a strong willingness as well as an expectation that they as teachers should be held accountable for their children's learning. They do not use their children's lack of background experiences in content areas which give advantaged children a head start in school as a way of avoiding accountability. As one observes the school and its ongoing curriculum, it is clear that the teachers actually seek to provide the life experiences they feel their children need. Field trips, resource people, special materials, and numerous other activities demonstrate that the teachers feel it is part of their job to provide whatever background experiences they feel the children lack and which are within the power of the school to provide. In cases where this is not possible, vicarious experiences (e.g., video or computer programs) are utilized. Again, it is typical in impoverished schools for teaches to justify and rationalize their lack of accountability on the basis of their children's limited life experiences. The Buffalo Creek faculty do the reverse. They seek to provide these experiences and hold themselves accountable for doing so.

Principal Protects Teachers' Time and Energy

The role of the principal, not in theory but as practiced, is an important indicator of this school's success. Specifically, the behavioral demonstration of what the principal does in this regard is that she absorbs stress. She does not pass on the demands of the state or the district to the teachers. She protects the teachers from the continuous paper flow, deadlines, and demands for reports which she receives. To a great extent she meets the demands of the bureaucracy in ways which do not break into teachers' time or their work with the children. The teachers at Buffalo Creek have a general notion of the fact that the principal is doing this but because they are protected by the principal they cannot always give details. The principal can give numerous examples of how she protects teachers' time and energy in order to allow them to concentrate on teaching and children. When it is not possible to avoid involving the teachers in doing some paperwork, there is a clear effort to find the most efficient ways in which to get the task accomplished. Buffalo Creek is not a school in which teachers' mailboxes are constantly crammed with things that teachers must set aside their teaching to accomplish.

Interruptions Are Minimal

In action research studies with practicing urban teachers, it is not unusual for them to report up to 125 interruptions per week. The squawk box, children coming late, notes from the office or other teachers, and students in their room making constant requests to leave are the norm. On a verbal level, school staff will claim that the children's learning time comes first. In practice however many schools do the reverse. It is not uncommon to observe teachers who do not begin the lesson until 15 or 20 minutes into the period and who never get to complete the lesson in the way they had planned.

Anyone in the office, school safety aides, or visitors feel it is permissible to interrupt a classroom. After all, it is just a brief interruption and the teacher and children are assumed to have all day together. This is not a common pattern in Buffalo Creek. The stated value that learning time is to be protected is also the practice. There are rarely announcements over the intercom, and children's coming and going for extraneous reasons are kept to a minimum.

Children in the halls are rare. The common expectation is that while this is a pleasant, friendly place, it is also a place of work where people are busy and purposeful. Schools characterized by constant interruptions cannot possibly achieve the climate of Buffalo Creek. Here the work ethic is clearly demonstrated by the great amount of on-task time of the staff and the children.

Faculty Has Not Made Tests the Curriculum

Buffalo Creek teachers are concerned about the mandated tests their children must take but they do not let these tests control the school curriculum. In many failing schools the faculty has given up and has substituted the tests for the curriculum. They then follow a drill-and-kill format trying to teach the children how to respond to similar questions and formats to those on the tests. Unfortunately, children do not learn this way and the test scores don't improve.

The faculty at Buffalo Creek is well aware of the fact that the first criterion which will be used in evaluating the school, the children and themselves will be the achievement scores. Nevertheless, they hold their anxieties in check and continue to offer a curriculum that is relevant to their children's lives, that will engage the children, and that includes what the teachers believe are the most important concepts and skills to be learned. This takes both courage and commitment on the part of the faculty. Bombarded as they are by state and district mandates they hold fast to the idea that the curriculum must connect with their children's lives and that the children must derive personal meaning from their learning. The faculty are able to resist the pressures of the test mania which engulfs them for several reasons: they each derive strong support as members of a communal faculty, and they have a principal who is willing to risk that if the teachers really teach the knowledge of most worth the test scores will take care of themselves. They now have lived through their first year and have generated good test scores after having taught their way and not drilled for the tests; this is a great reward for the faculty.

A Precollege Curriculum for All

Growing out of their commitment to teaching in accordance with how children learn, the teachers continue to offer the curriculum in terms of its stated objectives rather than as test items. What this means in practice is that the teachers' classroom programs are an amalgam of key concepts from the various subject matters taught in thematic units. Basic skills are taught as part of and in addition to these units. The success of this approach, as perceived by the teachers and demonstrated by the test scores, leads the whole faculty to hold high aspirations for their children. As the children experience success from their achievements, the school program itself becomes a continuous source of encouragement and reward for them. In effect, there is a positive cycle in motion: the fact that the teachers keep finding legitimate ways for the children to be successful leads the children to try even harder tasks, which in turn leads to the accomplishment of more difficult learning. Observing the positive cycle they have set in motion, the teachers at Buffalo Creek seriously expect that the children they teach will all be able to go to college if they so choose. They see the children as future successes, not barred from options because of school failure. I know of no school serving this population of children in which the faculty as a group expects that their children will get to college and beyond. It is as if the assumed expectations of a faculty in an advantaged suburb have been transplanted into an impoverished school. This is a remarkable condition because it not only reflects the expectations of the Buffalo Creek faculty but the reality of what they see themselves and their children accomplishing every day.

Administrative "With-It-Ness"

Every good school administrator knows what's going on in the school. In Buffalo Creek, the principal knows what's going on in every classroom. She is even aware of what is happening to a large number of individual children; what they are doing, their problems and victories, and how they feel today. But this level of awareness is characteristic of many administrators, including some who are heading unsuccessful schools. What's happening in Buffalo Creek is that administrative sensitivity and awareness are only the beginning of the principal's leadership. The critical question is, "What does the principal do with all the input and firsthand knowledge she gains from being in the classrooms and corridors?" In most cases she takes little or no overt action and serves as a source of encouragement and support. This builds a sense of empowerment among staff who feel that they not only can solve most of their problems but that the principal is aware of and appreciates what they are doing.

In other instances, however, the principal helps resolve problems by working on the setting or conditions of work and allowing the teachers and children to feel they have taken care of things themselves. By providing materials, a part-time aide, a free period, a piece of equipment, or by helping with special events, the principal works on improving the conditions under which teachers work rather than trying to change the teachers directly. Again, teachers feel they have resolved their own problems (and they have), but the principal's role in altering the setting has made these teacher resolutions possible. In addition to not interfering directly but changing the conditions under which teachers work, this principal uses her knowledge of what is going on in the school in other ways: she is willing and able to deal with emergencies; she communicates thoroughly and well so that everyone feels they know what is going on; and she connects the school to health, human services, and law enforcement agencies.

None of these functions could be performed if the principal did not maintain a thorough ongoing knowledge of what is happening to the teachers and children in the school. The lesson of leadership here is that because everyone in the Buffalo Creek school community (staff, teachers, children, parents, community, central office staff) knows that this principal has a high level of awareness; they control, modify, and shape their own behavior in ways they would never do if they thought she was less knowledgeable. Knowing that she knows what faculty are doing, some teachers are motivated by a need for approval, others by a fear of failure, some by a need to demonstrate independence, and others by a desire to share good work. While the motivations of the faculty and staff vary, it is clear that the principal's deep knowledge and sensitivity exert a powerful leadership impact whether she takes any direct action or not.

Consensual Decision Making

The question that predicts most about teacher morale in a school is, "How are disagreements handled?" In Buffalo Creek, staff are not shy about expressing their concerns. This means that teachers feel no pressure to stifle themselves and simply cope with things they may not understand or agree with. They do what is typical in communal groups. They talk things over until they reach consensus. This requires time for sharing, understanding others' points of view, and considering options together. The principal may participate in these discussions, but her voice does not override any others. This cooperative behavior is not much different from what happens in a supportive family. Teachers honestly want to know why colleagues may agree or disagree with them because their professional self-concept is derived from these "family" members. As teachers explain their ideas to each other, they are doing so to colleagues who care about them as well as the children. In such a situation, each teacher has a built-in reward for suggesting things that will keep meeting children's needs as the ultimate value to be preserved.

Once an individual teacher feels respected and appreciated, s/he wants to remain a part of the group providing these rewards. In this way, the group's approval exerts some influence over each member's behavior. And in groups like Buffalo Creek, where people care about each other, they seek to reach consensus because they want every member of the group to feel comfortable and enhanced. It would be unimaginable for this faculty to simply follow orders from the principal or to take formal votes in which the majority wins and the minority loses. A communal group is like a family in which the participants know they will remain linked and committed to one another beyond any immediate decision. They also know that the total school and each of them as individuals can continue to succeed only if they all succeed. This recognition impels them to constantly seek consensus and move ahead as a group. In effect, the unit of analysis is the school not the individual teacher.

Climate of Teacher Encouragement

There is much discussion and analysis about what motivates people and controls their behavior as professional practitioners. Learning theory focuses on rewards which can readily be observed: power, status, money. One of the most powerful and least understood motivators is the absence of punishment. Much of the behavior in the workplace is influenced by what appears to be no reward but which in reality is a great one for many people: the absence of criticism.

In teaching there is little consensus on what constitutes goodness but great agreement on poor teaching. For example, denigrating children or deprecating their culture are universally agreed upon as undesirable. Specific teaching behaviors such as yelling, not providing any positive feedback, or not listening to children are readily agreed upon as negative acts of teaching. In any school, the faculty shares a greater body of knowledge regarding the things they should not be doing than what they can agree on as positive acts. For teachers in typical schools it becomes a source of tacit approval and motivation to avoid the criticism of peers. The typical school environment supports teacher isolation so that teachers who do perform negative acts of teaching may perform them in private. It is also common in many school environments for teachers to not be rewarded for sharing positive achievements. One teacher's positive accomplishments may be met with feelings of jealousy or perceived as threats by other teachers who cannot demonstrate such achievements. As a result, teaching has been a profession most teachers prefer to practice in private. Recently, with the growth of team teaching, this professional credo is starting to be challenged but it is difficult to move teachers into risking open practice.

Teachers Practice in the Open

Everyone knows what others are doing. Much recognition, praise, and encouragement are mutually shared by the teaching staff. What makes this situation different and special however is more than its openness. These teachers work in the absence of threat and without a fear of punishment for having tried something and failed. They work proactively, seeking to do better because they will not be criticized for efforts that may prove to be less than perfect or even unsuccessful. In this environment, the rewards do not come to those who do little in order to avoid criticism.

Recognition and approval are given teachers for all the extra efforts they expend and for all the special things they try. For teachers as well as children, effort is regarded as the best explanation of success. In opposition to typical school climates, the teacher who would feel most threatened and unrewarded in Buffalo Creek would be a teacher whose motivation was to not rock any boats, to not risk anything, to never discuss what she is trying in her classroom, and to simply avoid criticism.

The Children Feel Needed

The children feel it is a special privilege to be in this school. The basic reason they feel it as a special place is that the staff believe it is. The process by which teachers accomplish this is by making each student feel needed. "We couldn't do this project without you" is, in essence, the message sent to the children. In many schools serving children in poverty, the teachers continuously give students the message that "you are not needed here unless you shape up and stop interfering with my teaching." In such typical situations, it is the teacher's classroom and the teacher's work that is the focus of concern. In Buffalo Creek, it is the children and their work which is the focus. By using a high degree of teaming, cooperation, and peer assistance, the feeling that permeates the student body is that their contributions and efforts are needed to make things work. The Tribes management program and the use of thematic teaching units also serve to make the children interdependent and places them in mutual roles rather than in the position of isolated learners. The impact of these practices on the total school environment is the widespread belief among the children that Buffalo Creek is their school, that it exists for their benefit, and that it wouldn't work except for their efforts.

Teachers Are Students of Learning

There is an ongoing interest among the teachers regarding how their children learn and what conditions in this particular school can best facilitate it. The staff does not view learning as a course they took once at the university. They regularly think about and discuss with each other the processes by which their children are learning. This interest focuses on two attributes: the children's ages and their Hispanic background. The teachers regard their students as children first. They seek better and more effective ways of increasing the learning of the particular pupils in their classrooms.

At the same time, the teachers are extremely sensitive to the fact that these are also Hispanic children, living in this particular area, who have had specific kinds of life experiences and missed others. The teachers recognize their quest as a series of questions and concerns that they will ask themselves and each other for as long as they remain in Buffalo Creek. "What more can I learn about how my kids learn, about what interferes with their learning, and what makes it easier for them?" This is a critical and extremely valuable set of questions for a teaching staff to be asking itself. It shows that they perceive themselves as learners. It indicates that they expect to do better each year and not have one year of experience over and over. Most of all, the questions of these teachers regarding how their specific children learn best is that they see the learning process as driving the curriculum and their teaching practices. In typical schools, the faculty seeks to implement their favorite teaching strategies and the required curriculum without regard for how their children learn best. The operating norm in Buffalo Creek is the reverse; as teachers gain insight into how their children learn best, they adjust their teaching methods and connect the curriculum to the children's learning.

Teachers Act as if They Are Important

The teaching staff in Buffalo Creek seems to have many individuals with high positive self-concepts. The total faculty appears to be a group of confident, optimistic, "can do" people. It is typical in schools serving children in poverty for teachers to feel pessimistic about all the negative life conditions faced by the children over which the school has no control. As a result, it is common for teachers of children in poverty to feel there is little they can do to turn life around for their students. Such perceptions make many teachers feel helpless and therefore unaccountable.

The general feeling communicated by the Buffalo Creek faculty is one of optimism. They feel they are helping their children become successful learners and that they are thereby having a powerful impact on their children's lives. Success sets up a cycle whereby teachers feel even more hopeful, which in turn helps lead them to more success. When teachers such as those in Buffalo Creek enjoy a high self-concept about themselves and their work, it is inevitable they will model these feelings of efficacy to the students. And because "it takes somebodys to make somebodys; nobodys don't make somebodys," the teachers' feelings about themselves exert a powerful influence on the children's self-concept.

Children Reluctant To Go Home

A solid indicator of a successful school is that on any given day many of the children do not want to go home. They want to finish some work or they simply want to stay in an environment they find pleasant. Many of the children feel the teachers want them there; others simply enjoy being with their friends. For the children in Buffalo Creek, school is an inviting, engaging place. They arrive with enthusiasm and leave with reluctance.

Faculty Planning Includes Out-Of-School Objectives

While it is typical for school faculties to feel helpless in counteracting many of the debilitating life conditions their children encounter in the school community, the Buffalo Creek faculty feels they should at least try. One indicator of this commitment is the faculty developing an antigangs plan. There is a low-income housing complex where many of the children live. This housing area is known for recruiting young children into gangs. The Buffalo Creek faculty believe that their school plan should include some means for counteracting such activity. When a school staff believes it should make this kind of effort, it indicates first that they feel accountable for their children's total well-being, and second, that they feel important enough to have an impact on conditions which occur outside of school.

Children Expect Teachers To Be Good

Teaching in Buffalo Creek is made more challenging by the fact that there are so many good teachers. Children have come to expect that teachers will care about them, seek to generate their interest, try to connect the curriculum to their lives, provide engaging materials, use a wide range of equipment, employ exciting teaching strategies, and evaluate them fairly. In more typical schools, the few really good teachers receive strong student cooperation because most of the other teachers do not treat children in these ways. In Buffalo Creek, where outstanding teaching has become the norm, the children have come to expect it. As a result, there is a constant form of professional pressure on the teachers to keep up a very high level of superior teaching. They must continue to plan, seek out creative activities, and work hard since last week's or even yesterday's successes will not be sufficient. Teaching is an activity which requires each new day to stand on its own and to generate success all over again. In a place where all the teachers are caring and respectful of children, the children come to regard such treatment as their right. In a very real sense it becomes a great challenge to remain a good teacher in Buffalo Creek because everyone on the staff is constantly doing things which in typical schools would be viewed as exceptional. What an observer senses in Buffalo Creek is that in spite of the faculty being an excellent one, they must work exceptionally hard just to keep up with the high level of expectations they have set for themselves. Fortunately, it is a communal group and rather than compete, they cooperate and help each other meet the constant pressure to maintain a high standard of teacher performance.

Pervasive Bilingual Program

Most of the faculty is Anglos, but over half, including the principal, are bilingual. This means that the bilingual program at Buffalo Creek actually goes on all day in informal ways as well as in formal class periods. As in all bilingual programs, the ultimate goal is to make all the children reach a level in standard English which will enable him/her to be an independent learner working at grade level in English in all subject areas. Getting there is the great challenge. In Buffalo Creek a teaming between bilingual and ESL teachers allows them to use bilingual methods throughout the day in all subject matters and activities. This ensures that students become proficient in English. There is a definite feeling of comfort and competence which is communicated by the faculty because of their own acceptance and/or proficiency in both languages.

A FINAL NOTE

It is certain that there are more than these 33 indicators of success in the Buffalo Creek School. State laws, district policies, financial support, the curriculum, and many other things contribute to the school's success. But the primary explanation for what makes Buffalo Creek an outstanding school is to be found in the quality of its teachers and principal. While it is true that the staff has much content knowledge (including Spanish and ESL) and much know-how regarding teaching strategies, it must be remembered that faculty in many other impoverished schools who may know as much as the Buffalo Creek teachers have created only mediocre or failing schools. What these teachers (and principal) have is in addition to subject-matter knowledge and teaching know-how. The Buffalo Creek staff has an additional expertise, which includes the 33 themes presented in this chapter.

First, every one of the success indicators is primarily a function of the staffs' ability to relate to the children, the parents, and each other. Second, the staff shares a common ideology of why the school exists, what is supposed to happen to the children, and their role as teachers (and principal) to make it happen. Third, the Buffalo Creek staff is gifted at relationship skills—and this is key. Studying Buffalo Creek leads to the conclusion that children in poverty must have teachers who can connect with them. The teachers' desire and ability to want to live with the children all day, every day, is prerequisite to the children's learning.

UPDATE ON BUFFALO CREEK ELEMENTARY SCHOOL

By 2007, according to school leaders at Buffalo Creek, 27 of the original 29 teachers hired using the Star Teacher Selection Interview in 1997 were still teaching at Buffalo Creek Elementary School, and an additional 10 staff members were employed. They too were hired using the Haberman Star Teacher Selection Interview, for a total of 37 Haberman Star Teachers. The student demographics of 680 students at Buffalo Creek still show a largely Hispanic population: 80.6% Hispanic, 8.22% African American, 7.2% white, 3.5% Asian/Pacific Islander, 85% economically disadvantaged, and 61.6% with limited English proficiency. The Texas Assessment of Knowledge and Skills (TAKS) score award in 2004–2005, Buffalo Creek received the "Acceptable" rating, and were the "Recognized" status in 2006. These statistics further affirm the research of Dr. Haberman, which now spans five decades.

A 2016 inquiry found two critical changes at Buffalo Creek. First, the present school administrator is the fourth principal of BCE and took the reins in 2008, and the new teachers were not hired using the Haberman Star Teacher Selection Interview. In 2015–2016, there were 32 first-through fifth-grade teachers at Buffalo Creek and only 15 of the teachers were hired by the prior three previous principals. Therefore, a little less than half of the teachers at Buffalo Creek were Haberman star teachers. Second, in 2012 the TAKS test was replaced with the State of Texas Assessments of Academic Readiness (STAAR); a test that is less cumulative in terms of subject-matter content, but more rigorous (Weiss, 2012). The Texas Education Agency's (TEA) 2015 Report Card confirms some subtle student demographic changes since Buffalo Creek's 1997 opening; 89.3% of the 638 students are Hispanic, 68.3% are economically disadvantaged, and 72.6% are English language learners. Buffalo Creek's 2015 STAAR accountability rating of "Met" Standard appears satisfactory. "In 2015, to receive Met Standard accountability rating, districts and campuses must meet targets on three of four indexes: Index 1 or Index 2 and Index 3 and Index 4" (TEA, 2015a, p. 1). The indexes for 1–4 are Student Achievement, Student Progress, Closing Performance Gaps, and

Postsecondary Readiness, respectively. The "Met" Standard "indicates acceptable performance and is assigned to districts and campuses that meet the targets on all required indexes for which they have performance data" (TEA, 2015b, p. 1). As we drill down into Index 1 (average Student Performance), we find that 66% of all Buffalo Creek's students, as an average for all subject areas, met the satisfactory standards for the 2014–2015 STAAR exam (TEA, 2015a). While one may be tempted to compare Buffalo Creek's post-2008 achievement results with its pre-2008 achievement outcomes, it is unfair to compare TAKS and STAAR campus scores and such an appraisal is not within the scope of this update but worthy of future study.

The Haberman Educational Foundation (HEF), Inc. is pleased to have been affiliated with such dedicated staff and principals for nearly a decade. HEF wishes Buffalo Creek great success with its deserving learners.

ACKNOWLEDGMENT

"Victory at Buffalo Creek" first appeared in the May 1999 issue of *Instructional Leader*; volume 12, number 2, pages 1–5. It is reprinted with permission of the Texas Elementary Principals and Supervisors Association (TEPSA).

CHAPTER QUESTIONS

1. How is the setting of Buffalo Creek Middle School similar to, or different from, other suburban school districts with diverse learners?

2. One of the indicators for academic success among the Hispanic learners for Buffalo Creek Elementary School is widespread peer teaching. Please explain this criterion and your experience with it.

3. One of the indicators for academic success among the Hispanic learners for Buffalo Creek Elementary School is teachers as risk-takers, not change agents. Please explain this criterion and your experience with it.

4. What role does the principal play in the overall effectiveness of an underserved school?

5. What was the retention rate of teachers at Buffalo Creek Middle School? At your school? And what is the impact of teacher attrition on student achievement?

REFERENCES

Texas Education Agency. (2015a). *Buffalo Creek Elementary School report card.* Retrieved from https://cms.springbranchisd.com/Portals/333/ BCE%20School%20Report%20Card.pdf?ver=2016-05-31-151257-933

Texas Education Agency. (2015b). *Chapter 2—Ratings criteria and the index targets.* Retrieved from https://rptsvr1.tea.texas.gov/perfreport/account/2015/manual/ Chapter%2002_Final.pdf

Weiss, J. (2012, March 19). STAAR vs. TAKS: Texas' new standardized tests come to schools next week. *Dallas Morning News.* Retrieved from http://www.dallasnews.com/news/education/headlines/20120319-staar-vs.-taks-texas-new-standardized-tests-come-to-schools-next-week.ece

CHAPTER 9

TEACHING IN THE WINDY CITY

A Mixed-Methods Case Study
of Seven Star Teachers in Chicago

**Nicholas D. Hartlep, Christopher M. Hansen,
Sara A. McCubbins, Guy J. Banicki, and Grant B. Morgan**

Chapter Objectives

The learner will

1. understand how Star Teachers bear the responsibility of their
    teaching and their students' learning regardless of their students'
    life situation;
2. recognize the ways in which Star Teachers seek opportunities to
    affect educational change beyond their classrooms, which some-
    times includes leaving the K–12 classroom; and
3. critique the behaviors of Star Teachers who find ways to work,
    often within suboptimal schools/school systems, for the sake of
    their students.

Our nation's K–12 urban schools are in need of highly effective teachers. In addition to urban school districts needing stellar teachers, an

Better Teachers, Better Schools: What Star Teachers Know, Believe, and Do
pp. 161–176
Copyright © 2017 by Information Age Publishing
All rights of reproduction in any form reserved.

interrelated need is retaining the highly effective teachers it already has. National statistics indicate that a significant percentage of K–12 teachers will leave the classroom within their first 5 years of teaching. According to the National Commission on Teaching and America's Future (2010), "After five years over 30% of our beginning teachers have left the profession" (p. 4). Failure to retain teachers is financially burdensome for urban school districts. In addition to being expensive, teacher turnover has also been found to negatively impact student academic achievement (Ronfeldt, Loeb, & Wyckoff, 2013). In summary, not retaining K–12 teachers is a problem worth solving.

In this chapter we share the results of ongoing research that continues to be carried out in Chicago, Illinois. We first share information about the city of Chicago and its public schools. We then present our multiple case study which sought to investigate the dispositions of seven highly effective K–12 urban teachers who were teaching in Chicago Public Schools (CPS) at the time of the study. Before describing their professional dispositions and teaching practices, we examine what the literature finds about the teaching practices of effective urban K–12 teachers. We conclude our chapter by sharing what we discovered when interviewing and observing the seven participants. We also share what these findings hold in terms of implications for future research and practice.

Chicago Public Schools

The setting for this mixed-methods case study was Chicago, Illinois. Chicago Public Schools (CPS) is an urban school district and is the third largest school district in the United States. At the time of this study, CPS had 462 elementary and 106 high schools, serving 400,545 students. Chicago, the "Windy City," is home to a diverse group of people. According to Hartlep (2012b), "Despite that its school landscape and students are predominately African American and Latino, 12.2% of its student are Limited English proficient, 86% are from low-income families, 45% are African American, 41% are Latino, 9% are White, 3.6% are Asian/Pacific Islander, and 0.2% are Native American" (p. 14). Hartlep notes that "Chicago is unique in its own right; it loses more Black kids than soldiers in Iraq and Afghanistan to gun violence" (p. 14).

A root cause of urban violence is inequity, and its taproot is inadequate teaching and school opportunities. Chicago, like many urban cities (i.e., Los Angeles, Milwaukee, New York), has a difficult time retaining its K–12 teachers. The Consortium on Chicago School Research (Allensworth, Ponisciak, & Mazzeo, 2009) notes that "in a typical CPS school, half of the teaching staff turns over within five years" (p. 10). It is not uncommon for

K–12 teachers who teach in underresourced schools and urban districts to bide their time until they escape to a suburban school system where they will be paid more and where they will be able to teach in (segregated) schools that resemble the schools they attended as students. This tacit reality is problematic, especially in light of research that documents racial imbalances between the K–12 teaching force and the children that these teachers serve (see Toldson, 2011). According to the National Center for Educational Statistics (2012a, 2012b), 81.9% of our nation's K–12 teachers are non-Hispanic white, and 76.3% are female. Making matters worse, and reinforcing segregated schooling and racial imbalances between teachers and students, research suggests that K–12 teachers desire teaching in school environments that resemble where they were schooled (Achinstein & Ogawa, 2011). This means that segregated schools reproduce segregated schools.

STATEMENT OF PROBLEM

In addition to the problem of the demographic imperative (the racial and cultural imbalance between those who teach and those who are taught; Sleeter, Neal, & Kumashiro, 2015), we also feel that an insufficient amount of attention has been paid to the in-service K–12 teaching population. The implications are numerous. First, it means that research that examines the practices of in-service teachers is equally important as research that examines preservice teachers. It also means that although it is important to hire more racially and culturally diverse K–12 teachers, it is equally important (if not more so because of the mismatches between who teaches and who is taught) to study persistent and effective in-service urban K–12 teachers. As a result, the present case study sought to investigate the dispositions of seven highly effective K–12 urban teachers (four of whom were white) who were teaching in the Chicago Public Schools at the time of this study. Before we share more about these seven teachers, we review what the literature finds in terms of effective urban K–12 teachers.

REVIEW OF THE LITERATURE

Effective Urban K–12 Teachers

Stronge (2007) states that there are "common attributes that characterize effective teachers" (p. ix). Some of these attributes are that effective teachers care deeply, recognize complexity, communicate clearly, and serve conscientiously. Stronge writes that a "central theme that resonates throughout the research and literature regarding effective teachers is that of a caring teacher" (p. 100).

Morrison (2006) described effective teachers as those who "accept responsibility for teaching, allocate most of their time to instruction, organize their classroom for effective instruction, … maintain a pleasant learning environment that is student centered, and provide opportunities for practice and feedback on performance" (p. 13). Another definition was provided by Wong and Wong (2005), who defined an effective teacher as "one who has positive expectations for student success, is an extremely good classroom manager, and knows how to design lessons for student mastery" (as cited in Aleccia, 2011, p. 87). Some researchers break down the defining characteristics of an effective teacher even further, separating teacher effectiveness into distinct categories. According to Aleccia (2011), there are four criteria for being an effective teacher and/or teacher educator: (a) being clear about your professional mission, (b) having the appropriate background/training, (c) keeping current in your classroom practice by bridging theory with practice, and (d) modeling what it means to be an "accomplished teacher" for preservice teachers, including getting your National Board certification.

Paying particular attention to the effectiveness of teachers in urban schools, Haberman (2004) identifies dispositions, core beliefs, and ideologies of urban teachers who flourish teaching children in poverty. Through extensive research on effective urban teachers, Haberman (1993, 2004) developed both quantitative and qualitative instruments that place teacher dispositions into 10 subcategories: (a) persistence, (b) organization and planning, (c) valuing student learning, (d) translating theory into practice, (e) approach to students, (f) approach to at-risk students, (g) survival in a bureaucracy, ways of explaining both (h) teacher and (i) student success, and (j) fallibility.

METHODOLOGY

Haberman Star Teacher Live Interview Protocol

We used the Haberman Star Teacher Pre-Screener to identify and the Haberman Star Teacher Live Interview Protocol to interview the seven CPS teachers in this case study. The seven teachers were identified as part of a larger study of Chicago Public School teachers. In Table 9.1 we provide profiles of the seven teachers who were interviewed. Star Teacher Prescreener results are placed into four quartiles based on the proprietary scoring system the Haberman Educational Foundation uses to rank

Table 9.1.   Demographic Information, Prescreener Scores, and Interview Scores for Seven Star Teachers

Teacher (Education level)	Gender	Race	Age	Years of Experience	Prescreener Score (45)	Interview Score (45)	Teaching Assignment
Janet (Working on Doctorate)	F	AA	53	17	40.00	36.25	K–8 librarian
Mary (Master's)	F	AA	28	7	40.00	41.00	PK
Collette (Bachelor's)	F	W	23	2	40.00	43.50	10–12 English
Anna (Master's)	F	W	29	7	41.00	38.00	7–8 special ed
Bailey (Bachelor's)	F	W	23	1	42.00	36.25	5
Michael (Bachelor's)	M	W	33	1	42.00	39.25	H.S.
Ryan (Bachelor's)	M	L	23	0	42.00	40.00	9–10 special ed

Note: AA = African American; W = White; L = Latino; E.S. = Elementary School; M.S. = Middle School; H.S. = High School.

teacher candidates; candidates who score in the upper quartile (38–50) are considered Stars by the Haberman Foundation.

Once identified by the online Prescreener, these seven high-scoring teachers were invited and agreed to participate in the Star Teacher Live Interview Protocol. Previous research has found this protocol to be statistically reliable and valid (see Baskin, Ross, & Smith, 1996; Lesniak, 1969; Storey, 1995).

Interviews using the established protocol were recorded and later transcribed by the researchers. Transcription was carried out by graduate research assistants, producing "clean transcripts" (Elliot, 2005). Clean transcripts are a form of transcription that eliminates pauses, intonations, false starts, and utterances that are common in everyday speech. Clean transcripts allow the content of what is said to be read and understood easier. This decision was made in light of literature that indicates that verbatim transcription is unnecessary, especially in mixed-methods investigations, such as ours here (e.g., see Halcomb & Davidson, 2006). Interviews varied in time, lasting from 25–50 minutes. Interview scores were generated by the interviewers by using a Haberman Foundation proprietary method of analysis: interview answers were weighted evenly, and participants whose score fell within the first quartile (33.75–45) were considered to be Star Teachers.

Teacher Participants

A total of 9 CPS teachers were initially identified as being stars from a larger sample of 191 CPS teachers who participated in a different larger study; however, the research team was only able to schedule interviews with 7 of those nine teachers. Teacher participants ($n = 7$) included high school, middle school, and elementary school teachers. The majority of the participants (71%) identified as being female ($n = 5$), and 29% of participants identified as being male ($n = 2$). Three of the participants were 23 years old, three were between 28 and 33 years old, and one was 53 years old at the time of the case study. The majority of the teacher participants were white ($n = 4$), followed by African American ($n = 2$), and Latino ($n = 1$).

Although our sample size is small in comparison to the teaching staff of CPS, our Star Teacher group appears to be similarly represented by teachers of color in comparison to all CPS teacher demographics (see Table 9.2). Like CPS teachers, our Star Teacher group underrepresents the racial and ethnic makeup of students of color in the CPS student population. This racial-ethnic imbalance between both CPS and star teachers (primarily white, non-Hispanic) and the students they teach (primarily students of color) has deep implications for both the current makeup of

Table 9.2.   Chicago Public School (CPS) Student Demographics Compared to Star Teacher Sample

Racial Category	2013–2014 CPS Student Representation ($n = 400,545$)	2013–2014 CPS Teacher Representation ($n = 11,519$)	Star Teacher Representation ($n = 7$)
Hispanic	45.2%	18.6%	14.3%
African American	39.7%	24.6%	28.6%
White	9.2%	49.7%	57.1%
Asian	3.5%	3.4%	0.0%
Asian/Pacific Islander	0.32%	0.1%	0.0%
Native American	0.0%	0.4%	0.0%

Source: Adapted from http://www.cps.edu/about_cps/at-a-glance/pages/stats_and_facts.aspx

the CPS teaching corp, and the actual CPS student population: mostly the need for more diverse teachers.

Data Coding and Analysis

The research team followed the consensual qualitative research (CQR) method while analyzing the structured interview data. The Haberman Star Teacher Live Interview has high levels of interrater reliability; however, the CQR method also increased reliability because of its consensual nature (Hill et al., 2005; Hill, Thompson, & Williams, 1997). We followed Hill et al.'s (1997) categories of "general" (applies to every case, 7), "typical" (applies to at least half of the cases, or 3+), and/or "variant" (applies to less than half, but more than one case, 1–2).

Two researchers, the first and second authors, served as the interviewers. The two of them interviewed all 7 teachers in person in Chicago (see Table 9.1). These interview sessions were recorded and later transcribed. However, the research team all served as analysts. Meeting as a team, the transcripts were initially reviewed using an open-coding format. The two original interviewers also reviewed their memos in order to develop initial themes for the analysis. This approach to conducting interviews in pairs was ideal, and according to the training manuals the team received from the Haberman Educational Foundation, "promotes inter-rater reliability, helps interviewers recall the details of the [interview] and builds *consensus*" (p. 30, emphasis added).

Research Team Composition and Reflexivity of Researchers

The first author, the principal investigator (PI), was a pretenure assistant professor of educational foundations. He had experience conducting focus groups and carrying out qualitative research (e.g., see Chapman, Joseph, Hartlep, Vang, & Lipsey, 2014; Hartlep, 2012b), as well as conducting quantitative (e.g., see Hartlep, 2012a) and mixed-methods studies (e.g., see Hartlep & Ellis, 2013; Hartlep & McCubbins, 2013; Hartlep, McCubbins, & Morgan, 2014). As a Korean transracial adoptee, he was disappointed that no Star Teachers were identified as Asian American, but he was excited to interview Latino and African American teachers because he supports the diversification of the teaching force and he also speaks Spanish.

The second author was a pretenure assistant professor of teaching and learning. He had previous experience carrying out teacher-practitioner research, art-based research in education, scholarship of teaching and learning (SoTL) of teacher education, and feminist methodology (e.g., see Hansen, 2012).

The third author was an advanced doctoral student at the time of this study. She was studying science education and had a master's degree in science education. Her previous experience included conducting survey research and carrying out mixed-methods research (Hartlep & McCubbins, 2013; Hartlep et al., 2014).

The fourth author was a pretenure assistant professor of educational administration and was a former school teacher, principal, and superintendent. He, like the third author, had limited qualitative research experience. His background, like the fifth author, was in quantitative research methods (Banicki, 1987).

The fifth author was a pretenure assistant professor of educational psychology. He had extensive experience carrying out methodological research using advanced multivariate procedures (e.g., see DiStefano & Morgan, 2014; Morgan, 2015; Morgan, D'Amico, & Hodge, 2013) as well as simulation studies.

FINDINGS

In this section of the chapter, we share our findings. First, we share the major codes followed by the themes that were most salient within each code. Last, we share actual quotes from the Star Teachers that speak to these salient themes. We end our chapter with a discussion of what these findings hold in terms of implications for future research and practice.

Major Codes

Some 21 major categorical codes were found: (1) persistence, (2) school organization, (3) teacher characteristics and/or endorsements, (4) "throw-away" kids, (5) classroom experience, (6) family literacy, (7) student disengagement, (8) student motivation, (9) resistance to schooling, (10) myth/reality of urban teaching, (11) burnout, (12) respect, (13) school culture, (14) behavioral management, (15) classroom management, (16) learning, (17) community, (18) relationships, (19) at-risk, (20) cultural awareness, and (21) subversive teaching. From these codes, sub-themes were created, the most salient ones being presented below. As was already mentioned, we followed Hill et al.'s (1997) categories of "general" (applies to every case), "typical" (applies to at least half of the cases, or 3+), and/or "variant" (applies to less than half, but more than one case, 1–2). Theme #1 was found to be general, while themes #2 and #3 were found to be typical. Due to space restrictions, we do not share variant themes.

THEMES

Three themes were identified: (a) Personalized Teaching, (b) "Throw-Away" Students, and (c) At-Risk is Situational.

Personalized Teaching

Five of the seven star teachers mentioned something that spoke to the ethos of personalized teaching. The theme of personalized teaching referred to a dynamic of teacher-student relationships. For instance, Janet mentioned that knowing names was extremely important. She said the following:

> So I see, like, five classes a day and I see anywhere from first grade to eighth grade in a day so I see about 600 kids. One of those weaknesses is not being able to know 600 children's names. So every day when I come to work, I'm thinking about "Okay, who am I getting, how do I make sure, you know, whose names do I need to know today" because once you know the names it makes life a lot easier instead of going "Excuse me dear, pardon me sir, young man what's your name, young woman."

Meanwhile, Collette added additional insight into the importance of being personal with her students. She said,

> If that doesn't work, I will wait until we get started and go over to their table for a second. Just stop and talk and ask them how they are doing that day. Talk to them about something else for a little while and then kind of reintro-duce what we are doing.

Michael added his thoughts why personalized teaching is effective. According to Michael, "I found that when I built relationships with students they worked with me, not against me."

"Throw-Away" Students

Five of the seven Star Teachers alluded to the notion that urban schools have children who are considered to be "throw-aways." Theme 2, throw-away students, referred to how urban students become seen and treated as being disposable. The majority of the Star Teachers opposed such a view, perceiving all children to be valued and important. Mary offered pointed insight, saying the following about how students become stereotyped as being at risk:

> I think there are students who can come from poverty and not be at risk. I think that society kind of puts them in that category and stereotypes them as such but I think just the at-risk student is the student that does not enter school or is in school in a grade and they're not meeting the expectations of that particular grade.

Janet shared two stories to explain her approach to throw-away kids:

> So, going back to the kids that nobody wanted to work with, as an example, I had a little boy who was on the autistic spectrum and one of the things I do not like is when someone walks in and says "Put that down, don't touch that, he's not listening." I'm like, "Yes he is." But he was playing with his imaginary toys. He's not bothering anybody. He's just playing with his imaginary toys, but I learned he's listening; so to demonstrate that the kid is listening and I know what I'm doing with the kid, we did a spelling test. So the [other] kids who were doing the "right" thing, they had the words for a week. I didn't give the other kid the words. I gave him the words that day just before we took the test [because I knew] he had been listening all week. The principal came in; he's playing with his imaginary toys. I said, "Okay, let's take this spelling test." They took the spelling test,"; he scored 100 points. The other kids didn't. They had a week to learn the words. I said, "So when you make him stop playing with the imaginary toys, he's not listening because … it cuts off his ability to do what he needs to do to process stuff." He also needed to walk around the room so when he takes his test I give him a clipboard. I let him walk around the room.
>   I had another kid … he was a big kid. He was in a gang. He didn't want his crew to know he couldn't read. I knew the secret. I said, "Look, you can't read and you're in my homeroom and I need you to succeed so what can we do? So how about this, if you come to school every day before everybody else gets here, I will work with you on the reading." That kid comes to school every day, every day before everybody else gets there and we work on his reading. It took him a year to read that book but he read it."

"At Risk" is Situational

Five of the seven Star Teachers indicated that they felt that "at risk" was something that could be conceptualized as being situational; meaning that they disagreed with the commonly held belief that at risk was something pathological or tied to some form of deficit. Anna provided the following insight about students being considered at risk:

I think that I see the child a lot more holistically, so an "at-risk" child could also be at risk socially-emotionally through their family, through kind of their general disposition we can see … and then of course their academics as well.

Ryan added his perspective, commenting on why being at risk was a phenomenon he saw as being situational:

I think it depends on the demographics of the student, so where they were raised. Does the student have a socioeconomic status where the parents make an okay living? Do they have—the students that I work with that are behind or have IEPs or are learning at a third-grade, fourth-grade level [while in high school], the students that I ask, "Hey do you have a computer at home?" And they are like, "No I don't." And I ask, "Do you know how to get to a library?" And some students are like, "Yeah, but my parents won't let me." And does that hinder their learning? I think it does."

Bailey commented that circumstances cause children to be at risk in schools. She stated the following:

For me, for teaching it means that there are certain areas or gaps laid in or there are areas that they need to work on probably more than some of the students at the level. But mostly, especially in my school, it means that they have other circumstances going on. I have a kid with two alcoholic parents who just moved in with his grandma and is hopefully going to move in with his less angry alcoholic father now that they are separated. Sometimes it is newcomers. We have a lot of mostly ELL kids—out of the 1,200 kids in our school only 100 speak English as their primary language. That they come in with backgrounds that may not be assumed, that the label may not be seen—because usually when it's used it's used as a thing that they are behind. That they are behind, that they are deficient in something that they are missing something, that they are "at risk" of not being what they are supposed to be and it usually means that they have either other things to deal with or their strengths lie in other areas, or both usually.

Mary also saw the at-risk label as circumstantial, but explained schooling's responsibility in maintaining it when she explained,

I will say statistically speaking, it does kind of start in neighborhoods [i.e., families]. I think it's still about exposure. So if you're not exposed to vocabulary, you're not exposed to ways, books or counting or those basic skills at an early age, you already enter school—whether it's in kindergarten or first grade—at a disadvantage. And then if as time progresses, you're still not getting those opportunities, it [academic performance] still doesn't progress. So then you cannot just fault a home environment, you can fault a school or teacher of the same thing because *once they enter school, why are they now still at risk?*" (emphasis in original)

DISCUSSION

Overall, the seven Star Teachers whom we interviewed in CPS displayed common Star ideologies and core beliefs. They were more persistent than their non-Star peers. In our quantitative analyses we found a statistically significant relationship between Star Teachers and fallibility. The difference between Star Teachers and their non-Star peers is that Stars recognize and own up to mistakes in the classroom that break teacher-student rapport. In other words, Star Teachers readily admit their mistakes, and "apologize and rectify the situation publicly" (Haberman, 2004, p. 187). Michael, Collette, Janet, Anna, Ryan, Bailey, and Mary all understood this quite well.

We also found that there was a statistically significant relationship between Star Teachers and their approaches to at-risk students. While both Star Teachers and non-Star Teachers understand the factors that affect at-risk students, the key difference between the two are that Star Teachers "seek more effective teaching strategies, regardless of youngsters' backgrounds" (Haberman, 2004, p. 169) in order to make their teaching and their students' learning more meaningful and relevant. In other words, non-Star Teachers use the label of "at risk" to prove "the child cannot be taught or doesn't belong in their classroom" (Haberman, 2004, p. 169), while star teachers take responsibility and "find ways of involving [their] students in learning no matter what their out-of-school lives are like" (Haberman, 2004, p. 168). Star Teachers do not blame students, while non-Star Teachers do quite often. Star Teachers are not judgmental or moralistic and they believe in effort rather than ability. The Star Teachers in our study saw "at risk" as something that was situational and not deterministic. Hill-Jackson and Lewis (2010) write that "the study of dispositions has failed to receive the type of serious scrutiny it deserves in teacher education and is neglected in the teacher selection process" (p. 84); we couldn't agree with them more, which is why we carried out this mixed-methods case study of Star Teachers in Chicago.

IMPLICATIONS FOR FUTURE RESEARCH AND PRACTICE

In the beginning of this chapter, we indicated that urban schools need to do a better job at identifying and retaining their effective K–12 teachers. Based on the results presented in this chapter, we recommend that urban school districts, like Chicago, not only recruit K–12 teaching candidates whose dispositions indicate the potential for effective urban teaching (responding to the demographic imperative), but also continue to use dispositional data to identify and support their in-service teachers in order to better serve the needs of their teaching force and in so doing serve the needs of their students (having star teachers in the classroom would be responding to the democratic imperative). From the standpoint of practice, we recommend that school principals must have a respect for learners (and teachers) of all ages, with special appreciation for the dispositions of the people they serve, and use dispositional information in a way that strengthens the teaching staff by relying on the dispositional strengths of teachers and providing professional development that focuses on dispositional areas needing improvement.

At the same time that our survey data indicates that those teachers surveyed who performed in the top half of Haberman Star Teacher Pre-Screener dispositional rankings are more likely to leave the profession or leave CPS schools more quickly than their counterparts who scored in the bottom half of the rankings; this points to a grievous situation for urban school districts like Chicago. If those teachers most likely to succeed are the same ones most likely to leave teaching or leave the urban school setting, then reform efforts have a challenging problem: What are the chances of successful reform in the urban setting if current school conditions are driving out the very teachers most likely to lead and succeed in their efforts to help their students toward academic success? We believe very little.

Both at the level of the school district and the academic research institute, we believe that focused energy (time and financial resources) must be devoted to identifying, supporting, and cultivating the potential of those teachers who show the greatest dispositional potential for success in the high-poverty, urban schooling community. This mixed-methods case study shows that both "good" and Star Teachers exist in our school system, and that many of those teachers appear to succeed despite the challenges of bureaucratic school institutions that have grown up in our large, urban communities. At the same time, we know that more needs to be done to support their efforts and find ways to grow those efforts into school- and systemwide dispositions of success. Research into dispositional characteristics of success can be one method of leading practical reform efforts in dynamic school systems that are ready for change. The scholarly work of Dr. Martin Haberman is a key to unlocking the lock of retaining and recruiting highly effective urban K–12 teachers, something this volume, edited by Dr. Valerie Hill-Jackson and Delia Stafford, has taken up.

CHAPTER QUESTIONS

1. How might schools and school systems use Haberman screening tools to aid in professional development of teachers?
2. Discuss the implications of using tools like the Haberman screening tools to identify teachers as potentially exemplary in working in underresourced, high-need urban schools.
3. How might including dispositional measures like the Haberman tools expand a school system's understanding of teacher quality?
4. A number of the teachers identified as Stars in this study explain that they go above and beyond typical expectations for the teaching profession. How might these efforts inform a school's personnel choices, its support for faculty, and its expectations for what efforts might be needed to assure student success?

REFERENCES

Achinstein, B., & Ogawa, R. T. (2011). *Change(d) agents: New teachers of color in urban schools.* New York, NY: Teachers College Press.
Aleccia, V. (2011). Walking our talk: The imperative of teacher educator modeling. *The Clearing House, 84*(3), 87–90.
Allensworth, E., Ponisciak, S., & Mazzeo, C. (2009, June). The schools teachers leave: Teacher mobility in Chicago public schools. *Consortium on Chicago School Research.* Retrieved from http://files.eric.ed.gov/fulltext/ED505882.pdf
Banicki, G. J. (1987). *The study of potential voter behavior to an educational tax referendum* (Unpublished dissertation). Northern Illinois University, Dekalb.
Baskin, M. K., Ross, S. M., & Smith, D. L. (1996). Selecting successful teachers: The predictive validity of the urban teacher selection interview. *Teacher Educator, 32*(1), 1–21. Retrieved from http://dx.doi.org/10.1080/08878739609555127
Chapman, T. K., Joseph, T., Hartlep, N. D., Vang, M., & Lipsey, T. (2014). The double-edged sword of curriculum: How curriculum in majority white suburban high schools supports and hinders the growth of students of color. *Journal of Curriculum and Teaching Dialogue, 16*(1/2), 87–101.
DiStefano, C., & Morgan, G. B. (2014). A comparison of diagonal weighted least squares robust estimation techniques for ordinal data. *Structural Equation Modeling, 21*(3), 425–438.
Elliot, J. (2005). *Using narrative in social research: Qualitative and quantitative approaches.* London, England: Sage.
Haberman, M. (1993). Predicting the success of urban teachers (the Milwaukee trials). *Action in Teacher Education, 15*(3), 52–56.
Haberman, M. (2004). *Star teachers: The ideology and best practices of effective teachers of children and youth in poverty.* Houston, TX: Haberman Educational Foundation.

Halcomb, E., & Davidson, P. (2006). Is verbatim transcription of interview data always necessary? *Applied Nursing Research, 19*(1), 38–42.

Hansen, C. M. (2012). *A gendered study of men elementary educators through collective memory work* (Unpublished dissertation). University of Georgia, Athens. Retrieved from https://getd.libs.uga.edu/pdfs/hansen_christopher_m_201208_phd.pdf

Hartlep, N. D. (2012a). *A segmented assimilation theoretical study of the 2002 Asian American student population* (Unpublished dissertation). University of Wisconsin, Milwaukee. Retrieved from http://books.google.com/books/about/A_Segmented_Assimilation_Theoretical_Stu.html?id=GhmxmAEACAAJ

Hartlep, N. D. (2012b). Teachers' pet projects versus real social justice teaching. In A. Honigsfeld & A. Cohan (Eds.), *Breaking the mold of education for culturally and linguistically diverse students: Innovative and successful practices for the 21st century* (pp. 13–22). Lanham, MD: Rowman & Littlefield.

Hartlep, N. D., & Ellis, A. L. (2013). Rethinking speech and language impairments within fluency-dominated cultures. In S. Pinder (Ed.), *American multicultural studies: Diversity of race, ethnicity, gender and sexuality* (pp. 411–429). Thousand Oaks, CA: Sage.

Hartlep, N. D., & McCubbins, S. (2013). What makes a star teacher? Examining teacher dispositions, professionalization, and teacher effectiveness using the Haberman Star Teacher Pre-Screener. *Department of Educational Administration and Foundations, Illinois State University.* Retrieved from http://www.habermanfoundation.org/Documents/WhatMakesAStarTeacher.pdf

Hartlep, N. D., McCubbins, S., & Morgan, G. B. (2014). Revealing the myth of the "fully qualified" bright young teacher: Using the Haberman Star Teacher Pre-Screener to teach and assess professional dispositions and core beliefs in education. In J. A. Gorlewski, B. Porfilio, D. A. Gorlewski, & J. Hopkins (Eds.), *Effective or wise: Teaching and assessing professional dispositions in education* (pp. 37–56). New York, NY: Peter Lang. Retrieved from http://dx.doi.org/10.1177/0022487102053002002

Hill, C. E., Knox, S., Thompson, B. J., Williams, E. N., Hess, S. A., & Ladany, N. (2005). Consensual qualitative research: An update. *Journal of Counseling Psychology, 52*(2), 196–205. Retrieved from http://dx.doi.org/10.1037/0022-0167.52.2.196

Hill, C. E., Thompson, B. J., & Williams, E. N. (1997). A guide to conducting consensual qualitative research. *Journal of Counseling Psychology, 25*(4), 517–572. Retrieved from http://dx.doi.org/10.1177/0011000097254001

Hill-Jackson, V., & Lewis, C. (2010). Dispositions matter: Advancing habits of mind for social justice. In V. Hill-Jackson & C. Lewis (Eds.), *Transforming teacher education: What went wrong with teacher training and how we can fix it* (pp. 61–92). Sterling, VA: Stylus.

Lesniak, R. J. (1969). *Predicting classroom behavior of urban teacher candidates through the use of a classroom behavior task* (Unpublished doctoral dissertation). University of Syracuse, NY.

Morgan, G. B. (2015). Mixed mode latent class analysis: An examination of fit index performance for classification. *Structural Equation Modeling, 22*(1), 76–86.

Morgan, G. B., D'Amico, M. M., & Hodge, K. J. (2013). Major differences: Modeling profiles of community college persisters in career clusters. *Quality & Quantity, 49*(1). Advance online publication. Retrieved from http://dx.doi.org/10.1007/s11135-013-9970-x

Morrison, G. S. (2006). *Teaching in America* (4th ed.). Upper Saddle River, NJ: Merrill-Pearson.

National Center for Educational Statistics (NCES). (2012a). *Schools and Staffing Survey (SASS): Table 1. Total number of public school teachers and percentage distribution of school teachers, by race/ethnicity and state: 2011–12*. Retrieved from http://nces.ed.gov/surveys/SASS/tables/sass1112_2013314_t1s_001.asp

National Center for Educational Statistics (NCES). (2012b). *Schools and Staffing Survey (SASS): Table 2. Average and median age of public school teachers and percentage distribution of teachers, by age category, sex, and state: 2011–12*. Retrieved from http://nces.ed.gov/surveys/SASS/tables/sass1112_2013314_t1s_002.asp

National Commission on Teaching and America's Future. (2010, January). *Who will teach? Experience matters*. Washington, DC: Author. Retrieved from http://nctaf.org/wp-content/uploads/2012/01/NCTAF-Who-Will-Teach-Experience-Matters-2010-Report.pdf

Ronfeldt, M., Loeb, S., & Wyckoff, J. (2013). How teacher turnover harms student achievement. *American Educational Research Journal, 50*(1), 4–36. Retrieved from http://dx.doi.org/10.3102/0002831212463813

Sleeter, C., Neal, L., & Kumashiro, K. K. (Eds.). (2015). *Diversifying the teacher workforce: Preparing and retaining highly effective teachers*. New York, NY: Routledge.

Storey, R. S. (1995). *Utility of the modified Haberman Interview in higher education* (Unpublished doctoral dissertation). University of Texas at Austin.

Stronge, J. H. (2007). *Qualities of effective teachers* (2nd ed.). Alexandria, VA: ASCD.

Toldson, I. A. (2011). Diversifying the United States' teaching force: Where are we now? Where do we need to go? How do we get there? *The Journal of Negro Education, 80*(3),183–186.

CHAPTER 10

SELECTING AND PREPARING URBAN TEACHERS

Martin Haberman

Chapter Objectives

The learner will

1. discover the factors that attract individuals to teaching;
2. interpret the characteristics of mature adults who become effective urban teachers; and
3. rate the conditions under which urban educators teach.

Three thousand youth drop out of school every day. The achievement gaps between racial groups and economic classes continue to widen. The persistent shortage of teachers who can be effective in 120 failing urban school systems guarantee that the miseducation of seven million diverse children in urban poverty will continue. Traditional university-based teacher education has demonstrated for over half a century that it cannot provide teachers who will be effective and who will remain in these schools for longer than brief periods. Recruiting and preparing teachers for the real world will require teacher education programs to focus on selecting mature, diverse adults who can be prepared on the job as teach-

Better Teachers, Better Schools: What Star Teachers Know, Believe, and Do
pp. 177–199

ers of record with the help of mentors and with access to technological support. These teacher education programs cannot claim that the negative conditions of work in urban schools must first be improved before they can be held accountable for providing competent teachers for diverse students in poverty. The likelihood is that these failing school systems will get even worse as they continue to miseducate current and future generations. Since the models for preparing effective teachers for diverse children in poverty already exist, they can and should be replicated now. This chapter focuses on this promise.

WHAT ATTRACTS PEOPLE TO TEACHING?

It is now typical for Americans to change jobs and career paths throughout their working lives. The old paradigm of school-to-work in which individuals were trained for one job or career which they then pursued for a lifetime is long gone. The new paradigm is an iteration of school-to-work-to-school-to-work-to-school-to-work as people require constant retraining for new roles and careers. While much has been written about this new pattern of individuals moving through many jobs and roles over a lifetime, the emphasis of this literature is top-down and external: it deals with how economic forces demand that individuals retool themselves for the global information age (Humphrey & Wechsler, 2004). While these demands are real and accelerating, the fact is that adults also respond to internal needs as they move through the stages of adult development. What a 20-year-old thinks is a satisfying job reflects a different set of needs and expectations than what a 35- or 50-year-old regards as a satisfying job.

In spite of denigrating terms such as "job changers," "retreads," and "career switchers" (Stoddard & Floden, 1995), mature individuals seeking new roles and careers in teaching is a predictable, natural, desirable response to maturation and development. Indeed, it is a healthy response. Those who are comfortable in precisely the same jobs at age 60 that they held at age 20 are fixated in a pattern of nongrowth (Heath, 1977). While American society is clearly the most flexible in allowing and supporting shifts in life choices, there are nevertheless both reasonable limits as well as unfortunate rigidities controlling the options open to people. If an individual decides at age 20 that repairing motorcycles is an "awesome" job, it will be easier for him/her to start a technical career at age 30 than it will be to become a psychiatrist. Similarly, the individual at age 20 who is motivated to become a kindergarten teacher might find it easier at age 35 to develop a chain of daycare centers than to become a veterinarian.

People are driven to search for meaning at all life stages (Bronoski, 1971; Frankl,1984); but what seems meaningful to them changes markedly in succeeding stages of maturity. And even in the world's most open society, the constraints and limits placed on individuals become harder to overcome as they mature and take on greater responsibilities. In the end, the choice of a job or career is a compromise between what the individual in a particular life stage wants with what he or she perceives as a realistic option. Many who have analyzed the young adult stage of life characterize it as the age of "me-ness," in which the focus is on self. In contrast, middle adulthood can be characterized as a time when many desire to put meaning in their lives by helping others find meaning in theirs (Erickson, 1963). As adults shift from a focus on self to more social concerns, they are motivated to reconsider their job and life opportunities. Many careers such as law, medicine, and public administration provide opportunities for helping others but require long periods of expensive preparation. Other jobs, in the health and human service sectors, offer the opportunity to serve others after relatively brief periods of training. Many adults pose the question to themselves in this way: "What can I do that will put more meaning in my life by helping others, without making my own family suffer from my becoming a student again with no income or health insurance?" For many the answer to this question is becoming a teacher through a program of paid, insured, on-the-job training.

ATTRIBUTES OF URBAN TEACHERS

While the search for meaning is the primary attraction of teaching to mature adults, there is a set of background factors which are predictive of what kind of people will be effective and remain in schools serving diverse students in poverty. Many who can become effective teachers will not have all of these attributes, but the population of mature adults who become effective and remain in these classrooms tend to have many of the following characteristics, they

- live in or were raised in a metropolitan area,
- attended schools in a metropolitan area as a child or youth,
- are parents or have had life experiences which involved extensive relationships with children,
- are African American, Latino, members of a minority group, or from a working class white family,
- earned a bachelor's degree from other than a highly selective or elitist college (many started in community colleges),

- majored in a field other than education as undergraduates,
- have had extensive and varied work experiences before seeking to become teachers,
- are part of a family/church/ethnic community in which teaching is still regarded as a fairly high-status career,
- have experienced a period of living in poverty or have the capacity to empathize with the challenges of living in poverty,
- have had out-of-school experiences with children of diverse backgrounds,
- may have had military experience but not as an officer,
- live in the city or would have no objection to moving into the city to meet a residency requirement,
- have engaged in paid or volunteer activities with diverse children in poverty,
- can multitask and do several things simultaneously and quickly for extended periods such as parenting and working part-time jobs.

The aforementioned attributes do not guarantee success as an urban teacher; they raise the probability that individuals with these attributes will succeed and remain. The reverse of these attributes describes a pool of people who are unlikely to remain in impoverished schools. Unfortunately, many districts still recruit and hire only the traditional pool (i.e., middle class, white, monolingual, late adolescent females who graduated from suburban, small town and parochial schools, who were full-time undergraduate majors in education, with little or no work or life experiences, without families or child-rearing experience, who lack commitment or roots in the particular urban area). Again, all of these characteristics are not required but having a cluster of them is typical of individuals who succeed and stay in urban schools. Nonetheless, these attributes describe "the best and the brightest" population for teaching diverse students in poverty.

While teaching will remain a predominantly female career, more mature males can and should be recruited and prepared. As with females, the most powerful predictor is age; as more mature males are recruited, the number who succeeds and remain increases substantially. In addition to the characteristics outlined above, the males who succeed in urban teaching need nine additional attributes. They are willing and able to

- multitask and perform several functions simultaneously,
- work in feminine institutions where procedures and human relationships with other adults are of greater importance than outcomes,

- take directions and accept evaluations from female principals and female supervisors,
- implement criticism not stated as direct orders but as "suggestions" or "concerns,"
- spend a good part of every day encouraging and nurturing children and youth as well as teaching them,
- interact positively with mothers and female caregivers,
- maintain class control by motivating and relating to children rather than trying to dominate them,
- regard children's misbehavior as a professional problem to be resolved rather than a threat to their authority or manliness,
- make personal sacrifices of time and energy to meet students' needs.

Men with all or most of these attributes succeed as urban teachers. They are men who are able to understand and overcome the way males are typically socialized in our society. In all teacher education programs, a higher percentage of males than females quit or fail, but by selecting men who have the nine additional attributes cited above, the programs I have developed over the past 46 years have produced as many as one third male graduates.

SHORTAGE OF TEACHERS IN URBAN SCHOOLS

To understand the opportunities and challenges facing career-changing adults, it is important to review the complex nature of the well-documented current teacher shortage. The National Commission on Teaching and America's Future estimates a need to hire up to 5 million full-time teachers between 2008 and 2020. The preponderance of these new hires are teachers needed to serve 16 million diverse children in urban and rural poverty (U.S. Department of Education, 2015). The phenomenon of an urban district needing thousands of teachers surrounded by suburbs and small towns where there are hundreds of applicants for one position has been well documented for over half a century.

Although the typical age of college graduates has risen from age 22 to age 26, it is still generally true that most of those preparing to teach are college-age youth, that is, late adolescents and young adults. This analysis is not an advocacy for preventing all such individuals from becoming teachers but to shift the balance. The current emphasis remains approximately 80% still being youngsters below age 26 and only approximately 20% being older "nontraditional" postbaccalaureate students or adults in alternative certification or on-the-job training programs. Given the needs in urban poverty districts, this balance should be reversed so that the majority of those in teacher training would be adults over age 30. Denigrating labels such as "retreads" or "career changers" indicate the power of the misconceptions and stereotypes regarding the age at which it is generally believed that individuals should become new teachers. My best estimate is that of the approximately 500,000 traditionally prepared teachers under age 26 who are produced annually, fewer than 15% seek employment in the 120 major urban districts serving approximately seven million diverse children in poverty. In my state, Wisconsin, the figure is 10%. This represents approximately 75,000 of the college and university's annual output. The research based on my Star Teacher Selection Interview indicates further that of the 15% who are willing to apply to work in urban school districts that only one in ten (or 7,500) of those under age 26 will stay long enough (three years or longer) to become successful teachers in urban schools. What this means is that the approximately one half million youngsters under 26 in over 1,200 traditional programs of teacher education provide the 120 largest urban school districts with about 1.5% of their annual teacher output. While this is obviously a very small output from traditional teacher preparing institutions it does represent a block of young people who do have the potential for teaching diverse children in urban poverty and for whom the doors of the profession must remain open. But, should this population of young teachers represented by this 1.5% contribution remain as the predominant pool of future teachers? So should school systems be looking for other constituencies from which to draw and develop the teachers America needs?

Several factors contribute to the "shortage" of teachers where they are needed most; that is, in urban schools. First, the length of an average teaching career is now down to 11 years. Teachers who pursue lifelong careers as classroom teachers are now clearly in the minority. Second, in many states, the majority of those graduated and certified in traditional programs of teacher preparation never take jobs as teachers. In 1998, in Wisconsin, 71% of those graduated and certified by colleges and universities did not take jobs as teachers (Schug & Western, 1998). In 2001, of newly certified graduates, 65% did not take teaching jobs. This lower figure does not mean that more teachers entered classrooms since the total number produced in 2001 had declined by almost 20%. These nonteaching certified graduates are frequently referred to by many experts in teacher education as "fully qualified." But, if they do not take teaching positions because the jobs are primarily in urban schools serving diverse children in poverty, for what and for whom are these graduates "fully qualified?" The state licenses issued them should contain codicils or reservations such as "is prepared to teach white children not in poverty in small town or suburban school districts." Instead, all 50 states issue only unrestricted, universal licenses pronouncing the bearers qualified to teach all children of a given age, or all children in a given subject matter or all children with particular exceptional conditions. The staggering percentage of the newly certified teachers choosing to not waste their own time or the children's time is actually a benefit since it does not inflict potential quitters and failures on children in desperate need of competent caring teachers. Newly certified graduates not taking jobs are also a clear indication that the bearers of these licenses are being much more honest about themselves and their lack of competence than those who prepared them and who insist on pronouncing them "fully qualified." In 1999, the SUNY system prepared 17,000 "fully qualified" teachers. The number who applied for teaching positions in New York City that year was zero. In 2004, the State of North Carolina met its need for 10,000 teachers (only 3,500 were certified by in-state colleges and universities) by hiring teachers from abroad through a private company that receives $11,500 for each teacher it finds. The City of Greensboro recruits for teachers in Capetown, South Africa.

The third reason for the teacher shortage is the number of beginners who take jobs in urban schools but fail or leave. Using data from the National Center for Educational Statistic's School and Staffing Survey, Ingersoll (2001) concluded, "School staffing problems are primarily due to excess demand resulting from a revolving door—where large numbers of teachers depart for reasons other than retirement" (p. 3). This churn of teachers into and out of schools serving diverse children in poverty results in approximately 50% of new teachers leaving urban districts in less than 5 years. In my own city, Milwaukee, 50% of the more than 1,000 new teachers hired annually will be gone in three years or less. Many quit in the first year (Haberman & Rickards, 1990).

The fourth major reason for the teacher shortage in urban schools is the shortage of special education teachers. This shortage is exacerbated by the fact that many suburbs, small towns, parochial and private schools contract out the education of their children with special needs to their nearby urban school districts. This not only increases the teacher shortage in urban districts but also raises their costs. For example, in Wisconsin and in many others, the state makes a deduction in aid to the urban district for every special education class not taught by a fully certified teacher. No state imposes such a fiscal penalty when a district employs an uncertified teacher in math, science, or other areas of continuing shortage. But there is a more fundamental reason for this shortage of special education teachers. In effect, "fully qualified" teachers prepared in traditional university-based programs are systematically trained to view many of their children as somehow lacking, deviant, or having special needs. New teachers unable to connect with and manage their students will see things that are wrong with the children and their families rather than the inadequacies in themselves. Trapped by biased, limited, cultural definitions of how a normal child should develop, behave, and learn language, it is inevitable that teachers would refer children they cannot connect with for testing to equally limited school psychologists who then provide the backup test scores and psychological evaluations to show that these children are not capable of functioning in normal ways.

A fifth reason for the teacher shortage results from greater career opportunities now available to women outside of teaching at the time of college graduation. Many, however, soon discover that they encounter glass ceilings and can only advance in limited ways. After age 30, this population includes many who decide to make more mature decisions than they did at age 20 and seek to become teachers of diverse children in poverty. The sixth reason for the shortage deals with college graduates of diverse racial and cultural backgrounds who have greater access into a larger number of entry level career positions than in former times. As with the population of women who perceive greater opportunity for careers of higher status and greater financial reward outside of teaching, this population also frequently experiences glass ceilings after age 30. For instance, African Americans compose fewer than 6% of all undergraduates in all fields and substantially fewer who decide as youthful undergraduates to pursue traditional university-based programs of teacher education. But as career-changers after age 30, racially diverse college graduates (particularly women) become a primary source of teachers for children in urban school districts. The school district employs more African American college graduates than any business in Milwaukee, and this is true in many other cities. The continuing and worsening teacher shortage must also take note of the special nature of teaching fields such as math and science. Math and science teachers leave at a higher rate than others; they tend to be men seeking better opportunities in other fields (Murnane, 1996). While the causes of the shortage in these areas have some distinctive dimensions, they are not discussed separately since the solutions proposed for the general shortage also impact these high-needs specializations.

In studies of quitters and leavers, the most commonly cited reasons refer to poor working conditions and the difficulty of managing the children. A typical list includes the following reasons: overwhelming workload, discipline problems, low pay, little respect, lack of support, and the clerical workload. The difficult working conditions in many urban schools discourage beginning (and experienced) teachers, but such complaints raise questions about the validity of these responses, the maturity of the leavers making these responses, and the quality of the teacher preparation offered those who give these reasons for leaving. Indeed, interviews of high school students indicate quite clearly that even young adolescents are well aware of the negative conditions under which their teachers work (Florida State Department of Education, 1985).

Quitters and leavers who offer these reasons for terminating their employment and those who accept and analyze these responses as authentic explanations, make the findings of studies on why teachers quit or fail highly problematic. While poor working conditions do contribute to teacher losses, in-depth interviews I have had with quitters and failures from schools serving diverse children in urban poverty over the past 45 years reveal other explanations for leaving than those gleaned from superficial questionnaires, surveys, and brief exit interviews. My final classroom observations of teachers who are failing also support the existence of more basic reasons for leaving than those gained from typical exit interviews. Leavers are understandably chary about having anything on their records that they believe might make it difficult for them to get a reference for a future job. They are also savvy enough to not say things that might make them appear prejudiced toward multicultural children and their families. It takes an hour or longer for a skilled interviewer to establish rapport, trust, and an open dialogue in order to extract more authentic and fewer superficial reasons for why teachers leave. For example, the quitter's citation of "discipline and classroom management problems" as the reason for leaving takes on new meaning when one learns what the respondent is really saying. In typical surveys, quitters and failures frequently mention the challenge of working with "difficult" students, and this comment is simply noted or checked or counted. During in-depth interviews where rapport has been established, this cause is amplified by leavers into more complete explanations of why discipline and classroom management are difficult for them. They make statements such as, "I really don't see myself spending the rest of my life working with 'these' children," or "It's clear that 'these' children do not want me as their teacher." When the reasons for the disconnect between themselves and the children are probed further, leavers will frequently make statements such as the following: "These kids will never learn standard English" or "My mother didn't raise me to listen to 'm.f.' all day" or "These children could not possibly be Christians," or "These kids are just not willing or able to follow the simplest directions."

The comments of quitters and leavers which may have at first appeared to indicate a simple, straightforward lack of skills on the part of a neophyte still learning to maintain discipline, can now be recognized as actually representing much deeper issues. Rather than a simple matter which can be corrected by providing more training to caring beginning teachers who understandably just need some tips on classroom management and more experience, it is clear there is a disconnect and an irreconcilable chasm between these teachers and their students. Teacher attrition increases as the number of minority students increases (Rollefson, 1990).

Quitters and leavers cannot connect with, establish rapport, or reach diverse children in urban poverty because at bottom they do not respect and care enough about them to want to be their teachers. These attitudes and perceptions are readily sensed by students who respond in kind by not wanting "these" people as their teachers. Contrary to the popular debates on what teachers need to know to be effective, teachers in urban schools do not quit because they lack subject matter or pedagogy. Quitters and leavers know how to divide fractions and they know how to write lesson plans. They leave because they cannot connect with the students, and it is a continuous, draining hassle for them to keep students on task. In a very short period, leavers are emotionally and physically exhausted from struggling against resisting students for 6 hours every day. In my classroom observations of failing teachers, I have never found an exception to this condition: if there is a disconnect between the teacher and students then no mentoring, coaching, workshop, or class on discipline and classroom management can provide the teacher with the magic to control children he or she does not genuinely respect and care about. In truth, the graduates of traditional programs of teacher education are *fully qualified* only if the definition of this term is limited to mean they can pass written tests of subject matter and pedagogy. Unfortunately, while knowledge of subject matter and pedagogy are absolutely necessary, they are not sufficient conditions for being effective in urban schools. Knowing what and how to teach only becomes relevant after the teacher has connected and established a positive relationship with students.

Many who give advice on how to solve the teacher shortage in urban schools frequently assert that "these" children need to be taught by the "best and the brightest." Unfortunately, the typical criteria used to define "the best and the brightest" identify teachers who are precisely those most likely to quit and fail in urban schools. The majority of early leavers are individuals with higher intelligence quotients, grade-point averages, and standardized test scores than those who stay; more have also had academic majors (Darling-Hammond & Sclan, 1996). Teachers who earn advanced degrees within the prior 2 years leave at the highest rates (Boe, Bobbit, Cook, Whitener, & Leeber, 1997). Those who see teaching as primarily an intellectual activity are eight times more likely to leave the classroom (Quartz, Thomas, Hasan, Kim, & Barraza-Lawrence, 2001).

In 1963, the Milwaukee Intern Program became the model for the National Teacher Corps. In the ten years (1963–1972) of the Corps' existence, approximately 100,000 college graduates with high GPAs were prepared for urban teaching. While many stayed in education, fewer than 5% remained in the classroom for more than 3 years (Corwin, 1973). This was the largest, longest study ever done in teacher education. The fact that the shibboleth "best and brightest" still survives is testimony to the fact that many prefer to maintain their pet beliefs about teacher education in spite of the facts. In effect, the criteria typically used to support the "best and brightest" are powerful, valid identifiers of failures and quitters. While being an effective teacher of diverse children in poverty has some intellectual and academic aspects, it is primarily a human relation's activity demanding the ability to make and maintain positive, supportive connections with diverse children, school staff, and caregivers. Those threatened by this view misconstrue my advocacy to mean that I believe knowledge of subject matter and knowledge of teaching are unimportant. Not so! There is substantial research evidence that teachers who know more English usage and who have greater knowledge of the subject matters they teach, have children who learn more (Zeichner & Schulte, 2001). But it is only after the propensity to relate to diverse children in urban poverty has been demonstrated that the teacher's knowledge of subject matter and how to teach can become relevant.

This raises the more basic issue of whether future teachers (or anyone) can be taught to connect with diverse children in poverty or whether this is an attribute learned from mature reflection about one's life experiences after one has had some life experiences. If it is, as I believe, the latter, then it is an attribute that must be selected for and not assumed to be the result of completing university coursework. Indeed, there is substantial evidence that college courses and direct experiences reinforce rather than change teacher education students' prejudices and abilities to connect with diverse children in poverty (Haberman, 1991). This is also true of in-service teachers (Sleeter, 1992). Selecting people with the predispositions to connect with diverse children in poverty rather than assuming that training programs will change students' basic values and perceptions is the greatest weakness in traditional teacher education and my strongest advocacy for change.

By studying great urban teachers and quitter/failures, I have been able to identify fourteen functions which discriminate between the two groups. I have found that they perceive things differently and consequently, hold different beliefs and values regarding the nature of childhood, the ways people learn best and the purposes of schooling. They also have different beliefs regarding the value and importance of ethnic diversity and issues of equity and access to high-quality educational opportunity. For example, the ideology of successful teachers leads them to view effective schooling as a matter of life or death for diverse children in urban poverty. This perception impacts everything effective teachers do and the consequences of their practices for children and youth. Clearly, teachers who remain in urban schools and are effective exhibit the following attributes:

1. **Persistence** refers to the effective teacher's continuous search for what works best for individuals and classes. Part of this persistence involves problem solving and creative effort. The manifestation of this quality is that no student goes unnoticed or can stay off-task for very long. Effective teachers never give up on trying to engage every student.

2. **Protecting learners and learning** refers to making children's active involvement in productive work more important than curriculum rigidities and even school rules. Effective teachers not only recognize all the ways in which large school organizations impinge on students but find ways to make and keep learning the highest priority.

3. **Application of generalizations** refers to the teacher's ability to translate theory and research into practice. Conversely, it also refers to the teacher's ability to understand how specific behaviors support concepts and ideas about effective teaching. This dimension predicts the teacher's ability to benefit from professional development activities and grow as a professional practitioner.

4. **Approach to at-risk students** deals with the teacher's perceptions of the causes and cures for youngsters who are behind in basic skills. Effective teachers see poor teaching and rigid curricula as the major causes. They are also willing to assume personal accountability for their students' learning in spite of the fact that they cannot control all in-school and out-of-school influences on their students.

5. **Professional versus personal orientation** to students refers to whether teachers might use teaching to meet the their emotional needs rather than those of the students. Quitter/failures have a different set of expectations than effective teachers on how they expect to relate to children. They find it difficult to respect and care about children who may do things they regard as despicable.

6. **Burnout—its causes and cures**—predicts the likelihood that teachers will survive in an urban school bureaucracy. Those with no understanding of the causes of burnout who hold naïve expectations of working in school systems are most likely to be victims.

7. **Fallibility** refers to the teacher's willingness to admit mistakes and correct them. This dimension of teacher behavior establishes the classroom climate for how students respond to their mistakes in the process of learning.

Seven other functions also discriminate between greatness and failure in urban teaching. Following are these functions:

1. **High expectations:** The demonstrated belief that all the children can be successful if appropriately taught.
2. **Organizational ability:** The skill to plan, gather materials and set up a workable classroom.
3. **Physical/emotional stamina:** The ability to persist with commitment and enthusiasm after instances of violence, death, and other crises.
4. **Teaching style:** The use of coaching rather than direction and information giving.
5. **Explanations of success:** An emphasis on student effort rather than presumed ability.
6. **Ownership:** The willingness to lead students to believe it is their classroom not the teacher's.
7. **Inclusion:** The acceptance of accountability for all the students assigned to the classroom.

Presently, more than 200 cities across America utilize the Urban Teacher Selection Interview, which includes the first seven functions outlined above. This very large, ongoing sample provides the database for claiming that mature adults are three times more likely than younger candidates to demonstrate these functions.

IMPACT OF EFFECTIVE
TEACHER ATTRIBUTES ON URBAN SCHOOLS

A critically important attribute of teachers who are effective in urban schools is how they respond to the ceaseless pressure of preparing students for a school career. These mandates for what experts pronounce must be included in a basic education. The second curriculum is what teachers actually teach. This is markedly less than the district's stated curriculum. The third curriculum is what children actually learn. This is much less than the stated curriculum and what teachers have taught. The fourth curriculum is what is tested for. This is the narrowest of the four curricula and represents only a sampling of what students supposedly learned. As one considers the relationship among these four curricula in urban school districts, it is clear that what is tested for is the dominant curriculum. Indeed, urban schools take pride in aligning their curricula with the tests. What alignment means, in effect, is that what is advocated, taught, and learned is continually narrowed and limited to what is tested for. This trend will continue and will increase the pressure on urban schools and teachers in them. In Wisconsin, as in all of the other states, the majority of schools identified as Schools in Need of Improvement (failing schools) are in major urban areas.

In suburban and wealthy private schools, the professional staff and parents agree on many broad school goals that include basic knowledge in all areas of learning; skills of learning and using technology; citizenship; aesthetic development; health and physical education; emotional health; environmental studies; interacting positively with people of all backgrounds; and ethical behavior. In schools serving the urban poor, the general public (80% of whom have no children in schools) has narrowed these grand school goals down to two: get a job and stay out of jail. This narrowing of goals in schools serving the urban poor presents several challenges for effective, caring teachers: how to help students do well on tests but still offer a deeper curriculum that will take students beyond what is tested for and how to include all the grand goals offered advantaged children in urban schools where aspirations and expectations for the staff and students have been lowered. It is clear that more mature beginning teachers are more able to deal with these pressures for several reasons. They are in a stage of development that enables them to see beyond absolutist thinking, such as "My principal says to get them ready for the test so I can't teach them other things." More mature adults, particularly those who are parents, are more prone to asking themselves what kind of curriculum and teaching they would want for their own children. They are also more likely to have had work experiences where they negotiated with superiors regarding how to get the work done more efficiently by doing it somewhat differently. In teacher education programs, more mature teachers are consistently rated higher than younger beginners by their principals, even though they are constantly negotiating with them to offer the children a more expanded, richer curriculum (Haberman, 1999).

There is substantial evidence from our Urban Teacher Selection Interview that one out of three candidates over 30 years of age will pass this interview, while only one out of ten candidates under 25 years of age passes. This interview compares candidate's answers to the responses of the most effective urban teachers. A critical question on this interview deals with "protecting the learning of children" and refers directly to this issue of teaching and learning beyond the curriculum that will be tested for. More mature applicants are three times more likely to specify behaviors for themselves that require putting the children first and then negotiating with superiors to protect that learning. Less mature candidates advocate following directives, even if they believe the results might narrow children's learning, because they dare not risk discussing directives with superiors. In short, if a district seeks beginning teachers who will function primarily as test tutors, it would seem they would also negotiate for expanding and enriching the curriculum. In addition, more mature teachers are more likely to teach issues of equity and social justice. Since this teacher population is composed primarily of women, minorities, and whites from low-income backgrounds, many of them have actually experienced discrimination, prejudice, or glass ceilings in the workplace. They are sensitive to such issues in their schools and in the lives of their students. They initiate a broad range of learning activities with their students that involve all types of environmental problems, the criminal justice system, the actions of elected officials, and consuming products manufactured by child labor. Mature teachers are more likely to offer a curriculum in which students are involved as active participants now rather than a curriculum for becoming active citizens after graduation.

THE SCHOOL ENVIRONMENT, WORKING CONDITIONS, AND THE RETENTION OF URBAN TEACHERS

Although teachers leave primarily because they cannot connect with diverse children and youth in poverty, it is necessary to recognize that the conditions under which teachers work can present formidable obstacles. In some urban schools, conditions teachers face are so horrific that they drive out not only those who should never have been hired but many who have the potential for becoming effective teachers and even stars. Because these conditions are likely to worsen, the strategy of recruiting and training more mature people who can succeed in schools as they now are is a more responsible social policy than continuing to prepare traditional populations of new teachers on the naïve expectation these conditions will improve. In many of these districts, beginning teachers are often expected to work under conditions that are medieval: rooms without windows; over 30 students in a class including six or more students with exceptionalities; insufficient, outdated textbooks; no dictionaries; no paper; no access to a copier that works; no computers connected to the Internet; science rooms without running water; little or no consumable materials; no parking; no closet the teacher can lock or even a hook to hang up his/her coat. Teachers spend an average of $650 dollars a year of their own money on supplies (Haberman, 1998). There are teachers who use their own funds to buy chalk. When I recently asked a principal to provide a teacher with some chalk he replied, "The teachers knew how much money we had for supplies and they chose to use it up by January. What do you want from me?" Observing the equipment, supplies, and materials that urban teachers typically have to work with frequently leads one to question whether these teachers are working in the United States of America.

In 2001, I visited schools in New York City on behalf of the New York State Department of Education. These classrooms were exactly like the ones I was in as a child in the same city 65 years earlier. The only difference I could see was that there was an electric clock on the wall. In this financial and cultural world center, I observed many caring, well-intentioned beginners whose only teaching material was chalk, a blackboard, and paper already used on one side. Many of our urban schools function as isolated third-world outposts in the midst of a 21st century technological society. In addition, getting through urban school's archaic personnel systems for an initial appointment, securing an assignment to a particular school and classroom, and then meeting the never-ending paperwork and clerical demands would wear any reasonable person down in short order. Added to this is the problem of trying to teach in classrooms which experience an average of 120 interruptions per week (Delgadillo, 1992). The mindless, overpowering bureaucracies of urban school districts seem organized for the express purpose of driving out the beginners who care the most and retaining only the "strong insensitives" (i.e., those who are inured to how mindless bureaucracies ignore the needs of children in poverty). Unfortunately, status studies and summaries of these conditions do not change or improve them. Advocating what should be does not change the nature of what urban schools are or will be. All may agree that the conditions of work faced by beginners are a critical determinant in driving out many with high potential, but the critical question remains, Is it likely that these conditions will improve or worsen? Following is a prognosis based on the five most important conditions of work (i.e., salaries, safety, class size, principals, and testing).

Salaries

In my city, Milwaukee, a single mother with two or more children (a typical profile of one pool who are likely to succeed and stay in urban teaching) will earn a starting salary that is low enough to meet the state's poverty criterion and will entitle her to food stamps. In the future, I believe teacher salaries will not increase in real dollars. Much worse than the annual rate of inflation are the out-of-control costs of health care, which double every 3 years. Urban school districts are negotiating greater contributions from teachers to help cover these costs but will still be forced to put whatever monies they might have used for salary raises into health care. In Milwaukee, the teachers' benefit package is already 63% so that a beginning teacher paid $29,000 costs the district $47,200 with benefits. In 2012, the benefits package was roughly 75%. This means that a beginning teacher paid $40,000 will cost the district over $70,000 per year, and this assumes that the teachers will be paying for a greater share of their health care, thereby decreasing their real income. As long as health costs double every 3 years, there will never be enough funds to give teachers more than nominal salary increases which cannot keep up with the cost of living.

School Safety

I believe the amount that urban districts pay for school safety personnel and equipment will continue to increase. Many cities' expenditures for safety make them the second or third largest "police" force in their state. This not only diverts funds from educational purposes but also seriously alters school climate, transforming them from educational institutions into custodial ones. In many urban middle schools, there is more invested in hall cameras than in computers or computer-assisted instruction. As more time of professional staff is directed to issues of control, it casts a pall over the self-concepts of teachers who have a great need to perceive themselves as educators rather than as safety personnel.

Class Size

Class size has great impact on teacher morale and effectiveness. In those states which mandate smaller classes, there will be a sharp decrease in class size for primary grades and increases in class size for teachers in all the higher grades. In urban districts, class size will increase in response to budget cuts and higher birth rates among the urban poor. These increases in class size will be worst in urban middle schools where many students who cannot pass the 8th grade tests to get into high school remain until they drop out. In urban middle schools, teachers may work with between 100 and 150 students daily. This age group is an especially challenging one for teachers who must deal with high levels of student frustration, explosive physical maturation, and the tremendous peer pressure exerted on students, particularly on males, to not learn in school. These conditions of work in urban middle schools will not improve even in districts that return to a 1-8 school organization. Recognizing that this is the last chance for many youth, caring teachers work especially hard. Teacher burnout and dropout rates are high. Such conditions make it more likely that teachers who stay longer than 5 years will be the "strong-insensitives" rather than those who are caring and committed.

Supportive Principals

There is a growing shortage of effective urban school principals. The growing expectation that the principal can no longer be a building manager but must be the instructional leader of a community organization will deepen this shortage. In addition, an increasing number of urban districts now hold the principal accountable, on an annual basis, for raising test scores. Raising these expectations for principals cuts down on the pool of those who can be effective in such demanding roles. It is noteworthy that beginning teachers frequently cite "having a supportive principal" as a critical factor in their professional development and whether or not they leave. There is also a continuing and growing shortage of racially and culturally diverse school leaders who can function effectively in African American and Latino communities. Principals are still drawn from the ranks of former teachers in the same urban pool of racially and culturally diverse teachers; the pool from which future principals will be drawn will not increase. One obstacle to turning this situation around is that every urban district has a shortage of effective principals now. This means that most of the teachers and assistant principals who will compose the pool of future principals may never work for or ever see an effective principal functioning as an accountable, instructional leader. Without such models of success to emulate and mentor them, the prognosis is that tomorrow's principals will function in essentially the same ways as today's. This makes the likelihood that teachers will be getting more support from an increasing pool of more effective principals problematic.

Tests

The number of tests taken by students in urban schools is not likely to diminish. District and state mandates have now made testing a fact of life for urban teachers. In some districts, the curriculum is so tightly aligned with the mandated tests that teachers actually follow scripts in order to cover all the topics on which students will be tested in the exact same way. This is a critical condition of work for many beginners who are misled into believing that as teachers they would be professional decision-makers rather than script readers and test tutors. The very strong likelihood is that the pressures felt by teachers to prepare their children for tests will continue and increase since so many will be assigned to schools officially designated as failing. On the positive side, there has been an increase in several conditions which beginners rate as critical conditions of work. First, there is more teacher teaming than in the past. This means that teachers have greater access to other teachers' ideas and experiences. Second, there is more mentoring of beginning teachers by experienced teachers with released time. Both of these factors are expensive because they involve greater costs for staff development; and while implemented in a few urban districts, they are more likely to be cut than expanded.

FINAL THOUGHTS

This chapter has discussed problems and prospects regarding personnel preparation for urban schools. As it appears, there is no shortage of young teacher candidates in traditional programs of teacher education whose primary motive is to secure licenses that will enable them to be hired in any state. The need is for effective teachers in urban schools to serve diverse students in poverty. Mature adults who begin with a focused local, urban commitment are more likely to not only succeed but also survive. Securing teachers whom diverse children in urban poverty deserve requires changing some of the institutional values in traditional university-based teacher education.

First, the clients of teacher preparation are not students in programs of teacher education but the diverse children in poverty in urban schools who need effective teachers. This change of perception regarding who the clients are will cause many shifts in practice; the most notable being that teacher candidates will be put through selection and training procedures that result in significantly more of them self-selecting out or being failed before they are licensed.

Second, the long-term, continuing shortage of effective urban teachers does not mean that standards should be lowered but that they must be raised. Teachers who will be effective and who will remain are individuals who not only have knowledge of subject matter and pedagogy but who can connect with diverse children in poverty and can function under adverse working conditions.

Third, candidates should not be admitted into programs of teacher education because they have passed the traditional selection criteria at a college or university. Urban school districts must first process candidates through their selection procedures. Only those whom the district would be willing to hire should be admitted into preparation programs.

Fourth, the locus of preparation must be urban school classrooms in which the candidates function as teachers of record. The various pools of adults who can be recruited, selected, and prepared to be effective in urban schools envision themselves changing careers in order to function in the role of teachers. They are not willing to take on the role of students in teacher education programs and have demonstrated clearly, over decades, they will not be recruited if their primary role is to become college students rather than teachers. This means alternative certification programs, intern programs, and on-the-job training must be used to recruit and prepare mature candidates.

Fifth, the traditional practice of young college students deciding they would like to be teachers of a particular age or subject matter and then seeking employment after graduation must be abandoned as a strategy for preparing urban teachers. The starting point for creating the pools of teachers to be trained in the various specializations should be based on the projections of teacher need in the local urban school districts. Only those who can fill a specific school need for a particular teacher specialization should be recruited, selected, and prepared.

Sixth, for teachers to remain and be effective, their training program cannot focus on universal truths (i.e., the nature of children, teaching, and learning). Training programs cannot be preparation for teaching in the best of all nonexistent worlds. From the outset, preparation must focus on serving particular groups of children from specific local cultures attending schools in a particular urban district. Assuming that preparing candidates for no place in particular prepares them to teach all children everywhere will only perpetuate the current system of turning out "fully qualified" graduates not taking jobs, quitting, or failing. There is no shortage of teacher candidates whose primary motive is to secure licenses that will enable them to be hired in any state. The need is to prepare teachers for specific urban schools to serve particular constituencies. Mature adults from a specific urban area who begin with a focused local, urban commitment are more likely to not only succeed but remain.

Seventh, the tradition of waiting for young undergraduate students to apply to a university to be prepared as teachers must be replaced with aggressive and targeted marketing programs directed at pools of local, adult college graduates, particularly those of different races and cultures. Traditional forms of nationwide recruitment by urban school districts competing with each other for a limited pool of young graduates need to be replaced by strategies which focus on mature residents in a specific metropolitan area. Local churches, businesses, governments, and community organizations are basic sources for the recruitment of African American and Latino applicants. While women are the primary target, ways of reaching local male pools must also be utilized. New ways of explaining the work of a teacher in an urban school district need to be an integral part of honest, realistic marketing that lets applicants know what they are getting into from day one. Urban school districts must accept the fact that new teacher recruits need to be oriented and prepared to work in inefficient, dysfunctional bureaucracies.

Eighth, specific attributes of great urban teachers should guide the selection of new teachers into preparation programs. State-mandated skills of subject matter and pedagogy are necessary but not sufficient. All programs of preparation should utilize both interviews of applicants that compare them to effective teachers and the direct observation of candidates actually relating to children and youth. These are the two most powerful predictors of success with diverse children in urban poverty.

And ninth, offering inducements for candidates who are hesitant about teaching diverse children in urban poverty do not recruit the appropriate population. Signing bonuses, reduced apartment rentals or down payments on homes will attract quitter/failures. Funds used for such inducements should instead be used for mentors and tuition remission. This is the financial aid that helps mature candidates the most. Such support will be most effective in keeping the pathway into teaching open to adults with financial responsibilities and low-income candidates.

Considering the working conditions teachers say they need versus those they regard as debilitating, the likelihood is far greater that the negative conditions under which teachers work are likely to worsen. What this means for securing teachers who will stay and become effective is clear. While all constituencies must do everything possible to try and improve the conditions under which urban teachers work, the students cannot be held hostage waiting for change agents who have been completely unsuccessful up to now. The need is to recruit and retain teachers who can be effective with today's children and youth in today's schools. Teacher educators should not be allowed to take the pious position that it is unfair or even immoral for beginning teachers to function in today's schools and therefore those who prepare teachers cannot be held accountable for the quality of their training programs until the urban schools are first transformed. There are real children and youth spending the only lives they will ever have being miseducated in these schools every day. Demanding that the schools improve before effective teachers can be prepared for such places will sacrifice still another generation. The most prudent course is to scale up the successful models of urban teacher education we now have and recruit, select, and prepare caring, effective, mature teachers who will make a difference immediately.

ACKNOWLEDGMENT

This chapter was originally published online in 2005 by the Haberman Educational Foundation (HEF), Inc. and was entitled "The Rationale for Preparing Mature Adults as Teachers of Diverse Children in Urban Poverty." It is reprinted with the permission of HEF.

CHAPTER QUESTIONS

1. As you review the factors that attract individuals to teaching, identify those that you agree with and those you do not.

2. Review the list of characteristics of mature adults who become effective teachers. Do you agree with this list? Why or why not? If the recruitment and selection of mature teachers is critical to teaching success, why aren't more districts engaging in initiatives to identify and retain this type of educator? What is your district doing to identify and retain mature educators?

3. In your experience, and making reference to new sources, evaluate the credibility of the five reasons for the teacher shortage.

4. The five most important conditions of work have been identified as salary, safety, class size, principals, and testing. Summarize these conditions at your school. Next, argue whether or not these circumstances will change for major urban school districts in America and at your school.

REFERENCES

Boe, E. E., Bobbit, S. A., Cook, L. H. Whitener, S. D., & Leeber, A. L. (1997). Why didst thou go? Predictors of special and general education teachers from a national perspective. *The Journal of Special Education, 30*, 390–411.

Bronoski, J. (1971). *The identity of men.* New York, NY: American Museum Science Books.

Corwin, R. G. (1973). *Organizational reform and organizational survival: The Teacher Corps as an instrument of educational change.* New York, NY: Wiley.

Darling-Hammond, L., & Sclan, E. M. (1996). Who teaches and why: Dilemma of building a profession for twenty-first century schools. In J. Sikula (Ed.), *Handbook of research on teacher education* (pp. 67–101). New York, NY: Macmillan.

Delgadillo, F. (1992). *A qualitative analysis of an alternative master's program for practicing teachers engaged in action research* (Unpublished doctoral dissertation). University of Wisconsin-Milwaukee.

Erikson, E. (1963).Childhood and society. New York, NY: Norton.

Florida State Department of Education. (1985). *Teaching as a career: High school students' perceptions' of teachers and teaching.* Tallahassee, FL: Education Standards Commission. Retrieved from http://files.eric.ed.gov/fulltext/ED266088.pdf

Frankl, V. E. (1984). *Man's search for meaning.* New York, NY: Washington Square Press.

Haberman, M. (1991). Can cultural awareness be taught in teacher education programs? *Teaching Education, 4*, 96–104.

Haberman, M. (1998). How much of their own time and money do teachers spend on their students? *Kappa Delta Pi Record, 35*, 71–79.

Haberman, M. (1999). Increasing the number of high quality African Americans in urban schools. *Journal of Instructional Psychology, 26*(4), 208–212.

Haberman, M., & Rickards, W. (1990).Urban teachers who quit: Why they leave and what they do. *Urban Education, 25,* 297–303.

Heath, D. (1977). *Maturity and competence.* New York, NY: Macmillan.

Humphrey, D. C., & Wechsler, E. M. (2004). *The status of the teaching profession.* Santa Cruz, CA: Center for the Future of Teaching and Learning.

Ingersoll, R. (2001). *Teacher turnover, teacher shortages and the organization of the schools.* Seattle, WA: Center for the Study of Teaching and Policy.

Murnane, R. J. (1996). Staffing the nation's schools with skilled teachers. In E. A. Hanushek & D. W. Jorgenson (Eds.), *Improving America's schools: The role of incentives* (pp. 241–258). Washington, DC: National Academies Press.

National Commission on Teaching and America's Future. (2010). *Who will teach?: Experience matters.* Retrieved from http://nctaf.org/wp-content/uploads/2012/01/NCTAF-Who-Will-Teach-Experience-Matters-2010-Report.pdf

Quartz, K. H., Thomas, A., Hasan, L., Kim, P., & Barraza-Lawrence, K. (2001). *Urban teacher retention: Exploratory research methods and findings* (Technical report of the Center X/TEP Research Group, #1001-UTEC-6-01). Los Angeles, CA: UCLA, Institute for Democracy, Education, and Access.

Rollefson, M. (1990). *Teacher turnover: Patterns of entry to and exit from teaching.* Washington, DC: National Center for Education Statistics.

Schug, M., & Western, R. (1998, June). Deregulating teacher training in Wisconsin. *Wisconsin School News,* 8–14.

Sleeter, C. E. (1992). *Keepers of the American dream: A study of staff development and multicultural education.* London, England: Falmer Press.

Stoddard, T., & Floden, R. E. (1995).Traditional and alternative routes to teacher certification: Issues, assumptions and misconceptions. In K. Zeichner (Ed.), *Reforming teacher education in the United States.* New York, NY: Teachers College Press.

U.S. Department of Education, National Center on Education Statistics. (2015). Condition of education, racial/ethnic enrollment in public schools, 2012. Washington, DC: Author.

Zeichner, K., & Schulte, A. K. (2001).What we know and don't know from peer-reviewed research about alternative certification programs. *Journal of Teacher Education, 52,* 266–282.

ABOUT THE CONTRIBUTORS

ABOUT THE EDITORS

Dr. Valerie Hill-Jackson received her interdisciplinary doctorate in educational leadership degree, summa cum laude, from St. Joseph's University in Philadelphia, Pennsylvania. She is a clinical professor in the Department of Teaching, Learning, and Culture at Texas A&M University and teaches in its Culture & Curriculum and Urban Education programs as well as the Educational Leadership for Curriculum and Instruction's online program. She is also a senior researcher, a volunteer position, for the Haberman Educational Foundation. Dr. Hill-Jackson's research interests include social justice leadership, service-learning and community education, STEM education for the underserved, ethnography, urban education, and gifted education.

Dr. Hill-Jackson has several publications in *Multicultural Education Perspectives*, *Urban Education*, *Kappa Delta Pi Record*, and the coeditor of *Transforming Teacher Education: What Went Wrong in Teacher Training and How We Can Fix It* (Stylus, 2010) and *Better Principals, Better Schools: What Star Principals Know, Believe, and Do* (Information Age, 2016). She is a university and internationally recognized educator and scholar, and has many prestigious awards and recognitions to her credit, including the American Educational Research Association/Spencer Fellowship; and the Childhood Lead Poisoning Star Award for her research in K–12 community education and outreach. In 2013, Hill-Jackson was conferred with the Upton Sinclair Award and won a Traditional Core Fulbright Award to conduct research in the United Kingdom.

Delia Stafford, known as the practitioner's practitioner, is the president and chief executive officer of the Haberman Educational Foundation, Inc. in Houston, Texas, and was named a 2015 *Elite American Educator*, a recog-

201

nition for her achievements and leadership in developing educational programs for impoverished and at-risk youth. For nearly a decade, Ms. Stafford directed the nation's largest school district-based alternative teacher certification program in the Houston Independent School District. She was twice recognized at White House ceremonies for her success in that program and her advocacy in finding good teachers for children at risk and in poverty. In addition to research interests in alternative teacher certification and teacher selection, Ms. Stafford's publications include urban school district-based teacher education, violence prevention, beliefs of effective teachers, student resilience, and research implementation. Ms. Stafford began the Haberman Educational Foundation in 1994 for the purpose of making visible and lasting improvements in the education of America's 16 million diverse children living in poverty.

ABOUT THE AUTHORS

Dr. Robert H. Audette (1938–2014) was associate professor in the Reading and Elementary Department at the University of North Carolina in Charlotte. He was an excellent teacher, mentor, and community leader.

Dr. Guy Banicki is an associate professor at Illinois State University. He earned his EdD from Northern Illinois University in Educational Administration. Prior to his tenure at the university, Dr. Banicki was a school superintendent, elementary principal, and teacher for 36 years. Presently, Guy is teaching Building Community Engagement through Collaboration as part of the principal preparation program. Dr. Banicki's research agenda includes papers and presentations on social and emotional learning, teacher and principal dispositions, and emotional intelligence. He has chaired and served on several dissertations on educational leadership and school finance.

Dr. Sherell Fuller, assistant professor at Winthrop University, began her career in education as an elementary and middle school teacher in Fairfax County, Virginia. She served as a fourth-grade general education teacher and a seventh/eighth-grade English teacher. Her career in higher education began at the University of North Carolina at Charlotte, and she spent 9 years there serving in various capacities such as clinical assistant professor, undergraduate program coordinator, teacher education learning community coordinator, and liaison for the Children's Defense Fund Freedom Schools Program. Dr. Fuller's service and teaching areas of interest include preparing pre- and in-service teachers to work with diverse populations, supporting educators in the understanding and implementing culturally responsive pedagogy, differentiation of instruction, recruiting underrepresented populations into education, mentoring preservice teachers, and preparation of STAR teachers.

Dr. Martin Haberman (1932–2012) began as a teacher of preschool and elementary children in New York and completed a doctorate in teacher education at Teachers College, Columbia. He holds honorary doctorates in human letters from Rhode Island College and the State University of New York for his contributions to teacher education in America. Over the past 50 years he has pursued a research agenda that established the knowledge base for his Star Teacher Selection Interview, Star Administrator Selection Interview, and the online prescreeners related to these interviews. These instruments are now used in school districts. He received countless awards and recognitions which include Distinguished Alumnus of T.C. Columbia, the Pomeroy Medal from American Association of Colleges for Teacher Education, a Lifetime Contributions Award from the American Educational Research Association, a Standard Oil Award for Excellence in College Teaching, and an award from the Corporation for Public Broadcasting for special service in the advancement of public broadcasting in education. He was a Laureate of Kappa Delta Pi. Professor Haberman's extensive research and demonstration efforts have influenced certification laws in several states, admission procedures in many universities and selection decisions in hundreds of school districts hiring teachers and administrators in rural and urban schools serving students in poverty. Professor Haberman is a former editor of the *Journal of Teacher Education*, the author of more than 250 invited papers and articles, 40 chapters, and 8 books. Kappan selected his "Pedagogy of Poverty" as one the most influential articles of the last 20 years. Professor Haberman has made over 350 presentations of his work to academics, educational leaders, and elected officials.

Dr. Martin Haberman will be remembered for his contributions to the American community of educators. He was a legend in his own time and leaves a legacy that has the potential to ensure that the children and youth of America will have the opportunity to have a great teacher and a great principal. It is his lasting gift to those charged with educating future generations.

Dr. Stephen D. Hancock, is an associate professor of multicultural education in the Department of Reading and Elementary Education at UNC Charlotte, where he also serves as the assistant director of the Urban Education Collaborative. He is an international visiting professor at the Pedagogische Hocshule in Ludwigsburg Germany, where he teaches diversity and globalization in education. Dr. Hancock's research interest supports, academic relationships in urban school context, reading practices and strategies for urban students, ethnographic and autoethnographic methodologies, and White teacher effectiveness in multicultural spaces. He is the editor of *Autoethnography as a Lighthouse: Illuminating Race, Research, and the Politics of Schooling* and *White Women's Work: Examining the Intersectionality of Teaching, Identity, and Race.* In addition, he has published in top journals, including the *Harvard Education Review.*

Dr. Christopher M. Hansen, assistant professor of early childhood education at the University of Tennessee at Chattanooga, focuses his research efforts on dispositions of K–12 teachers, teacher education, and gender in the teaching corps. His research into teacher dispositions attempts to complicate the discourse around ideas like teacher effectiveness and teacher quality. He studies teacher identity formation among preservice teachers in clinical-immersion courses and in-service teacher professional development as part of their collaboration with teacher education programs in order to highlight the good work of teachers and teacher education and to advocate for more inclusive relationships between teacher preparation programs and school communities. One final research interest is a critical examination of the recruitment, preparation, hiring, and supporting of male elementary teachers, with particular focus on the privileged positions that men occupy in elementary schools.

Nicholas D. Hartlep is an award-winning assistant professor of urban education at Metropolitan State University. Before coming to Metropolitan State University he taught at Illinois State University for 4 years and before that he was an advanced opportunity program fellow at the University of Wisconsin-Milwaukee, an "Urban 13" University, where he earned a PhD in the social foundations of urban education and was named an "Outstanding Doctoral Student." Dr. Hartlep also has a master of science degree in K–12 Education and bachelor of science degree in teaching, both conferred from Winona State University. As a former public school teacher he has taught in Rochester, Minnesota and Milwaukee, Wisconsin, as well as abroad in Quito, Ecuador. Dr. Hartlep's research interests include urban in-service teachers' dispositions, the impact neoliberalism is having on schools and society, the model minority stereotype of Asian/Americans, and transracial adoption. He has received several awards for his scholarship. He received the University Research Initiative (URI) Award in 2015 from Illinois State University in 2015 and a Distinguished Young Alumni Award from Winona State University in 2015, which recognizes graduates who are 45 years old or younger and have distinguished themselves in their work or in their community. In 2015 he also received the Upton Sinclair Award for consistently impacting the field of education. In 2016 the University of Wisconsin-Milwaukee presented him with a Graduate of the Last Decade (GOLD) Award for his prolific amount of writing. His scholarly books include *Going Public: Critical Race Theory & Issues of Social Justice* (2010), *The Model Minority Stereotype: Demystifying Asian American Success* (2013), *Unhooking From Whiteness: The Key to Dismantling Racism in the United States* (2013), *The Model Minority Stereotype Reader: Critical and Challenging Readings for the 21st Century* (2014), *Killing the Model Minority Stereotype: Asian American Counterstories and Complicity* (2015), *Modern Societal Impacts of the Model Minority Stereotype* (2015), and *Unhooking from Whiteness: Resisting the Esprit de Corps* (2016). He is currently finishing a coauthored book with Daisy Ball entitled *Asian/Americans: A Critical Analysis of the "Model Minority" as Perpetrators and Victims of Crime* to be published by Rowman and Littlefield. You can follow his work on Twitter @nhartlep or at the "Model Minority Stereotype Project" (www.nicholashartlep.com). He lives and writes from St. Paul, MN.

Ms. Sara McCubbins is a doctoral student at Illinois State University, where she engages in educational research. She received her MS in chemistry education at Illinois State University and holds a teaching certificate for secondary science and English, as well as middle level science and language arts. She has published numerous books on topics relating to interdisciplinary project-based curriculum and performance assessment-based curriculum. Her interests include curriculum development, professional development for teachers, university and community outreach, analyzing the role informal science plays in scientific knowledge acquisition, and student attitudes toward science.

Dr. Sueanne McKinney is associate professor of elementary education at Old Dominion University in Norfolk, Virginia. Her research includes preparing teachers for high-poverty schools, which led to several publications, including *Teacher Education and Practice* (2014), "Urban Students" in C. Berube's *STEM and the City: The State of STEM Education in American Urban Public Schools* (2014) and *Urban Education* (2008). Dr. McKinney has been awarded grants worth over a million dollars, including a National Science Foundation grant focusing on at-risk students and STEM education. Additionally, she has received numerous teaching awards, such as the Virginia Council of Teachers of Mathematics and the 2009 William C. Lowry University Professor of the Year Award.

Dr. Sherese Mitchell is the chairperson of the Education Department at Hostos Community College in South Bronx, New York. She has an extensive background working with children in various settings—classroom, Sunday school, hospital playroom, and a day camp. Dr. Mitchell has brought that experience to her current instructional position to future educators enrolled in methods courses at Hostos. She has also utilized those interests in research with learning styles and tactual resources. She is passionate about student accountability and classroom management and provides staff developments on such. She is a board member of the National Association of Community College and Teacher Education Programs and the Children's Center at Hostos. Dr. Mitchell's research includes many paper presentations at local, regional, and national conferences.

Dr. Grant B. Morgan is currently associate professor in the quantitative methods graduate program in the Department of Educational Psychology at Baylor University, and he is also the coordinator of the quantitative methods specialization graduate program (MA and PhD). Morgan has authored over 70 articles, manuscripts, book chapters, proceedings, and technical reports, including one book. He earned a PhD in educational research and measurement from the University of South Carolina in 2012. Morgan has parallel lines of research that involve methodological investigations of advanced models using Monte Carlo methods and applications of advanced quantitative modeling in a variety of areas via transdisciplinary collaboration. His methodological works have been published in such journals as *Structural Equation Modeling, Computational Statistics & Data Analysis, Methodology*, and *Language Assessment Quarterly*. His transdisciplinary collaborations have appeared in such journals as *Journal of Applied Measurement, Journal of Healthcare Management*, and *Women's Health Issues*. Morgan has numerous awards and nominations, including three distinguished paper awards from American Educational Research Association-affiliated organizations, Cornelia Marschall Smith Professor of the Year nomination, and Division D Early Career Award nomination. Morgan is member of American Educational Research Association, Division D, Structural Equation Modeling, Multilevel Modeling, and Rasch special interest groups.

Dr. Jack Robinson has been involved with educational initiatives in urban and rural education for over 40 years. His research interests and focus in working with teachers is to enhance their use of assessment to promote student motivation and learning especially in schools with a high number of minority and/or economically disadvantaged students. He has worked with several doctoral students in examining issues related to urban education and has sought to enhance the preparation of preservice teachers for work in such environments. To guide that work he has been involved with a number of local school districts in funded and unfunded professional development projects. He participated in a joint 5-year College of Education and local urban school district professional development schools project, worked with a model inner city math magnet school for 3 years, was a principle investigator on three major year-long teacher professional development grants, and a coprincipal investigator or participant on several other related grants working with teachers in urban and rural school districts at the elementary, middle, and high school levels. Related work has been published in *Teacher Development* (2014), *Teacher Education and Practice* (2014), *Teaching and Teacher Education* (2009), and *Urban Education* (2008).

Lauren Ashley Williams received her MEd in curriculum and instruction at Texas A&M University. After teaching as a secondary English/language arts and reading teacher for 3 years, she decided to focus on her interests in urban education, multicultural education, and the cultural beliefs of in-service teachers to drive her research and continued education as a doctoral student at Texas A&M University in the Department of Teaching, Learning, and Culture. Her personal and academic passions revolve around supporting students of poverty and the selection and retention of effective teachers and administrators for underserved students.

"Selecting Teachers and Principals of excellence for children and youth"

Announcing!
Haberman Star Teacher
Selection Interview Training

DATE:

PLACE:

TIME:

"Selection is more important than training"
The Haberman Educational Foundation offers superintendents, principals, site-based teams, and teacher leaders research-based strategies to select teachers and principals who will be unequivocally successful with at-risk students.

No school can be better than its teachers and leaders

For Two Decades, Research Has Shown That Teachers Drive Student Achievement:

1. The effect of teaching on student learning is greater than student ethnicity, family income, school attended by student, or class size.

2. The effect is stronger for poor and/or minority students than for their more affluent and/or white peers, although all groups benefit from effective teachers.

3. The effects accumulate over the years. ("Teacher Quality & Student Achievement Research" Center for Public Education. 2005, p. 2).

Teachers Who Succeed Know How to Build Relationships With Students

If a teacher candidate does not understand how to build relationships with students, it doesn't matter how much content knowledge, experience, or credential strength they may offer.

The Haberman Star Teacher Interview selects mature teachers who can build relationships with students.

The scenario-based interview assesses qualities like persistence, stakeholder focus, ability to translate theory into practice, perception of at-risk behaviors, personal vs. professional behavior, and fallibility. Each component reflects the effective school correlates.

Dr. Martin Haberman is author of the recently acclaimed 2005 publication <u>Star Teachers: the Ideology and Best Practice of Effective Teachers of Diverse Children and Youth in Poverty</u>. All training participants receive the new book and the interview tool which helps to identify excellent teachers. In the last 15 years, 260 districts have been trained in this research-based selection protocol. Principal Selection Training is also available. On-line pre-screeners are available for teacher/principals.

To Set a Date, Call 713-667-6185
or email us at dstafford@altcert.org
http://www.habermanfoundation.org

79442446R00130

Made in the USA
Lexington, KY
21 January 2018